QUEER ANXIETIES
of Young Adult Literature and Culture

Children's Literature Association Series

QUEER ANXIETIES
of Young Adult Literature and Culture

Derritt Mason

University Press of Mississippi / Jackson

The University Press of Mississippi is the scholarly publishing agency of
the Mississippi Institutions of Higher Learning: Alcorn State University,
Delta State University, Jackson State University, Mississippi State University,
Mississippi University for Women, Mississippi Valley State University,
University of Mississippi, and University of Southern Mississippi.

www.upress.state.ms.us

The University Press of Mississippi is a member
of the Association of University Presses.

First printing 2021

∞

Library of Congress Cataloging-in-Publication Data available

Hardback ISBN 978-1-4968-3098-2
Trade paperback ISBN 978-1-4968-3099-9
Epub single ISBN 978-1-4968-3100-2
Epub institutional ISBN 978-1-4968-3101-9
PDF single ISBN 978-1-4968-3102-6
PDF institutional ISBN 978-1-4968-3103-3

British Library Cataloging-in-Publication Data available

Contents

Acknowledgments

This book's queer childhood was spent in the Department of English and Film Studies at the University of Alberta, where Heather Zwicker, Nat Hurley, André P. Grace, and Margaret Mackey offered vital support, guidance, and critique. I remain deeply grateful to them, as well as those organizations that funded my research in its early phases: the Faculty of Arts, Graduate Students' Association, and Institute for Sexual Minority Studies and Services at the University of Alberta; the Social Sciences and Humanities Research Council of Canada; the Killam Trusts; and the Sarah Nettie Christie and Andrew Stewart Memorial Graduate Awards. During my graduate work, I participated in three summer institutes that were equally memorable and life-changing, not only for their intellectual stimulation but also for the many fabulous friends and colleagues they yielded: the ProLit Summer School at LMU Munich (2010), Cornell's School of Criticism and Theory (2011), and Banff Research in Culture (2014). I owe special thanks to Kathryn Bond Stockton, facilitator of our SCT seminar, for her generous and ongoing mentorship.

I am thankful for the family, friends, and colleagues I found in Edmonton, including Brent Bellamy, Sarah Blacker, Alex Carruthers, Cecily Devereux, Theo Finigan, Andrea Hasenbank, Susanne Luhmann, Todd Merkley, Clare Mulcahy, Emily Murphy, Mike O'Driscoll, Melissa Stephens, Brianna Wells, Liam Young, and Libe García Zarranz. The Jorgensen family fed me, housed me, provided me with transportation, and supported me throughout my doctoral work, and I will be forever grateful for the generosity of Senie, Per, Rhiannon, Jay, Louise, and Mark. Dean Jorgensen gave me the opportunity to write my dissertation from some of the most beautiful cities in the world, and he will always be a special part of this book.

Adolescence can be rough at the best of times, and this project was an unruly queer teen with a serious passion for delay. Fortunately, the University of Calgary provided an ideal home for my project's sideways growth into book form. The Faculty of Arts offered generous assistance that opened up the necessary time and space while making possible valuable research support from Jake Bews,

Paul Meunier, and Spencer Miller. I am grateful to the graduate students of ENGL 607 (Queer YA) from 2015 and 2019, and the undergraduates of ENGL 517 (Dystopian YA, 2016) and ENGL 472 (Advanced Studies in YA, 2017). Our conversations left me energized and inspired, and they truly transformed this project. I have wonderful colleagues in the Department of English, many of whom have enthusiastically shared advice, sample book proposals, and/ or friendship and delicious food over the years: thanks to Bart Beaty, Susan Bennett, Karen Bourrier, Faye Halpern, Jacqueline Jenkins, Larissa Lai, Suzette Mayr, David Sigler, Rebecca Sullivan, and Joshua Whitehead. I am so grateful to Morgan Vanek—my brilliant, steadfast writing buddy—for keeping me accountable (and endlessly entertained); and to Vivek Shraya, a trusty source of encouragement, keen insight, and laughter. I completed the final edits to this manuscript as the Wayne O. McCready Resident Fellow at the Calgary Institute for the Humanities; I'm much obliged to the CIH and its director, Jim Ellis, for such an enriching opportunity.

The broader University and city of Calgary communities have brought a number of delightful people into my life, all of whom have made the last five years a pleasure. Thanks to Daniel Voth, Melanee Thomas, Laura Hynes, Anthony Camara, and Pallavi Banerjee (business meeting associates); Caleb Donszelmann and Michael Hancharyk (my favorite queens); Marc Hall and Jerrod Oliver (meme and game buddies); Dawn Hamilton (superhero buddy); Adam Holman; and Jessalynn Keller and Naomi Lightman (brunch and coffee commiseration). He lives in Toronto, but Patrick David helped make my first-ever sabbatical totally unforgettable.

I feel fortunate to belong to the community of scholars working with children's and young adult literature—I'm especially beholden to members of the Children's Literature Association (ChLA) and the Association for Research in Cultures of Young People (ARCYP). I am indebted to Adrienne Kertzer for her decades of work establishing a resounding legacy of children's literature studies at the University of Calgary, and for our very first conversation at ChLA 2014. Michelle Abate, Kate Capshaw, Marah Gubar, and Gwen Tarbox have kindly shared their time and guidance over the years. Naomi Hamer is a superbly undisciplined co-conspirator and my favorite odd couple conference roommate. In addition to offering abundant support, Victoria Ford Smith wields a mighty GIF. Upon arrival at a conference dance party and/or karaoke bar, I will always be overjoyed to see the likes of Kristine Alexander, Josh Coleman, Cheryl Cowdy, Pete Kunze, Beth Marshall, Angel Matos, Kate Slater, Erin Spring, and Jason Vanfosson. Angel and Pete both read portions of this book and offered very helpful comments. A few stolen moments with Jules Gill-Peterson over the years have reoriented my thinking about this book. And I owe all of the heart emojis in the world to my favorite co-counsellor, Kenneth Kidd. Kenneth has read portions of this book more often than anyone else, and his feedback is always generous, sharp, and transformative. Mentors and colleagues don't get much better than Kenneth. I'm lucky to know him and our field is lucky to have him.

This queer teen of a book (no adulthood here, of course!) has found a perfect final home at the University Press of Mississippi. I'm thankful for the capable hands of Katie Keene and ChLA series editors Roxanne Harde and Jackie Horne. My anonymous reviewers pushed me to deliver my best work while stunning me with their generosity and thoughtfulness. Thanks to Malinda Lo and C. M. Ralph for permission to reprint images included in this volume, and to *Children's Literature Association Quarterly*, *ESC: English Studies in Canada*, and the editors of *Fictionalizing the World* for allowing me to revise some previously published material.

And finally, I'm eternally grateful for the love of my friends and family back in Ontario, including my parents, Bob and Sue, and my sister Tamara. Coming home to you is a privilege.

QUEER ANXIETIES
of Young Adult Literature and Culture

Notes on an Anxious Genre:
Queer Young Adult Literature and Culture

Storm, Stress, and Sex

In 1976, Frances Hanckel and John Cunningham posed the question "Can Young Gays Find Happiness in YA Books?" in response to the first four American young adult (YA) novels featuring gay themes, including John Donovan's *I'll Get There. It Better Be Worth the Trip*, published in 1969, and Isabelle Holland's *The Man Without a Face,* which followed in 1972. In their *Wilson Library Bulletin* essay, Hanckel and Cunningham celebrate homosexuality's newfound presence in YA while lamenting the fact that the eight primary characters in these four novels contend with five pairs of divorced parents, including two alcoholics; four deaths, one by violence; and four car crashes that culminate in "one mutilation, one head injury, and five fatalities" (534). The important work of positively role modeling gay youth and properly educating heterosexual readers, Hanckel and Cunningham claim, is undone by the persistent twinning of homosexuality and hopelessness. "Taken as a group," they conclude, "these novels have two salient characteristics: Being gay has no lasting significance and/or costs someone a terrible price" (532). For Hanckel and Cunningham, visible homosexuality in YA is important and ground-breaking. Potentially harmful, however, are the forms such visibility takes.

To rectify these alarming representational trends, Hanckel and Cunningham propose a series of criteria for writing and evaluating gay YA novels. Entitled "What to Do Until Utopia Arrives," this ambitious set of recommendations calls for more visibly gay and lesbian characters in YA; fewer stereotypical, harmful consequences to a character's coming-out; less emphasis on "gayness" as major plot point; more illustrated children's books about homosexuality; "more realistic portrayals of affection and falling in love"; and "accurate, sympathetic pictures of gays for nongays, so that they can learn to appreciate and not fear differences in sexual and affectational preference" (532–33). At the center of these recommendations lies a linear model of growth, wherein a period of adolescent "crisis or conflict" ultimately results in "a positive self-identity" in adulthood (528). It is crucial, Hanckel and Cunningham further claim, to combine the authentic experiences of gay youth with "a hope that is life-affirming and encourages the reader to consider and develop a workable moral philosophy" (528). This hope would ostensibly resignify what it means to be young and gay, providing readers with the non-pathological role models that are integral to representing the "growth and development of gay identity as a valid life choice" (532). However, Hanckel and Cunningham's essay concludes anxiously and with uncertainty about whether or not the genre is on a trajectory that will see these desires fulfilled.

Fast-forward thirty years: Michael Cart and Christine A. Jenkins co-author *The Heart Has Its Reasons: Young Adult Literature with Gay/Lesbian/Queer Content, 1969–2004*, a volume published in 2006 that assesses the pedagogical usefulness of the nearly two hundred queer YA titles that were in circulation at the time. As these authors point out, the publication frequency of queer YA had increased exponentially, "growing from an average of one title per year in the 1970s to four per year in the 1980s to seven per year in the 1990s to over twelve titles per year in the early years of the 21st century," indicating a growing market for and intensifying interest in the genre (xvi). While Cart and Jenkins provide updated language and criteria for evaluating the broader array of novels available, their anxieties are strikingly similar to Hanckel and Cunningham's despite the massive socio-political shifts that took place during the three decades that separate their studies. Utopia, it seems, had yet to arrive. Like Hanckel and Cunningham, Cart and Jenkins want to do away with stereotypes and representations of depressed and suicidal queer youth who are also the perpetual and inevitable victims of anti-queer violence—what Eric Rofes calls the trope of "martyr-target-victim" (41)—and foster greater acceptance for queer youth through the transformative potential of fiction. Cart and Jenkins espouse a "continued belief in the power of books to help teen readers understand themselves and others, to contribute to the mental health and well-being of GLBTQ youth, and to save lives," and like Hanckel and Cunningham, Cart and Jenkins favor texts that "offer positive portrayals of homosexual characters" while dealing "compassionately and honestly with homosexual themes and issues," navigating that delicate dyad of authentic realism and utopian hope (xviii). Cart and Jenkins also share with Hanckel and Cunningham a desire for queer YA to follow the same forward-oriented, linear, teleological trajectory as queer youth themselves: the transition from troubled adolescence to a stable and sexually resolved adulthood. "Suicide has already more or less disappeared from the pages of GLBTQ novels as this fiction has made the transition from problem novel to contemporary realistic fiction," they argue. "Now, like the rest of young adult literature, it must continue to come of age *as literature*" (166).

Cart and Jenkins conclude *The Heart Has Its Reasons* with more echoes of Hanckel and Cunningham: they offer a series of recommendations that evince persistent anxieties about enduring invisibilities and the degree and shape of existing queer visibility in YA. Calling for "more GLBTQ books featuring characters of color, more lesbian and bisexual characters, more transgender youth, and more characters with same-sex parents," Cart and Jenkins maintain that "the literature . . . needs to be more all-inclusive to offer a better reflection of the complexities of the real world and to insure that all young readers might see their faces reflected in it" (165). They continue:

> [GLBTQ YA] needs to be evaluated on the basis of the authenticity of its portrayal of GLBTQ adults and teens and the world they inhabit but it also needs to be evaluated as literature. Does it offer multidimensional characters? Does it have a setting rich in verisimilitude? Does it have not only an authentic but an original voice? Does it offer fresh insights into the lives of GLBTQ people? Does it offer other innovations in terms of narrative strategy, structure, theme? Or is it the same old story, told in the same old way that readers have encountered countless times in the past? (166)

Cart and Jenkins raise a number of crucial points about the lack of diversity in queer YA, which—like children's literature as a whole—has historically foregrounded White, middle-class, cisgender male protagonists. However, their questions also invite us to ask: what is an "authentic" and "original" GLBTQ voice? What constitutes "fresh insight" into queer lives? What is "the same old story," and why is it no longer of any use? What assumptions do Cart and Jenkins seem to make about how readers interpret the content of queer fiction for adolescents? Can these questions and objectives, resolute since the 1970s, ever be properly and completely answered and fulfilled, these anxieties entirely addressed?

My assertion is that no, they cannot. This does not mean, however, that we should stop exploring them. Instead, I want to shift focus and consider the stakes of these repeated attempts to pin down the most desirable representational strategies for the genre. How, in other words, can queer YA and its commentary function as illuminating indexes of anxieties about how adults do and/or should address queer youth? As the above examples illustrate, critics express several distinct concerns about queer YA, including its affective contours (the dominant affects should be hope and happiness), the visibility of its protagonists (young queer characters should be "out and proud") and the temporal trajectory of their narrative growth (by novel's end, any problems surrounding sexual self-identification should be resolved). I will suggest, however, that such calls for visibility and forward-oriented, teleological growth are not necessarily the most pedagogically rewarding or productive demands to make of queer YA. I argue instead that invisible, subtle, latent, and sideways queernesses are at least as worthy of attention as visible manifestations of nonheterosexual desires and identities. I will also demonstrate how queer YA texts and characters themselves often oppose the models of child development and visibility privileged by queer YA critics, instead valuing delay over growth and the infirm grounds of queerness over the stability and teleology of sexual identity. Indeed, I've found that those sites of intense anxiety surrounding queer YA also yield compelling queer models for reading and relationality. These sites of anxiety—queer visibility and sexual coherence; adolescent risk-taking; representations of HIV/AIDS; dystopia, horror, and "dark" YA themes; the promise that "It Gets Better" and the threat that it might not—are what I map and explore in this book.[1]

Central to my argument is a three-pronged approach to anxiety, which also provides the structure for this introduction: (1) anxiety's relationship to the histories of adolescence and YA; (2) anxiety's temporality, as embodied by YA characters themselves; and (3) an embrace of queer YA as an anxious genre. Anxiety is fundamental to understanding the past, present, and future of queer YA—so fundamental, I argue, that when attempting to characterize "queer YA," our analysis grows richer if we prioritize affect over subject matter and form. In this book, then, queer YA emerges as a body of trans-media texts with blurry boundaries, one that coheres provisionally around affect more than content. Additionally, I suggest that anxiety is both generated by and generative of queer YA. In other words, adult anxieties about queer adolescent crises produce queer YA as a possible remedy to these crises, while queer YA produces anxiety about whether or not its content is an adequate remedy.

The years 2010–11 marked a noteworthy turning point in contemporary queer YA discourse. It was during this time that we saw the longer history of anxiety and adolescence collide with contemporary concerns about queer youth and the content of texts for young people. Moreover, these conversations and cultural shifts related to queer youth seem to have had a very real impact on rapid subsequent growth in queer YA publishing. Here are three scenes that set the stage:

One. September, 2010. Suddenly, it seems, the media is saturated with images of young queers who are taking their own lives, driven to tragic extremes by relentless bullying. In the span of three weeks, five American teens kill themselves ("Raymond Chase"). Their names are manifest in print and digital ink, newspapers, magazines, and online memorials: Billy Lucas. Asher Brown. Seth Walsh. Raymond Chase. And in perhaps the most widely publicized case, Tyler Clementi, the Rutgers University student who leaps to his death from the George Washington Bridge after his roommate records footage of Clementi's sexual encounter with another man (McKinley). NBC News reports a "suicide surge" (Crary). Celebrity blogger Perez Hilton declares that "America [is] In CRISIS!" Although sociologists, health care workers, and educators have perceived queer teens as being at risk of suicide for decades, it seems that for the first time since Matthew Shepard's torture and murder in 1998 the general public is being made aware of the multiple forms of quotidian violence many young queers confront. Students fight difficult battles for the right to form gay-straight alliances at their schools (Wallace). Community leaders initiate anti-bullying policy and legislation reform. And on September 21, the day before Tyler Clementi would take his own life, writer Dan Savage and his partner Terry Miller launch the *It Gets Better* YouTube project, which invites adults to submit videos that offer messages of hope and encouragement to gay teens. As the *It Gets Better* website states, "The *It Gets Better* Project was created to show young LGBT people the levels of happiness, potential, and positivity their lives will reach—if they can just get through their teen years. The *It Gets Better* Project wants to remind teenagers in the LGBT community that they are not alone—and it WILL get better" ("What is . . . ?"). Before the end of *It Gets Better*'s first week, one thousand videos have been uploaded to the project's YouTube channel (Savage 1).

Two. September 28, 2011. In an interview on the Canadian Broadcasting Corporation's talk show *Q*, YA authors Rachel Manija Brown and Sherwood Smith claim that literary agents asked them to "de-gay" their novel to make it more marketable ("Is young-adult . . . ?"). In response, Brown and Smith go public. "There is a very real issue in young adult novels that there are very, very few books with gay characters," Smith asserts. Brown speaks at length about how she perceives fiction as having the power to save lives:

> I think that when you cut certain types of people out of fiction, . . . you're sending the message to teenagers saying that what they are inherently is so terrible that it can't be talked about and can't be portrayed, and I think that's really soul-crushing. There've been a number of [gay teen] suicides; LGBTQ teenagers do have a much higher suicide rate because of prejudice, and I don't want to add to that prejudice.

The *Q* interview is a follow-up to a post by Brown and Smith on the *Publishers Weekly* blog entitled "Say Yes to Gay YA," which receives the greatest number of single-day hits in the website's history and draws over forty thousand views in three days, as well as a defensive response from the agents in question (Fox, "Authors" and "Riposte"). "We would love to start this conversation," writes Joanna Stampfel-Volpe of the Nancy Coffey Literary Agency; "let's discuss" (Fox, "Riposte").

Three. October 9, 2011. In a *New York Times* op-ed entitled "No More Adventures in Wonderland," Maria Tatar decries the current state of children's literature as being too dark, too violent, too lacking in "imaginative play." "It is hard not to mourn the decline of the literary tradition invented by [Lewis] Carroll and [J. M.] Barrie," she writes, arguing that the *Harry Potter*, *His Dark Materials*, and *Hunger Games* series deliver unto children "an unprecedented dose of adult reality, . . . sometimes without the redemptive beauty, cathartic humor and healing magic of an earlier time." If only contemporary authors spent as much time with children as Carroll and Barrie did, Tatar asserts, their books would better reflect what children actually want in their stories. She concludes that unlike other authors, Carroll and Barrie "fully entered the imaginative worlds of children—where danger is balanced by enchantment—and reproduced their magic on the page. In today's stories, those safety zones are rapidly vanishing as adult anxieties edge out childhood fantasy."

The messages: queer youth are in crisis. Publisher constraints are limiting YA's effectiveness as a potential remedy. The genre of children's literature is doing the wrong thing. Together, these examples evince persistent anxieties about what children and youth are doing and reading, how what they read affects what they do, and how adult concerns and desires shape stories for young people. One product of these anxieties, it appears, was a boom in queer YA publishing. As Jenkins and Cart report in *Representing the Rainbow* (2018), an updated version of *The Heart Has Its Reasons*, "Ten young adult titles with LGBTQ+ content were published in the 1970s, forty in the 1980s, eighty-two in the 1990s, 292 in 2000–2009, and 513 titles in 2010–2016" (xi). Similarly, as seen in figure 1.1, Malinda Lo indicates that the number of LGBTQ YA books released annually by mainstream publishers more than quadrupled over a span of two decades, surging from fewer than twenty titles per year in the early 2000s to nearly eighty in 2016, eighty-four in 2017, and 108 in 2018.[2] Lo's statistics reveal a striking uptick in 2010–2012, when the number of titles published annually climbed from approximately ten to thirty-five and then continued to skyrocket.[3]

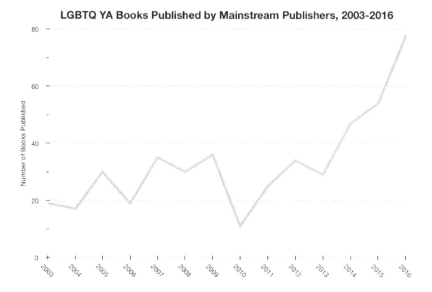

Figure 1.1. LGBTQ YA Books Published by Mainstream Publishers, 2003–2016. Statistics compiled by Malinda Lo. Retrieved from https://www.malindalo.com/blog/2017/10/12/lgbtq-ya-by-the-numbers-2015-16. Reproduced with permission.

In the above examples, we see the longer history of anxious YA criticism gaining cultural momentum through its intersection with queer youth advocacy. Simultaneously, Tatar's critique—although not explicitly invested in queer issues—speaks to enduring concerns about how adults address young people through literature. These are the same anxieties articulated by Hanckel, Cunningham, Cart, and Jenkins, and they appear particularly intense when it comes to questions about how sexuality—in particular, queer sexuality—should be represented in texts for young audiences. When hope and happiness seem absent from the queer popular imagination, when children's literature trends dark and disturbing, and when adolescents appear to be in crisis, many among us become quite anxious. Queer YA and cultural texts that seek to address queer youth proliferate as both an anxiety management strategy (a potential antidote to the fact that queer youth are in crisis) and a producer of additional anxiety (what if this address fails in its mission?). These persistent yet shifting anxieties should be recognized as generative, constitutive characteristics of queer YA and its commentary. Conversations about young people and the texts they (do or do not, should or should not) consume provide a useful lens for parsing a network of affective relations that has long haunted the histories of adolescence and literature for young people. I'll now offer a brief overview of that history.

The History of Adolescence as History of Anxiety

As Kent Baxter points out, early twentieth-century theorists of adolescence G. Stanley Hall and Margaret Mead "were both responding to a cultural need to define a (seemingly) new and growing segment of the population, a new theory of human development spawned by the works of Sigmund Freud, and a host of other anxieties related to the movement into the 'modern world'" (4–5). In his multi-volume *Adolescence* (1907), Hall famously develops two theories of this fledgling age category. First, he adapts a theory of "recapitulation," which presents the growth of a child into adulthood through adolescence as a mirror of the evolution of the human race. In cruder terms, children for Hall are savages who require indoctrination to become civilized adults, and adolescence is the appropriate time for schooling and various forms of discipline to take place, including corporal punishment (Cart 4). Bound up in recapitulation is a host of sexist, racist, homophobic, and colonial impulses, in addition to anxieties about adolescence becoming derailed from its normative developmental path. For Hall, White, male, heterosexual adulthood is the ideal telos of adolescence and the truest embodiment of civilization.[4]

Second, Hall coins the term "storm and stress" after the German *Sturm und Drang* to describe the emotional tempestuousness of adolescence. The three key components of storm and stress, according to Hall, are conflict with parents, a propensity for risky behavior, and mood disruptions. Although Hall's theories have been challenged and critiqued by many, the affiliation of teenagers, adolescents, and youth with storm and stress persists, especially in discussions about at-risk youth and teen angst more generally. Working contemporaneously with Hall was Freud, who famously offered his theories of the child's polymorphous perversity in *Three Essays on the Theory of Sexuality* (1905). Freud forced "the recognition that the child's inner life included all kinds of things that adults would wish weren't there," writes Nat Hurley: "aggressions, depressions, desires for the wrong kinds of objects, sexual desire, desire that could not be tamed into propriety" ("Childhood" 6). Like Freud, Hall both responded to and generated anxieties about the supposedly intrinsic characteristics of young people. The "invention" of adolescence, as Baxter describes it, occurred in tandem with this anxious impulse to rigidly define a category of age and discipline those who fall into it: "the process of inventing adolescence was a process of taming a threat," he explains, "and thus these definitions often reveal more about those who create them than the actual parameters of adolescence itself" (20). Indeed, "storm and stress" bears a double valence. It describes an ostensible form of adolescent anxiety and is simultaneously the source of tremendous anxiety for adults—such anxieties about power and control certainly surface as symptoms in Hall's work.

The "teenager" and the "young adult," on the other hand, came into being several decades after the adolescent. As Jon Savage indicates in *Teenage: The Prehistory of Youth Culture*, "teenager" wasn't used until the post–World War II era, when the word was coined by advertisers to describe a new market segment that reflected the increased spending power of young people between the ages of fourteen and eighteen years (xv). "Teenager" materialized—alongside the very notion of "identity," as Leerom Medovoi points out (56)—as a category that sat somewhat uneasily alongside adolescence. Baxter describes these two opposing figures: "the squeaky-clean 'ideal' adolescent, who is controlled, controllable, and will enable the human race to attain a type of moral perfection," and the teenager, "who represents a kind of cultural anxiety of the physical and sexual threat the adolescent can become if left to his or her own devices" (12). Cart flags that neither Hall nor advertisers used the term "young adult," however (4). Instead, this category was coined, like "youth," through the discourse of therapists, social workers, educators, and librarians. In 1957, "young adult" became primarily associated with the literary when the American Library Association formed a Young Adult Services Division, teenagers/youth/young adults became a desirable literary market, and YA was conceived as a saleable literary genre (Cart 7). "The young adult is associated with education, civic training, and cultural literacy," notes Kenneth B. Kidd, "such that 'young adult' has become shorthand for pedagogical programs and materials" ("A Case History" 167).[5] Similar to Baxter's distinction between "teenager" and "adolescent," Kidd flags an anxious tension between "young adult" and other permutations of this age category: "The term 'young adult' works to repudiate the chaos and perils of adolescence—the young adult is what we hope the adolescent or teenager will become" ("A Case History" 167).

Kidd also makes important distinctions between "the novel of adolescence" (roughly, a novel interested in coming-of-age that does not necessarily imagine a young audience for itself) and "the adolescent novel" (more or less synonymous with YA). Moreover, he demonstrates how anxiety has been central to the development of these genres:

> The novel of adolescence was coidentical with the naturalist novel and the proletarian novel through the first several decades of the century, but gradually split

off from those genres, looking more and more like something called the psychological novel, organized around the hypersensitive and anxious character. This,
in turn, became the problem novel, hence the general conversion of the novel of
adolescence into the adolescent novel. ("A Case History" 155)

The "problem" or "problem-realism" novel, a "storm and stress"-focused thematic subgenre of YA that foregrounds and often hyperbolizes social issues
confronting adolescents, offered fertile ground for the exploration of queer
themes as "gay youth" emerged as a social category in the 1970s. So, to offer a
rough summary, Anglo-American YA with visible queer content developed
from the convergence of the following forces, many of which stem from adult
anxieties: (1) the postwar identification of teenagers as a new target market
and the subsequent development of YA; (2) the "invention" of gay youth in the
1970s (see chapter two); (3) as Kidd points out, "the social movements of the
1960s and 1970s" ("Introduction" 114); and (4) the rise of the problem novel
in these same decades.

Julia Kristeva offers us a longer genealogy that, interestingly, reiterates
anxiety's position at the heart of the adolescent novel. For Kristeva, all novels
are adolescent novels, all authors are "perpetual subject-adolescent[s]," and
"novelistic psychology" has its roots in a fifteenth-century French work of
prose about an amorous young page (139–140). Kristeva makes her formulation
possible by understanding adolescence not as a category of age, but rather an
"open psychic structure" that, like "living organisms that renew their identity
by interacting with another identity," often "opens itself to that which has been
repressed" (136). Writing, in Kristeva's schema, is a manic defense triggered by
the subject's depressive position: the subject feels anxiety about possible object
loss or loss of self, and begins writing to "reconstruct their psychic space"
(137). "More real than a fantasy," Kristeva explains, "fiction generates a new
living identity" for its adolescent-author while simultaneously granting readers the narcissistic and voyeuristic pleasures of fantasizing about themselves
as adolescent subjects (137). "As a permanent witness to our adolescence," she
continues, "the novel would enable us to rediscover the state of incompleteness
(which is as depressive as it is joyful) that leads in some respects to what we
call aesthetic pleasure" (139). Kristeva's description of novelistic discourse as a
defense against a seemingly unstable or empty self offers a number of useful
threads: anxiety is a primary impetus for writing (adolescent) novels, anxiety
is central to adolescence as psychic structure, and this structure is available to
people of all ages.[6] The latter in particular might explain in part why YA, or
the adolescent novel—and its many narcissistic delights—enjoys tremendous
popularity across age groups.

When it comes to critics and commentators of contemporary queer YA, however, anxieties tend to be aroused by what Peter Hunt—in the context of children's literature as a whole—describes as "a tension between what is 'good' in the exploded abstract, what is good for the child socially, intellectually, and educationally, and what we, really, honestly think is a good book" (15). As with children's literature, questions about what is "good for" queer YA's imagined audience seem to be the most consistent source of critical anxiety and debate. What many of these critics tend to overlook, however, is the history I have just summarized, through which we see how notions of adolescence, queerness, and YA have long been braided with anxiety. Like Kristeva, I understand anxiety as a potentially creative force, in part because it maintains an "openness" to emotional and psychological experience including the pleasures of psychic "incompleteness." The promise of incompleteness, at odds with the sexual fixity that critics desire from queer YA, is further clarified through theories of anxiety's temporality.

Affect, Anxiety, and Temporality

Adam Phillips distinguishes between "worrying" and "anxiety" in *On Kissing, Tickling, and Being Bored*, in which he suggests that "worry always has an object, . . . worrying is beyond displacement, whereas one can feel anxious without knowing what the anxiety is about" (52). He offers a seventeenth-century *OED* definition of "anxious" as "'troubled or uneasy in mind about some uncertain event; being in painful or disturbing suspense; concerned; solicitous,'" but I am less interested in fine distinctions between worry and anxiety than I am in the compelling temporality suggested by both terms (52). For Phillips, "Worrying implies a future, a way of looking forward to things. It is a conscious conviction that a future exists, one in which something terrible might happen, which is of course ultimately true. So worrying is an ironic form of hope" (56). Yet Phillips also describes worrying for one particular child patient as "a form of emotional constipation, an unproductive mental process . . . among other things an attempt to arrest the passage of time," which echoes the *OED*'s description of anxiety as a state of "painful or disturbing suspense" (47–48).[7] A "halting" temporality is also central to Jacques Lacan's theory of anxiety as outlined in Book X of his *Seminar*; he identifies subjective "inhibition," which entails "the halting of movement," as an integral part of anxiety (10).[8]

Nat Hurley, who calls worrying a "discontent" of childhood, writes that Phillips is "encourag[ing] us to be open to the child's deployment of a sad passion as a future-management strategy" ("Childhood" 9). For adult YA critics (and, as

I've already discussed, theorists of adolescence like Hall), anxiety also emerges from attempts to manage the future: YA critics desire a version of the genre that will provide young readers with the fictional role models ostensibly necessary to their thriving. For queer YA's young protagonists, however, the future is often managed by anxiously delaying its arrival—arresting the passage of time, as Phillips and Lacan suggest—resisting growth into a coherent, stable sexual identity; lingering in a state of Kristevian adolescent incompleteness. Anxiety and worry in this context invite us to explore, as Hurley writes, "the temporal contradictions and dialectics that unsettle and reorganize the very ways we narrate the time of childhood and address childhood affects and attentions that move in multiple directions at once" ("Childhood" 19). This is a tension I will explore throughout this book: while YA critics insist that the genre look forward to a future rife with visibly queer characters, these characters seem more invested in delaying this future, in turning towards alternate relations without the kind of visibility critics describe. In addition to serving as the genre's affective center, anxiety describes a particular rhythm present in queer YA, a turning elsewhere to stall the present while simultaneously looking forward to an uncertain, queer future.

Hurley opens "Childhood and Its Discontents: An Introduction" with an image that speaks to this rhythm, what I call the "queer double-take." "Figure this: a child looking simultaneously forward and back," she begins, describing an illustration by Amy DiGennaro entitled *Running with M.E.,*

> oversized ear cocked down and back, oriented to what is clearly in the distance, but too far away for us to see. . . . Carrying the body of another, smaller child, this child's body moves forward, listens backwards but displays two faces: one peeks over her shoulder, as if following the ear backwards; the other peers fully forward, in profile, looking straight ahead into the rays that envelop the two small bodies in motion. (1)

For Hurley, DiGennaro's illustration is "a moving set of contradictions mobilized through a child looking forward and looking back, while being pulled and propelled into the space emanating from the vessel before her" ("Childhood" 2). Additionally, the image's stillness manifests a haunting stasis from which the child cannot (or does not wish to) escape in spite of the multiple directions in which she is simultaneously looking and being pulled. This image of the anxious child's anxious rhythm—looking forward, looking back, yet static—and the temporal tensions it evinces, is at the core of this book. The image and rhythm of the queer double-take also suggest Kathryn Bond Stockton's notion of "growing sideways," which she posits as a substitution for the forward-oriented metaphor of "growing up" that flattens the complexity of a child's desires, relations, and movements (*Queer Child* 11). Sideways growth, for Stockton, accounts for the many ways children delay growing up into the reproductive heterosexual adulthood that is their ostensible normative telos.[9] We can read DiGennaro's image as a picture of the queer child "growing toward a question mark," as Stockton writes, having a "[desperate] feeling there was simply nowhere to grow," a strong desire that "time would stop, or just twist sideways, so that one wouldn't have to advance to new or further scenes of trouble" (*Queer Child* 3). Recall, too, Kristeva's theory of adolescent novel-writing as a manic response to anxious subjectivity, wherein the "unity of the novel" becomes a space for managing self-proliferation while dwelling amongst the pleasures of incompleteness (148). Anxiety is the dominant affective form that surfaces through these various and varying intersections of adolescence, queerness, and writing: Stockton's notion of sideways growth, critics who describe the pedagogical function of queer YA, and histories of adolescence and the adolescent novel.

I envision the circulation of anxiety through and around queer YA criticism, discourse about queer youth and adolescents, and queer YA texts as an "affective economy," a term coined by Sara Ahmed in *The Cultural Politics of Emotion*.[10] In Ahmed's model, "feelings do not reside in subjects or objects, but are produced as effects of circulation. The circulation of objects allows us to think about the 'sociality' of emotion" (8). Further, speaking to the economic aspect of her formulation, Ahmed stresses that affect accumulates over time and through circulation: "signs increase in affective value as an effect of the movement between signs: the more signs circulate, the more affective they become" (45). I find Ahmed's concept useful since I do not see anxiety as being specifically located within any particular queer YA critic, text, or theorist; instead, anxiety is produced and accrues through the circulation of YA texts and discourse about queer youth and adolescence.[11] When I read the anxious rhythms of the queer double-take in a particular text, for example, this anxiety is not embedded in the text or its characters themselves, but it surfaces instead from the text's circulation in a web of discourse about queer youth, adolescence, pedagogy, the role of fiction and literature, and queer theories of childhood.

What affect theory further permits is a "bringing together" of sorts—first, in the sense that I draw on myriad texts across genre (fiction, theory, criticism), form and media. I analyze, for example, the video game *Caper in the Castro* in chapter three, the animated television series *Big Mouth* in chapter five, the YouTube project *It Gets Better* in chapter six, and online fanfiction in chapter seven. "Bringing together" also speaks to the relational impulse of affect itself. Brian Massumi writes that in affect, we are never alone . . . because affects in Spinoza's definition are basically ways of *connecting*, to others and to other situations. They are our angle of participation in processes larger than ourselves. With intensified affect comes a stronger sense of embeddedness in a larger field of life—a heightened sense of belonging, with other people and to other places. (214)

If we can locate potential for queer relationality in Stockton's description of growing sideways or "growing towards a question mark" (*Queer Child* 3), then perhaps there is a similar kind of world-making taking place in queer YA's affective economy. Perhaps, too, we can begin to think about the "ironic form of hope" that emerges from the circulation of anxiety through various media forms (Phillips 56). After all, does it not inspire at least a bit of hope that anxiety about the well-being of queer youth and the status of their representations in popular texts seems to connect so many of us? It may be that, in centering affect in our analysis of queer YA, we might better attune ourselves to the structures of feeling that attend adolescent queerness and those moments when our own anxieties, as adults, tend to shape our discursive interventions.

On Anxiety and "Not Defining" Queer YA

In this book, I depart from a strictly print-literature-based notion of queer YA to consider how and why anxieties that manifest themselves in queer YA criticism also surface in other media concerned with the adult/youth address. The anxious sites of queer YA, in other words, bleed beyond the scope of print literature and into cultural texts broadly conceived. I do not consider queer YA to be an easily defined set of texts that signifies in consistent ways and performs a specific didactic function. Instead of imagining queer YA as a cluster of novels that contain visibly queer themes and characters (as do Cart and Jenkins, among others), I want to contemplate how we can approach such texts from a perspective that foregrounds their affective ties instead of privileging genre, content, and imagined audience. In other words, what I call "queer YA" is not a set of narrative conventions, a marketing label, or anything reducible to content. It is instead a set of affects and effects with roots in the anxious emergence of adolescence and the "teenager," twentieth-century social and literary movements, theories of queer temporality, and the adult desire to both manage and support youth, queer and otherwise.

Integral to this approach is Marah Gubar's suggestion that any quest to define children's literature is ultimately a futile one. In her 2011 essay "On Not Defining Children's Literature," Gubar divides critics of children's literature into two categories—the "definers" and the "antidefiners"—and argues that the space of "not defining" is a productive middle ground between the two (210). Definers, Gubar argues, over-simplify and flatten the genre in a way that limits the breadth of potential criticism, whereas antidefiners "cut young people out of the picture entirely" (212). "The best approach we can take," Gubar concludes, "is to proceed piecemeal, focusing our attention on different subareas and continually striving to characterize our subject in ways that acknowledge its messiness and diversity" (212). Here, Gubar opens avenues for a nuanced and rigorous consideration of the multiplicity of threads—such as anxiety, in this case—that bind and divide texts for young people.

Outside the realm of adult criticism, young people are constantly in the process of producing queer children's and YA literature, defining on their terms what texts constitute the category. For one reader, the latent queernesses of *The Wizard of Oz*, for example—which would not, under the aegis of Cart and Jenkins, contain sufficient queer visibility to merit inclusion in their bibliography—might have far more significance than a text with characters who openly claim a gay or lesbian identity.[12] The same could apply to J. K. Rowling's *Harry Potter* books, an outwardly straight series that has become a source of many queer pleasures for young authors of fanfiction (see chapter seven). Although I owe much to Cart and Jenkins's work, I am uninterested in perpetuating a genre whose boundaries are delimited based on form (print literature) and imagined audience (young people), and whose critical approval is contingent upon content that disavows the negative affect of earlier queer YA titles.

I am also indebted to Roberta Seelinger Trites's *Disturbing the Universe: Power and Repression in Adolescent Literature* (2000) and Lydia Kokkola's *Fictions of Adolescent Carnality: Sexy Sinners and Delinquent Deviants* (2013), two important studies that consider the intersections of YA, age, power, and sexuality, and which I discuss at various points throughout this book. Both of these studies, in my view, simultaneously highlight and perform anxieties about the relationship between YA and its young readers, especially in their thoughtful analyses of the flows of power between reader, text, and the wider world. Trites's and Kokkola's works critique and reiterate persistent concerns about the balance of powers between YA text and reader: how much influence does a given text have on its reader's behavior? Do readers have the power to consciously subvert or absorb a given text's ideological content? Does a given text provide readers with strategies for negotiating or resisting power relations in the "real world," and/or does it encourage them to subject themselves to authority?

Inspired by the impulses of these studies, I understand queer YA as a genre anxious about its own constitution. Queer YA raises questions about how we teach and learn sexuality through reading, and often illustrates how queer reading practices exceed the way many critics assume young people interact with texts. The pedagogical imperative to teach readers "what queer looks like" is far less interesting and productive than an invitation to read queerly, to identify with and across and in opposition to sexual categories, to think queerness on queerer terms. So, I will not attempt to concretely define "queer YA," but I will track the anxious signifiers that accumulate around the term, putting literature, criticism, theory, and various cultural texts into conversation with one another. I hope to move beyond a conception of queer YA as a literary genre grounded in visibility and coherent sexual identity, arguing instead for an affective trans-media approach that complicates and enhances the way we—as readers, scholars, and teachers—think and write about queer YA, children's literature, and genre.

This somewhat sketchy approach to queer YA requires a similar take on "genre." If genre is constituted in part by audience expectations, as Steve Neale would have us believe (45), then I am establishing an expectation that the dominant affective structure of queer YA will be anxious. When I describe queer YA as a genre, I am referring to a very loose assemblage of cultural texts that cohere—perhaps only temporarily—around those sites of anxiety I discuss in this book.[13] In mapping these sites within and around queer YA, I bring together a number of key concepts, questions, and shifting forms of anxiety: the anxious critical dialogue that surrounds queer YA; theories of affect and temporality; the anxieties contained within the texts themselves, i.e. those characters and scenes of reading that exhibit the stall-and-start temporality of anxiety; and the instability and incoherence of queer YA as genre. Along these lines, my use of "queer" in this book follows queer theory's commitments to disrupting instead of reinforcing notions of stable and coherent identity, and to reclaiming texts and relational modes that queer YA critics have ignored and/or pushed to the margins.[14] Much queer YA commentary, I argue, overlooks queer theory's productive influence and instead privileges the visibility of hopeful, resolved LGBT identity. I also intend "queer" to inflect upon and *queer* (as a verb) YA itself. Queer YA as anxious genre is queer in its representation of nonnormative gender and sexuality *and* its resistance to easy description, definition, and coherence; queer YA is anxious in its perpetual turns back and forward in attempts to describe and define itself *and* its provocation of so much critical anxiety surrounding the way adults are (or should be) addressing and representing youth. Anxiety, here, both complements and supplements queerness. Anxiety speaks to the affective economy through which queer YA circulates, while itself manifesting a queer temporality that places delay and forward-oriented growth in tension with one another. Anxiety is also a relatively unaddressed affective dimension of queer theory, one I focalize—beginning in chapter one—through queer theories of childhood and temporality.

As I have attempted to illustrate thus far, critical expectations surrounding the function of fiction—as well as the critic's role in relation to fiction—are inherently anxious: what pedagogical or didactic function should queer YA fulfill? What future effects do we desire from queer YA? Is the role of the critic to find the "best" book for the child, or is it something else—something that includes, for example, an exploration of the complex and shifting dynamic between text and reader? Many critics, as I have pointed out, understand queer YA as a primarily didactic enterprise, or in Hurley's words, "a knowledge- or risk-management strategy" ("Childhood" 9). Similar to John Michael's idea that university English departments are structurally anxious, that is, constituted by texts that "necessarily do not form a peaceful community" (68), critics often imagine queer YA as pedagogically and generically cohesive, but it is ultimately unsettled.[15] And as Michael further suggests, we must remain "ever calculating" as we consider the stakes of our pedagogical and critical investments in a given genre along with the tools we use for defining its constitution and evaluating its texts (68). What I hope to begin formulating is an approach to queer YA that moves us beyond visibility and teleology, enhances our critical perspectives on YA and children's literature more broadly, and assembles a range of relevant discussions to enrich the ways we imagine teaching and learning in relation to queer YA. I believe that queer YA presents a great deal of positive, transformative potential for thinking relationality. Due to this potential, I maintain that we *should* be anxious about the content and circulation of queer YA, while remaining aware of how queer YA itself invites, produces, and makes manifest anxiety.

Sites of Anxiety

Each chapter of this book takes aim at a particular site of anxiety, yet these sites are not wholly distinct. My first two chapters reconsider and recuperate some early queer YA titles often seen by contemporary critics as too harmful, too laden with stereotype and negative affect to be of value to contemporary readers—specifically, John Donovan's *I'll Get There. It Better Be Worth the Trip* (1969) and Isabelle Holland's *The Man Without a Face* (1972). I draw the inspiration for these chapters in part from Heather Love's analysis of the ambivalent relationship between queerness and its painful histories. In *Feeling Backwards: Loss and the Politics of Queer History*, Love returns to early queer texts that are saturated with negative affect: self-loathing, loneliness, and isolation.[16] Unlike

Cart, Jenkins, and other critics, however, Love embraces "dark, ambivalent" texts, arguing that "such representations constitute a crucial 'archive of feeling,' an account of the corporeal and psychic costs of homophobia" (4). For Love, these "earlier forms of feeling, imagination, and community" enable us to critique "structures of inequality in the present" without subscribing unequivocally to a narrative of progression when it comes to queer rights and the normalization of LGBT identity (30). To this end, Love "insist[s] on the importance of clinging to ruined identities and to histories of injury" (30). Like Love, I am interested in how "queers have embraced backwardness in many forms: in celebrations of perversion, in defiant refusals to grow up, in explorations of haunting and memory, and in stubborn attachments to lost objects" (7). Queer YA teems with such backwards and sideways queer attachments, embodied by characters like Donovan's Davy and Holland's Chuck.

Much to the chagrin of some critics, Davy and Chuck don't "come out." Instead, they turn to alternative, "sideways" relations en route to—or in avoidance of—adopting a gay identity. Davy and Chuck grow sideways into creative forms of relationality, attaching themselves to queer objects that function as metaphors of delay and anxiety: a dog, in Davy's case, and pedagogy in Chuck's. In many ways, these two books are quintessential problem novels that establish gay YA conventions for years to come. They also, however, subvert problem novel tropes and the linear temporality of the "coming out novel"[17] through their anxious relationship to YA convention and their characters' reliance on texts without visible representations of queerness in order to make sense of themselves. Moreover, Donovan and Holland's novels challenge the linear narrative of progression in which many queer YA critics are invested. Donovan's novel, for example, fails to deliver on its title: its protagonist never arrives at a destination, a "there." Instead, this story focuses solely on the trip, which is filled with delay and a sideways relation with a very phallic dog. These two novels abound with fascinatingly messy "possibilities, gaps, overlaps, dissonances and resonances, lapses and excesses of meaning"—to cite Sedgwick on queerness (*Tendencies* 8)—that demonstrate how queer YA enacts its own anxiety regarding the way critics articulate its utility and establish its boundaries.

In chapter three, I consider the impact of HIV/AIDS on queer YA. Unsurprisingly, HIV/AIDS has been a source of tremendous anxiety for YA authors and critics, to the extent that the virus has been generally invisible in the literature. When HIV/AIDS is mentioned in YA, it is habitually (mis)represented in order to preserve the young protagonist's innocence. Uncles and other relatives are those living with HIV, not adolescents themselves; when young people do acquire the virus, it is typically through a blood transfusion or other statistically unlikely means. Moreover, HIV/AIDS is often depicted in YA as generationally and/or geographically detached from the main characters' lives. In an attempt to probe this generational chasm, this chapter puts into conversation two temporally and formally distant texts: C. M. Ralph's video game *Caper in the Castro*, created during the height of the AIDS crisis in 1989 and resurrected in 2017; and David Levithan's YA novel *Two Boys Kissing* (2013), which is set in the present-day but narrated by a ghostly chorus of gay men who died during the worst of the AIDS epidemic. As a video game, I argue, *Castro* allows us to play with and feel the anxieties about HIV/AIDS that continue to circulate in queer YA's affective economy. Together, *Castro* and Levithan's novel invite us to consider how affect associated with failure (helplessness and frustration, for example) tends to dominate discourse about HIV/AIDS in the context of young people's culture. These two texts indicate that dwelling with failure and loss—instead of striving for a teleological "win"—can potentially open us into new relational "networks." These networks, I claim, might entail more accurate representations of how HIV/AIDS endures in the present and remains an influential force in the lives of many young people.

Chapters four and five focus on anxieties similar to Tatar's—those surrounding dystopian, horrific, and otherwise "dark" themes in YA. In chapter four, I draw on Andrew Smith's novel *Grasshopper Jungle* (2014) to explore the representation of queerness as a locus of dystopian adolescent experiences and, by hyperbolic extension, the literal end of the world. Smith's novel satirically amplifies the "hideously distorted" darkness critics like Meghan Cox Gurdon attribute to YA, and simultaneously points to how queer sex is a kind of darkness—or invisibility—often "experienced as unbearable," in Lauren Berlant and Lee Edelman's words, by YA and its critics. Austin, *Grasshopper Jungle*'s history-obsessed narrator, records in astonishing detail the world's destruction by mutant bugs, yet Austin's moment of sexual intimacy with his male best friend remains a striking silence in his otherwise scrupulous account. This chapter concludes that *Grasshopper Jungle*'s excessive rendering of YA's storm, stress, darkness and violence ironically makes visible the novel's unwillingness to confront the unbearability associated with queer sex.

It feels important to note that aside from Avery (a trans character in Levithan's *Two Boys Kissing*) and Tracker McDyke (*Caper in the Castro*'s lesbian detective), the protagonists of the texts I examine in these first four chapters are all cisgender males. Furthermore, most of them are White—Levithan is the sole author to provide main characters who are people of color. The whiteness of children's literature as a whole, in fact, is disturbing: in 2015, an alarming 73.3 percent of books for young people centered White characters; the nonprofit and grassroots organization *We Need Diverse Books* was launched in 2014 in an attempt to address this longstanding deficiency.[18] The genre's sexism might be explained (but certainly not excused) by the fact that queer YA has inherited narrative conventions from "Bad Boy" books and the "feral tale," both of which Kidd explores in *Making American Boys* (2004).[19] As he signals, "The twentieth-century feral tale is preoccupied with boys and men," and earlier queer YA texts like Donovan and Holland's novels often rehearse feral tale tropes: young male protagonists have close relations with animals, and form intimate bonds with characters who serve as "foster father[s]" and subvert "the influence of the feral or den mother" (Kidd, *Making* 10).[20] Yet gender representation is not radically superior in the twenty-first century. As Lo reports, from 2003–13 a full 45 percent of queer YA novels featured a male cisgender main character; 33 percent featured cisgender female characters, 6 percent contained multiple LGBT protagonists, 4 percent had transgender protagonists, and 12 percent focused on a cis, straight character who was contending with some sort of LGBT "issue" (typically a queer family member or friend). The gender identification of characters is becoming increasingly diverse: Lo's 2015–2016 statistics include "gender-destabilizing," "nonbinary or genderfluid," and intersex protagonists, who alongside transgender characters make up around 10–15 percent of main characters in those years. However, 55 percent of queer YA protagonists in 2015 were cis males and only 31 percent were cis females ("LGBTQ YA"). In 2016, however, the balance shifted to 38 percent and 43 percent respectively, and these numbers have remained relatively constant: in 2018, 44 percent of protagonists were cis females and 39 percent were cis males. Moreover, Lo notes that 2017–2018 saw an "increasing number of books with multiple LGBTQ main characters . . . and this is often where you'll find transgender characters" ("A Decade of LGBTQ YA").

All of this is to say that, when working on a project that interrogates queer YA from various vantage points, it is often challenging to avoid the predominance of White, cis male characters. This, however, does not excuse the influence of my own desires, anxieties and blind spots on my text curation. As one of my anonymous readers correctly pointed out, I often ask the word "queer" to do some "heavy lifting . . . to cover multiple expressions of queer desire/sexuality" when, in fact, much of this book is a study of "the ways male queerness manifests in YA literature and culture."[21] When I began this research over a decade ago, I wasn't entirely conscious of how queer YA was serving as a kind of wish fulfillment for me, a means of both animating and grieving the gay adolescence I never lived, spent, as it was, deep in the closet. I have written about this elsewhere in an essay called "The Earnest Elfin Dream Gay," in which I describe my own anxious attachment to a particular, problematic gay YA character trope. My relationship to queer YA was clarified, beautifully, through words spoken by Jules Gill-Peterson, author of the extraordinary book *Histories of the Transgender Child*, at a 2019 conference. On the subject of working with problematic archives, Gill-Peterson referenced Sedgwick's classic piece on paranoid and reparative reading practices. "Sometimes we repair the [archival] objects," Gill-Peterson explained, "and sometimes they repair us."[22] Indeed, as I sought to be repaired by the objects of my study, I often connected—unconsciously or otherwise—with those protagonists who most closely resembled me: White, cis male, middle-class, gay. It is a privilege to have access to those mirrors that many others lack.

I therefore agree with my generous reader about, and take responsibility for, the limits of my archive and use of "queer." Nonetheless, I do hope my work will inspire readers to pursue their own intersectional examinations of queer YA, and I hope that the texts and criticism I have selected to represent particular anxieties offer methodologies that might be applied more broadly across other YA texts. I encourage those readers seeking a thorough catalogue of the genre to investigate Jenkins and Cart's *Representing the Rainbow in Young Adult Literature* (2018). This revised and updated version of *The Heart Has Its Reasons* (2006) provides an extensive bibliography of queer YA titles and a lucid history of the genre's development.

In chapters five through seven of this book, however, I shift outside the world of print literature and interrogate a wider variety of texts and characters. These chapters venture into the multimedia realms of Netflix's *Big Mouth*, the *It Gets Better* YouTube project, and those online fandoms that mash up *It Gets Better* with the television show *Glee*, whose peak popularity in 2010–11 coincided with that of Savage and Miller's campaign and the eruption of queer YA discourse and publishing. Chapter five moves us from Andrew Smith's adolescence-as-dystopia to *Big Mouth*'s adolescence-as-horror-show. Like *Grasshopper Jungle*, the popular animated Netflix series provides us with monstrous avatars for the *Sturm und Drang* of adolescence. Instead of horny, rampaging mutant mantises, however, *Big Mouth* offers us monsters, haunted houses, ghosts, and other Gothic tropes as embodiments of those anxieties that surround puberty and its horrifying humiliations. Unlike *Grasshopper Jungle*, however, *Big Mouth* does not relegate queerness to its margins. Quite the opposite: *Big Mouth* universalizes queerness, celebrates the polymorphous perversity of childhood, and uses camp to defuse many of the anxieties that attend representations of adolescent sexuality elsewhere in queer YA. Through its debauched mentor figure, the ghost of Duke Ellington, *Big Mouth* offers us a kind of camp with strong ties to shame—what Stockton calls "dark camp" in *Beautiful Bottom, Beautiful Shame*. Ultimately, I argue, *Big Mouth* unites its young protagonists through shared queer feelings, illustrating how shame and debasement can function as powerful models of relationality.

In chapter six, I take up the *It Gets Better* project as a site of convergence for children's literature and adult fictions. I argue that the circulation and adaptation of cultural texts like *It Gets Better* across and through multiple forms—what I refer to, after Stockton, as a text's "sideways growth"—challenge us to widen our theoretical lenses for the study of YA literature and culture. The book version of *It Gets Better* engages in a repetitive anxious rehearsal of its own metanarrative of "getting better" and renders the project (im)possible, I argue, drawing on Jacqueline Rose's *The Case of Peter Pan*. While *It Gets Better* fails politically, it succeeds nonetheless at generating critical cultural discourse about the adult/ youth address. In chapter seven, I examine how fans deploy characters from *Glee* in the context of *It Gets Better* to imagine scenarios where things do *not* get better, where the project's teleological narrative often fails to describe the lived experiences of queer youth. The traces in material culture of young people writing back to *It Gets Better*, I conclude, illustrate problems with Rose's argument about the untouched "middle space" between adult authors of children's literature and the genre's young audiences.

Throughout, I attempt to dodge the trap of children's literature criticism as described by Karín Lesnik-Oberstein, who argues that critics are often unable to relinquish the constrictive idea that "children's literature criticism is about how to choose books for children" (4). Theories of children's literature are "permitted to question or change everything about the criticism, at least apparently," she writes, "but the final goal of children's literature criticism itself—knowing how to choose the right book for the child—remains constant and unaffected" (5). While a partial aim of this book is to consider how children's literature criticism can benefit from an engagement with texts outside the purview of "children's literature" strictly defined, I do not seek to "improve" the usefulness of children's literature theory for selecting texts for young readers. Instead, I bring theories of children's and YA literature to bear on a video game, animated television show, YouTube project, and on fanfiction to illustrate children's literature's usefulness for reading a wide range of texts. This move springs from anxiety in two ways. I take up anxieties that attempt to keep children's and YA literature contained to a certain space on the shelf, both literally and figuratively, instead allowing children's and YA literature to bleed freely into other genres and forms; and I demonstrate the utility of children's literature and its theories for thinking more broadly about adult concerns and anxieties. In this vein, my conclusion draws on Beverly Lyon Clark's *Kiddie Lit* and a 2014 debate that sprung from the explosive popularity of YA to briefly consider how "immaturity" remains a source of unflagging anxiety for critics concerned about the reading habits of adults. If children's literature has been historically neglected by the academy, as Clark maintains, I argue that it's impossible to do so any longer given that the theoretical lenses of children's literature allow us to explore with such inventiveness the textual and cultural manifestations of that perpetually provocative and anxious relationship between adult and child.

As I conclude, recall Tatar's argument that "adult anxieties" are "edg[ing] out childhood fantasy" in contemporary children's literature. I find this claim intriguing for two reasons. First, without explicitly saying so, Tatar identifies anxiety as a primary locus of concern for children's literature, although in her view adult anxieties should not trump childhood fantasy in such books. Second, and paradoxically, Tatar's polemic against adult anxiety is itself a rehearsal of adult anxiety as it relates to children's literature. In a sense, I agree with Tatar's claim. While she maintains that the anxieties of adult authors are edging out spaces for childhood fantasy in children's literature, I argue that the anxieties of adult critics have edged out and failed to recognize the queer pedagogies and reading practices that cause texts to signify and circulate in ways that defy Tatar's interpretation, and these anxieties have further edged out those early queer YA texts that create space for fantasy and queer reading in excess of whatever stereotypes and negative affect they may also contain. The interventions of Tatar and other contemporary critics are not unlike those of anxious mid-Victorian fairy tale critics who "often found themselves defining the genre by a series of exclusions, by addressing everything the true tale was not: not trivial, not burlesque, not materialistic, not modern, not worldly, not adult" (Schacker 395). While positing a series of normative queer YA traits (hopeful, realistic, etc.), critics concurrently delineate exclusions: (good) queer YA is not hopeless, not stereotypical, not dark, not (too) unrealistic.

Queer YA is at its most fascinating and provocative, I believe, when it is given space to contain texts with visible queernesses *and* those latent queernesses that provide powerful opportunities for reading in all kinds of creative, nonnormative ways; when early titles aren't dismissed wholesale for their association of queerness with loneliness and despair, but are rather mined for the queer relations they represent; and when we leave the genre open for constant redefinition. This is an anxious and risky model: risky because it seeks to find queerness anywhere and everywhere, it threatens to disrupt how we often conceive of queer YA, it reclaims and reinvigorates titles that some critics have deemed harmful by contemporary standards, and it lends queer YA the capacity to disrupt sedimented models for relationality and imagine new ways of being. And these risks, no doubt, will continue to produce anxiety well into the future.

CHAPTER 1

Visibility: Growing Sideways in *I'll Get There. It Better Be Worth the Trip.*[1]

The era of "gay teen books" is over—has been over for several years now. Ask any editor. We're now in the era of "books where the characters happen to be gay." A character's homosexuality is usually no longer the central "problem" for the main character—the thing that's not resolved until the last few pages, or never resolved at all, as in *I'll Get There,* . . . because it couldn't be resolved in the world of 1969. Instead, a character's gayness is usually simply something that reinforces whatever the book's central theme happens to be, the other thing that has to be resolved. It sounds like a small shift, but it's not. It's huge.
—BRENT HARTINGER, *We Got There. It Was Worth the Trip.* (212)

The typical gay young adult fiction protagonist, according to author Brent Hartinger, is all grown up. The stereotypical lonely and troubled teen of yore whose sexual resolution was often perpetually forestalled has matured into today's role model, the character who just "happen[s] to be gay," whose sexuality is but one visible identity component among many. Hartinger conceives of this transition vis-à-vis the titular journey of John Donovan's groundbreaking 1969 novel *I'll Get There. It Better Be Worth the Trip*, which Michelle Ann Abate and Kenneth B. Kidd describe as "the first book for young readers that explicitly addressed the subject of homosexuality" (v).[2] Hartinger's playfully and teleo-logically titled short essay, "We Got There. It Was Worth the Trip," appears as an appendix to the fortieth anniversary edition of Donovan's novel. This reprint was issued just prior to the queer YA boom that began in 2010, thus fittingly permitting the book to retain its status as something of a queer YA urtext. In his essay, Hartinger assures readers that the "getting there" has been gotten, trip concluded, resolution achieved. Today, he infers, the novel itself is significant mostly as nostalgia, a historical document, a stack of faded photographs from the childhood of the now mature genre it spawned, a book that "academics are bound to value," as Rumaan Alam writes in a 2014 *Los Angeles Review of Books* column, "more as a sociological curiosity than [as a] work of literature."

This chapter revisits *I'll Get There*, now over fifty years old, to find value in that which Hartinger and others have critiqued over the years: those invisibilities, ambiguities, and nonteleological ways of conceiving growth that fill the pages of Donovan's novel. *I'll Get There* contains queer relations and scenes of reading that take place in intervals, in delay, in space where characters dilly-dally, dodge, and avoid growing toward a sedimented iteration of "gayness," to use Hartinger's word. Donovan's protagonist resists what Kathryn Bond Stockton calls "the vertical, forward-motion metaphor of growing up" (*Queer Child* 11), suggesting that this novel—so often lambasted for its hopelessness, stereotypes, and omissions—is a lot queerer than it may initially appear, and much more relevant to contemporary notions of sexuality and queerness than Hartinger's comments suggest.

Hartinger's version of queer YA's generic maturity, the "huge" shift that has taken place, rests on the assumption that certain kinds of contemporary visibility trump, ontologically speaking, the lack of sexual resolution in previous novels and the way in which those narratives position sexuality as a thematic problem. For Hartinger, as for many critics of queer YA, the value of contemporary novels lies largely in their rendering of unambiguous and unproblematic sexual identity. Indeed, as popular interest in queer YA has snowballed, so have critical opinions about what, precisely, these novels should make visible and what kind of pedagogical work they should aspire to do, and much of this criticism uses Donovan's novel as a springboard. In his 1994 essay "A Portrait of the Adolescent as a Young Gay," Kirk Fuoss points out how an increase in teen novels with "homosexual incidents or self-identified homosexual characters" does not diminish "the political implications of presences and absences" (163). As examples of significant absences, Fuoss draws on Donovan's novel and Isabelle Holland's *The Man Without a Face* (1972). Fuoss indicates that in both of these texts, "physical acts of male homosexuality (including hugging, kissing, and holding hands) are more often than not presented as occurring off-stage and out of sight" (163). "Holland's novel, like Donovan's," Fuoss maintains, "grants physical expressions of homosexual love all the presence of an ellipsis" (164). Moreover, Fuoss laments the lack of sexual resolution in the thirteen gay "problem-realism" texts included in his study, tracing the major characters' "trajectory of sexual identity, beginning with their sexual identity at the opening of the novel and ending with their sexuality at the close of the novel" (167). Fuoss notes regretfully that of the twenty-one "sexually suspect" characters he examines, a mere eleven "are self-identified as gay when their novel concludes" (167). The rest, he points out, lie somewhere on a spectrum between "not gay" and "truly ambiguous," with one character self-defining as "bisexual" (167). The primary problem, for Fuoss, is what Hartinger claims has been remedied in contemporary texts: a lack of visible, coherent manifestations of gay identity that are ultimately articulated as such by protagonists.

More recently, in an essay published in 2009, Thomas Crisp takes a somewhat different approach to the conversation about queer visibility in YA, interrogating the problematic literary tropes that associate realism with homophobia. Crisp points out that authors often use homophobic characters and themes to structure "realistic" stories about queer youth; such "realism" serves to perpetuate the troublesome notion that young queers inevitably will be subjected to various forms of violence. The problem, Crisp concludes, is that "because intolerance is so regularly heard and seen, readers and producers of children's and adolescent texts are conditioned to accept homophobia and homophobic discourse as a 'normal' part of life" ("From Romance" 339). In a 2011 article, Corrine Wickens addresses concerns similar to Crisp's, arguing that young adult authors often include homophobic antagonists "in order to problematize homophobia," but the result is that homophobia remains entrenched as their novels' central problem (153).

However, when critics assume that young readers learn about sexuality and queerness from books in a unilateral way (book contains visible representation of queerness, representation teaches the reader), they risk positing a reductive didactic relationship between text and reader. In other words, it is perhaps too easy to presume that because a book contains certain representations it will necessarily teach readers specific lessons about homophobia, identity, and/or queerness, or compel them to behave in certain ways. Lydia Kokkola addresses this issue in her study of sexuality in adolescent literature, noting that "there is no credible evidence that young readers will automatically fall into the identification fallacy, and emulate fictional characters" (161). Elsewhere, Crisp remarks that "accurate depictions of GLBTQ people are profoundly important for youth of all sexual identities," taking for granted that "accurate" might mean something radically different depending on the reader ("Trouble" 219). Claims to "accuracy," moreover, like Cart and Jenkins's call for authenticity in queer YA, require other representations to be held up as inaccurate, unrealistic, and pedagogically dangerous. Such representations, as in Hartinger's essay, tend to be older works that are deployed to shore up the authenticity and pedagogical efficacy of more recent titles, but rarely do critics account for alternative ways of reading queer visibility in books from *I'll Get There*'s era.[3]

I think that Crisp, Cart and Jenkins, Wickens, and others are right to highlight the dangers and risks of constantly representing homophobia and anti-queer violence on the pages of YA. Moreover, following Fuoss, I believe that absenting visibly queer characters and physical affection from such fiction speaks to systemic anxieties about the political and pedagogical implications of representing nonnormative sex and sexuality in books for young people. However, I want to shift the focus of conversations about visibility, realism, and their potential didactic effects to consider the multiple readerly possibilities presented by Donovan's novel. In addition to readings inflected by contemporary queer theory, I'm thinking of alternative reading strategies that include what Hurley in "The Perversions of Children's Literature" calls lingering in a text's "murky middle": a way of reading whereby readers disregard parts of a narrative that do not serve a particular interpretation or affective response—typically endings—while choosing to prioritize and dwell in other moments in the story (124). It is my contention that *I'll Get There* contains something of a guidebook for such lingerings, as well as instructions for reading the novel itself subversively and in defiance of interpretations that anxiously dismiss its (lack of) queer representations and relations as antiquated and potentially harmful.

Hartinger's declaration of the end of an "era of gay teen books" strikes me as a concomitant push for an end to ambiguous and occluded sexuality in young adult literature. As Hartinger maintains, today's characters simply "happen to be gay" (212), and their sexual identity should be writ large, transparently, and unproblematically on the pages of the novels in which they exist, leaving space for problems unrelated to "homosexual incidents." To supplement those critics who focus on the pedagogical dangers of omissions and ambiguities, I want to ask: what do omissions, invisibilities, and ambiguities allow and invite? Here, I refer not only to the glossing over of sexual encounters in fiction for the young, but also to moments such as the much-derided vague and "anticlimactic" (Cart and Jenkins 12) conclusion to Donovan's novel; "this ending," writes Alam, "which probably made the book more palatable to its contemporary readership, might gall some today."[4] These are moments, I contend, that invite readers to shift our focus, asking us to consider the potential queerness of *not* growing into a coherent gay identity, instead of focusing principally on how young people might learn—for better or for worse—from certain forms of "(un)realistic" or "(in)authentic" visibility.

As opposed to embodying a potentially harmful, retro version of gayness, Donovan's protagonist in my reading engages in the kind of "sideways relations" that Stockton theorizes in *The Queer Child*, those cultivated by children as they "approach their destinations, delay; swerve, delay; ride on a metaphor they tend to make material and so imagine relations of their own" (15). This notion of delay is central to how Stockton "prick[s]" the progressive and teleological narrative of "growing up" that dominates the popular imagination (*Queer Child* 11). En route to adulthood, she argues, children desire and form relations in ways that are not necessarily aligned with the normative trajectory toward reproductive heterosexual adulthood; Stockton describes these experiences and desires as moments of delay and spatializes them as sideways growth. "To be sure," she emphasizes about delay, queer adults in particular

> remember desperately feeling (when they were children) there was simply nowhere to grow, feeling a frightening, heightened sense of growing toward a question mark. Or growing up in haze. Or hanging in suspense—even wishing time would stop, or just twist sideways, so that they wouldn't have to advance to new or further scenes of trouble. (*Queer Child* 3)

This richly affective passage should recall, as outlined in the introduction, the temporality of anxiety: in particular, Adam Phillips's description of worrying as, simultaneously, "a way of looking forward to things . . . a conscious conviction that a future exists, one in which something terrible might happen" (56) and "an attempt to arrest the passage of time" (48). Although the queer child's desire for delay can emerge from this anxiety of growing into an unimaginable form of adulthood, Stockton further illustrates how the experience of delay also can be quite enjoyable: "Lingering," she writes, citing Freud, "is pleasurable 'for quite a time' and seems for even 'normal people' to 'find a place' 'alongside' getting to the ultimate goal" (*Queer Child* 25). Playing around *while* growing up—what Stockton calls the "sideways movements or suspensions in relation to the road of copulation to be followed"—is permitted, in other words, but the anticipated normative endpoint, at least in Freud's account, is always adult reproductive heterosexuality (*Queer Child* 25).

But what happens if Freud's "ultimate goal" is never attained? What if a queer child prefers the perversion of diversion—the pleasures, temporalities, and "ironic hopes," in Phillips's words, of its attendant anxieties—to whatever the question mark at the end of growing up might signify? Many YA critics expect an endpoint, but in their case, this telos is marked by the arrival of characters with a stable sense of LGBT identity. Donovan's protagonist, however, takes pleasure in various forms of delay that resist this progressive narrative of growth and development into coherent gay selfhood. The title of Donovan's novel is an unfulfilled promise, as we never learn where or what "there" is, only what the trip entails, and this particular trip is filled with delay, metaphor, and sideways relations with and through a reading of *Julius Caesar*, a phallic dog, and a lesson in reading for a text's "murky middle."

I'll Get There. It Better Be Worth the Trip. features two protagonists—introverted Davy and Altschuler, the charismatic "kid philosopher," as Davy describes him—whose relationship ignites during a class production of *Julius Caesar* (197). Davy and Altschuler first meet after Davy's grandmother, who raised him, passes away, and he is sent to live in New York with his alcoholic mother. Between his troubled mother and his distant father, Davy's closest friend prior to Altschuler is his precious dachshund, Fred. The two adolescents form their initial bond over *Caesar*, and the play's theme of betrayal also frames their relationship, which becomes physical when the boys kiss and again later when Altschuler spends the night at Davy's house (the sleepover specifics remain vague). Davy struggles with the event, narrating, "There's nothing wrong with Altschuler and me, is there? I know it's not like making out with a girl. It's just something that happened. It's not dirty, or anything like that. It's all right, isn't it?" (161). Shortly thereafter, Davy and Altschuler sample some of Davy's mother's whiskey and end up napping on the floor in close proximity. When the mother returns home and finds the boys asleep together, she assumes that she's catching them post-coitus and flies into a panicked rage. In the confusion that follows, she takes Fred outside; the dog slips off his leash and into the street, where he is struck by a car and killed. Davy becomes furious with Altschuler, interpreting Fred's death as a direct outcome of their tryst. Eventually, Donovan's novel "ends a bit anticlimactically," as Cart and Jenkins describe it, "with the two boys agreeing that they can 'respect' each other" (12).

Kathleen T. Horning writes that at the time of its publication, *I'll Get There* "was both highly regarded and recommended for young readers" and earned notices on the *New York Times* and *School Library Journal* Best of 1969 Book Lists (225). It's only recently, she continues, that "critics have been less kind to the book, pointing out that it falls into the same trap many early gay teen novels did, which was to punish the main character with a car accident leading to death or serious injury" (225). Horning further mentions that critics fault the book for "depicting gayness as a choice or suggesting that being gay is just a passing phase" (225), and emphasizing Davy's guilt after his elliptical sleepover with Altschuler, "especially when [Davy] feels responsible for his dog's death as a result" (226). Indeed, Frances Hanckel and John Cunningham's 1976 study identifies the ostensibly harmful "salient characteristics" of the first four YA novels with gay themes, including *I'll Get There*: "Being gay has no lasting significance and/or costs someone a terrible price. Not one plot has a happy ending in which the protagonists meet hostile pressures successfully and go on to find fulfillment and a supporting relationship based on love and respect." They conclude that "for gay adolescents the negative impact of these novels cannot be minimized" (532–33).[5] Cart and Jenkins's more recent critique is along these same lines. They point out how "a cause and effect relationship is implied between homosexuality and being the child of divorced parents" (14) and argue that the book's "most distressing" aspect is "the close—even casual—connection [the novel] makes between homosexuality and death" (15). Elsewhere, Roberta Seelinger Trites claims that "the novel implies that Davy's mother has somehow driven him to homosexual sex" (104); likewise, Kokkola argues that Davy "is characterized as a boy who has been damaged by his inadequate parents," and his relationship with Altschuler, in addition to being represented as "just a passing phase," is also "cast in the same light as bestiality . . . intrinsically wrong and utterly deviant" (140–41). The novel "suggests that homosexuality is," Kokkola concludes, "in some unspecified way, a result of poor upbringing and inadequate parental love" (140). In perhaps the most spirited critique of *I'll Get There*, British critic and novelist James Rees writes, "Donovan suggests that teenage homosexuality is so totally unacceptable, socially and psychologically, that any young homosexual is likely to have his fears and worries increased rather than reduced, and the prejudice of the heterosexual reader against homosexuals is reinforced" (quoted in Cart and Jenkins 14). While Cart and Jenkins find Rees's critique "a bit harsh," they concur that "it's hard to imagine any gay or lesbian teen finding much comfort or support in this novel" (14). The overall verdict from many critics, then, is that *I'll Get There*'s approach to sexuality—although groundbreaking for its time—is outdated and intensely problematic in the troubling, contradictory, and ultimately unresolved way in which it deals with Davy's experiences.

I'll Get There does indeed establish a number of stereotypical gay problem novel tropes and suggest an unfortunate causal connection between homosexuality and death, sadness, and loneliness. But while the novel may not satisfy the expectations of many contemporary YA critics, these same critics overlook the multiple queernesses offered by the book. We can also read *I'll Get There* as a story about Davy's desire for relations not reducible to "coming out" as gay, and his anxious relationship to the queer question mark toward which he is growing. Critics are quick to label Davy as "lonely" (as he is described on the book's back cover) or even, in Hartinger's words, "emotionally repressed" (204) and demonstrating "emotional disengagement with other human beings" (206). While we might infer that Davy is lonely due to an overall absence of friends in his life, he seems quite content with the sideways companionship of his dog, Fred, who serves as phallic surrogate for the queer question mark of Davy's (proto)sexuality. Theirs is a sideways relationship based on the temporality of anxiety, a central rhythm for Davy and the novel's other queer double-takes, including its exercises in reading for the "murky middle."

Recall Stockton's vivid description of what it feels like to grow toward a question mark, anxiously desiring the sideways twisting of time or its complete stoppage. Davy evinces such powerful desires for delay, stasis, and dwelling throughout the novel. This is a boy, after all, who befriends a stuffed coyote while visiting the Museum of Civilization with his father:

> I put my hand up to the glass in front of the coyote.
> "Hello," I say.
> "He's stuffed, Davy."
> "Sure, I know."
> I put my face against the glass.
> "Hello."
> Father walks away.
> "Hello, coyote," I say again. "What was your name?"
> The coyote just looks at me.
> "You must have had a name. You could have been a pet. Some Indian kid's pet. Were you?"
> He doesn't move, but I won't take my eyes off him. There's no one else in the corridor with the stuffed animals now.
> "Coyote," I say, "do you want to be petted?" Of course he just looks at me.
> "Do you?"
> I think he sees me. Honestly. There is something in his eyes which makes me believe that he understands that I am there and talking to him as a friend. I swear that he understands that I am his friend. (Donovan 67–68)

Here is Davy's ideal friend: one that is stuffed and static, that "sees" and "understands" Davy's longing for the same kind of stasis that it makes manifest. The repetition in the last two sentences—"that he understands that I am"—stretches the moment from fleeting communion into one that lingers, or "doesn't move," much like the coyote and Davy, the former stuffed, the latter still and alone with hand and face pressed up against the glass. Moreover, Davy imagines the coyote as "some Indian kid's pet," projecting onto the animal a kind of double stasis: the coyote is both literally frozen and preserved as an exoticized object of American prehistory.[6] Here, Davy demonstrates desires for delay and a backwards turn to a time far from his current position and trajectory.

However, it is Fred—our hero's other, more intimate canine companion—who remains the central vessel of Davy's longing for delay. For if Davy feels himself growing toward a question-marked "there" because of his desire for Altschuler, his present (the "trip") is defined in part by his eroticized sideways relation with a phallic dog that both foresees and forestalls his queer future. Davy and Fred have roots in a lengthy history of fictional child-and-dog relationships, "feral tales," and animal stories that have been explored by numerous scholars. Kokkola dedicates an entire chapter of her monograph to representations of sexual wildness in literature for young people. In "The Beastly Bestiality of Adolescent Desire," she unpacks the frequent, anxious displacement of teenage carnality onto animal figures that function to contain adolescent sexuality while simultaneously marking it as "wild, untameable, and decidedly more base than that of adults" (138). Kidd, on the other hand, illustrates how the feral tale's "abandoned boy is nourished rather than devoured by the beast, setting the stage for animal bonding as a theme in more modern accounts," which I would argue include Donovan's novel (*Making* 9). Moreover, Donovan's coyote scene also echoes conventions of the "Bad Boy book," a cousin of the feral tale, which "celebrate[s]," according to Kidd, "the pre- or early pubescent boy" as "primitive" and "attuned to nature" (*Making* 53). Davy's intimate relationship with Fred speaks to the boy's "natural" attachments, while his attraction to the (formerly) wild coyote—and Davy's association of this coyote with Indigeneity—links both Davy and the animal to notions of the feral and, problematically, "primitiveness," albeit a primitiveness that has been civilized through its containment and display in a museum.

In the chapter "A Boy and His Dog" from his 2009 study *Melancholia and Maturation*, Eric L. Tribunella theorizes "the enforced attachment-sacrifice paradigm" involving fictional canine companions (45). According to Tribunella, the "intense affectional attachment" between a (typically male) protagonist and his dog is, in fact, "a form of childhood sexuality that is often overlooked as such" (30). A boy's successful transition into adulthood and subsequent abandonment of what Freud might describe as a kind of perverse lingering with a canine friend, however, entails the ritualistic sacrifice of the animal. For Tribunella, killing a dog is "a way of (re)forming social subjects that are properly gendered and sexualized," of ushering in, in other words, appropriate and acceptable forms of heterosexual adulthood (30). Similarly, Kidd points out that the Bad Boy book's protagonist is ultimately compelled to "outgrow and incorporate his variously primitive tendencies" (*Making* 53).

In *The Queer Child*, Stockton also thinks through the affective intensity of animal-child bonds, arguing that these relations allow for "children's motions inside their delay, making delay a sideways growth the child in part controls for herself, in ways confounding . . . her future" (90). For Stockton, "the dog is a living, growing metaphor . . . for the child's own propensities to stray by making the most of its sideways growth. The dog is . . . the child's companion in queerness" (90). The queer child often enters "into an interval of animal," as Stockton writes (89), but Davy's dachshund is a different breed of interval-agent from Stockton's and Tribunella's dogs: Fred acts as a vessel for Davy's delay but also propels him forward into other queer relations. Fred is undoubtedly Davy's eroticized boyhood companion, but the dachshund departs from Tribunella's figuration and the Bad Boy genre by luring Davy into queer relations as opposed to enabling his growth into heterosexuality. Indeed, Fred "acts as the communicational medium for [Davy and Altschuler] in all the events that are narrated," as Kokkola points out (139). Moreover, Fred's martyrdom does not initiate Davy into adulthood; instead, he continues to crave delay while only ambivalently and ambiguously contemplating his future.

On numerous occasions, Davy's first-person descriptions of Fred are overtly sexual, reinforcing the dachshund's status as a kind of substitute penis, a place-holder for the real thing.[7] In transparently erotic terms, Davy recounts how he received Fred as a gift from his grandmother:

> when I came home from school, I heard a funny noise in the kitchen. I ran back to see what it was. There was Grandmother bending over a box filled with news-papers, stroking about ten inches of black dachshund. It was Fred. She picked him up and handed him to me.
>   "Happy birthday, David."
>   My eyes must have gotten as wide as two tennis balls. I reached over to get Fred. He was wiggling in Grandmother's hands. As I held him to me he squirted all over my jacket. Grandmother and I laughed. Fred, the nut, he just licked away at my face. (15)

The whole scene is indisputably coital, from Davy's grandmother's "bending over" to fluff or "strok[e]" the "ten inches" of "black" penis-puppy, to Davy's ecstatic response, to Fred's squirming and "squirting" when he first makes contact with Davy. Given racist Euro-American colonial ideology that hypersexualizes black-ness, Donovan's inclusion of the penultimate signifier "black" comes to connote a heightened eroticism; the racialization and thus deepened eroticization of Fred-as-penis recalls bell hooks's interrogation of the "unusual obsession with black male genitalia" on the part of White men, who have historically affiliated Black men with the "sexual primitive" (63).[8] The entire sequence establishes not only Davy's intimate sideways relation with his dog/lover, but also how the penis-puppy (a dachshund, to top it off: the breed frequently referred to as a "wiener dog") anticipates Davy's orientation toward a question mark that may itself be phallus-shaped. Davy's narration, in other words, transforms Fred into his lover and allows Davy to delay the arrival of a human male lover (namely, Altschuler) while experiencing and describing a level of intimacy with his canine companion that does not necessitate a confrontation with the looming question mark of the titular "there."

Elsewhere, Davy describes sweet-talk with Fred as "lovemaking" (52) and the dog's excitement at seeing him as "a state of ecstasy" (147), while his cuddle sessions with Fred are recounted in such a way that, taken out of context, they could be (mis)interpreted as describing a human lover: "[Fred] looks up at me, his dumb face begging for a kiss, so I bend over and pull him into my lap. He cradles his head under my chin, and in two seconds his eyes are closed and he's breathing heavily with the kind of instant and total sleep Fred seems able to fall into every time he's contented" (10). Here, Davy narrates with an attention to intimate detail otherwise absent; his voice during moments of contact with Altschuler remains aloof, while his intimacy with Fred is fluidly and richly described.

Ironically yet fittingly, the same Fred who enables Davy's delay also propels him forward into Altschuler's arms: in this moment, the link between penis-dog and male lover is firmly established. For it is Fred who seduces Davy and Altschuler into kissing for the first time, luring the boys into a human/canine ménage à trois that irreversibly reorients Davy's sideways movements and forces him to confront the question mark in spite of his attachments to delay. The kiss that broke new ground in YA occurs after Davy and Altschuler romp with Fred around Davy's mother's apartment, playing a game of tug-of-war that culminates in the boys lying side-by-side on the floor. Davy initially narrates the experience in staccato sentences that suggest a nervous heartbeat, syntax that stands in sharp contrast to the easy comfort with which he details his intimate moments with Fred:

> I close my eyes. I feel unusual. Lying there. Close to Altschuler. I don't want to get up. I want to stay lying there. I feel a slight shiver and shake from it. Not cold though. Unusual. So I open my eyes. Altschuler is still lying there too. He looks at me peculiarly, and I'm sure I look at him the same way. Suddenly Fred jumps in between us. First he licks my face, then Altschuler's, and back and forth between us. I think that this unusual feeling I have will end, but in a minute the three of us are lying there, our heads together. I guess I kiss Altschuler and he kisses me.... It just happens. And when it stops we sit up and turn away from each other. Fred has trotted off, maybe tired of both of us by now. (149–50)

Leading up to the kiss, Davy narrates with his characteristic penchant for repetition seen elsewhere in the novel: the recurrence of "lying there" and "unusual" suggests his desire to linger, to stay "lying there," not wanting to "get up" or move. Enter Fred, child's companion in queerness, who "jumps in" between the boys, disrupting Davy and Altschuler's locked gaze and the syntax of Davy's narration. Davy's sentences lengthen and his repetition diminishes; delay becomes motion and stasis fluidity, highlighting the temporal tension that underscores the entire novel and, fittingly, situating Fred in the middle of it all.

The production of *Julius Caesar* that initiates Davy and Altschuler's relationship and precedes this kiss triggers one of their many arguments that take place throughout the novel, many of which are debates about reading and interpretation that rely on turns to several historical texts. The two boys quarrel over who should be considered the protagonist in *Androcles and the Lion* (145) and spar over the catalyst of Fred's death, with Davy insisting, "It was because of what we did, you dumb bastard!" while Altschuler maintains that "It had nothing to do with us" (185). At one point early in the novel, Altschuler revealingly defines himself as an "agnostic" (84); like the novel itself, and his many disputes with Davy, Altschuler will never arrive at a definitive conclusion. When his class is rehearsing for *Julius Caesar*, Altschuler expresses his desire to read the play against the grain, resistantly: he wants to play Brutus as a hero and have Davy portray Caesar as a loathsome villain. Further, Altschuler proposes that the class truncate the narrative in such a way that Caesar's murder becomes the play's conclusion, so the audience would never witness Brutus's downfall and eventual death. "Altschuler spent so much time convincing everyone that Caesar was an old bastard," Davy narrates, "that the good-looking kid playing Mark Antony, who was dumb, couldn't think up any reasons for honoring Caesar's memory. The play would end with my death, everyone agreed. Everyone but [the teacher] Miss Stuart" (109). In addition to agreeing to an unconventional representation of its main characters, the class further consents to shorten the story in such a way that it ends with the middle, causing the narrative to signify quite differently.

The production of *Caesar* is followed by a dream sequence that takes place, notably, in the middle of the novel, immediately after the play and shortly before Davy and Altschuler kiss for the first time. This scene moves with the same anxious temporality and rhythm as Davy and Fred: a tension between delay and forward motion, sideways relations and forward growth toward a looming question mark; between a focus on the "trip" versus an investment in a destination, a "there." Davy narrates:

> I was walking along the beach at home, my real home, and I never seemed to stop walking. The beach isn't that long in real life, so it wasn't my very own and familiar beach. It was an imaginary beach. But I thought it was the very one I used to take Fred to. At least I thought it was that beach in the beginning of the dream because naturally the little bastard was trotting along beside me. Otherwise I wouldn't have been at the beach. It was late in the year, and the only time I went there was to walk Fred. So the dream started out to be a recollection of the good, free walks I used to have with Fred. We started out OK. (119–20)

Here, Davy takes a long time to go precisely nowhere as he establishes the setting for his dream. Just as he "never seemed to stop walking," he never seems to stop trying to determine what beach was represented in his dream and why. His repetition of the word "beach," the circular structure of the paragraph (he begins with a description of the dream, and then returns to "we started out" at the end), and the way his narration starts and stalls repeatedly all evince the familiar temporal tensions of the novel's queer double-take. Davy continues,

> But after a while, as the beach got longer and longer and less the beach I knew but some other beach, *the* beach, the one that rims the beautiful ocean that people think about, the one without seaweed and jellyfish, poor Fred wasn't in the picture anymore. I was. Just me. . . . I took off my clothes in the dream and then ran along the beach. I ran along the very rim of the tide, and it became windy and the sand blew all over me. I threw myself on the beach because the sand began to sting me as it blew against my body. . . . I think the wind stopped . . . [and] I did get up, and I did walk back, and Fred did trot into the picture I was dreaming about, and the beach did get smaller, and I must have found my clothes, and it all came out OK in the end. (120–21; emphasis in original)

In this latter portion of the dream description, we get much of the same starting-and-stopping, repetitive narration as we do in the first part: "the beach" is repeated, as is the verb "run" in various forms, yet the circular nature of the dream (always returning to Fred and being "OK" at the beginning and the end) gives a sense of motion without progress, of delayed movement, of a trip that dwells in the present, never arriving *there*, wherever there may be.

Also key is the way in which Davy introduces the dream, with instructions for readers about how they should read it, if at all: "The next part isn't part of the story," Davy claims, "so it is all right to skip over it. It's about what happened to me inside. . . . I dreamed some of these things, and some of them are real. It doesn't matter which are which" (119). Hartinger addresses this moment when he writes, "Unreliable narrator that [Davy] is, we ignore him, because we know instinctively that we're about to hear something that's key" (206). But what if we don't ignore Davy? What if we actually listen to him and choose to disregard certain parts of the text such as the dream sequence, Davy's mother's catastrophic negligence of Fred, or the novel's ambiguous ending? What if the narrative is actually encouraging readers to do precisely what Altschuler does with *Julius Caesar*: hack, slash, truncate, dwell, and delay as they see fit?

In her elaboration of the "murky middle," Hurley asks of Louisa May Alcott's classic novel, "What might it mean to read *Little Women* for what I like to think of as the murky middle of the book—those delicious places where Jo has fully organized an alternative world for herself where she alone gets to play the parts of boys and speaks in slang?" (124). This, I argue, is the kind of reading that *I'll Get There* invites: a dwelling in the narrative's center, broadly speaking (recall that the beach dream takes place in the middle of the narrative); a delayed or repetitive reading of moments that are most pleasurable (Davy's relationship with Fred, his exploratory intimacy with Altschuler); and an Altschulerian truncation of those points that the reader feels are like the second half of *Julius Caesar*—that is, irrelevant. Given that so many critics take issue with the ambiguity and seeming negativity of *I'll Get There*'s ending, what would it mean to disregard the ending entirely? Not only does Donovan's novel invite readers to do so, it literally shows us how through its deployment of Shakespeare's play.

When he initiates Davy and Altschuler's kiss, Fred sets in motion the events that will bring about his own death: Davy's sleepover with Altschuler that results in more intimacy (details omitted), the catastrophic incident with the whiskey, and the untimely walk with Davy's mother that sees Fred crushed under the wheels of a car, "not making the slightest move now," as Davy describes it; "He's not moving at all. I can feel him not moving" (176). Dead Fred comes to embody the stasis he has hitherto represented as metaphor. Although Davy can still "feel him," the sensation is no longer a sideways motion, but rather the stillness of death. While critics argue that the effect of Fred's death is to posit tragedy as the inevitable consequence of queer desire, or in Kokkola's words, that queer love is ultimately "transient" (140), the dog's demise also functions to expedite Davy's trajectory toward the novel's titular "there," eliminating the primary sideways relation that permits Davy's delay and forcing him to confront—at least momentarily—the queer question mark of his desire for Altschuler.

At the end of the novel, in spite of the elimination-castration of his most loving lateral relation and his quasi-reconciliation with Altschuler, Davy's forward motion remains hesitant. The story's end does not bring a "there," but simply more "trip." Readers bear witness to the return of the stuffed coyote, the novel's other motionless canine, this time with Davy in the company of a frustrated and disturbed Altschuler. When Altschuler insists that Davy shouldn't talk to the coyote, Davy retorts, "What the hell do you mean I shouldn't talk to stuffed animals? Look at that animal. Look into his eyes. He sees me. He understands me" (195–96). Altschuler points out that the coyote is dead and stuffed and has glass eyes, but Davy insists, "He's a pet. He was somebody's pet, and he will be a pet forever. Why don't you get lost in some dinosaur bones if you don't want to look at the coyote?" "You're nuts to think stuffed animals understand you," Altschuler concludes (195–96).

While Kokkola argues that this moment "breaks the tension and enables the boys to behave like friends again," I maintain that this isn't entirely the case (140).

Altschuler chastises Davy for his attachment to the stuffed coyote, while Davy insists doggedly on a mutual understanding between the permanently static animal and himself. It is significant that this episode occurs in the novel's last four pages and remains, in my view, unresolved. Altschuler does not succeed in convincing Davy that relationships with humans are superior to relationships with dead animals, and Fred's death does not reorient the trajectory of Davy's sideways growth. Immediately following the coyote incident, Davy and Altschuler discuss "this queer business" and the "peculiar night" that they shared (Donovan 197). While Davy draws a connection between their encounter and Fred's death, Altschuler replies, "Go ahead and feel guilty if you want to. I don't. . . . If you think it's dirty or something like that, I wouldn't do it again. If I were you" (197).

After a pause, Davy moves the conversation from the stasis of the coyote to the forward motions of growing up; "I guess some day we'll be old, like our parents," he says suddenly (198). The novel ends shortly thereafter with its much-criticized ambiguous ending:

> "Who do you want to be like?" Altschuler asks.
> "Me," I guess. "And guys like my grandmother. There was a great old girl. She was real stiff by nature, but she had respect for me, and I respected her. It was the same way with Fred too. We respected each other."
> "I respected Wilkins," Altschuler says [referring to his best friend who died of cancer].
> "I guess we could respect each other," I say. "Do you think so?"
> "Sure," Altschuler says. (198–99)

A perceptive reader might recognize that the boys have just used the word "respect" to describe their most intimate and loving relationships, which deserve far more effusive terms. Respect, here, means far more than it seems. But regardless, thus ends "the trip": a boy dwells among his sideways relations with a stuffed coyote, a "stiff" departed grandmother, and a deceased dachshund, while anxiously acknowledging that he will grow forward into old age; and two boy-lovers agree to "respect" each other when, in fact, they probably mean something else entirely. The novel concludes with the promise of more "trip" and nothing close to a "there," an unresolved and unresolvable juxtaposition of stasis and growth that leaves dangling a big, queer question mark.

Julius Caesar, Fred the dachshund, and Davy's dream all have the stall-and-start temporality of anxiety in common. *Caesar* is truncated so that it exists in a perpetual state of delay: its ending never arrives; it lingers in its own murky middle. The same could be said for *I'll Get There* itself, as its own ambiguous ending feels severed and incomplete, a "trip" with no "there." Alam suggests that Donovan's title, in fact, "completes the text." "The choice [Davy] makes," he writes, "is not between hetero- and homosexuality; rather, it's the choice to take his particular trip through life a bit more slowly. He'll get there, to queerness, when he's good and ready." Similarly, Kokkola speculates that the "'There' of Donovan's title is presumably adulthood. 'Getting There' is presented as the reward for the terrible trip one must make through adolescence to achieve this goal.... There/Adulthood is apparently a stable place where the causes of turmoil ... are no longer a problem" (110). To posit queerness and adulthood as transparent, "stable" endpoints, however, is to reinscribe a linear temporality that the novel subverts so well. Davy exists in an anxious space where his coming out and growing up are perpetually postponed, a space that sees him navigate sideways relations with a dog that launches him into a forward-oriented relation with another boy, while Davy nonetheless still craves delay and enacts this desire through the form of his narration. This tense temporal orientation disorients the normative, linear trajectory of growing up and coming out, enabling the text's queernesses to proliferate in tandem with the multiplicity of Davy's desires, pleasures, and longings.

In reading *I'll Get There*'s lack of resolution as paradigmatic of an underdeveloped and homophobic queer YA, critics ignore how Davy embodies motions, relations, temporalities, and desires that resonate with contemporary queer theory and suggest a model for creative and potentially subversive reading practices. As Heather Love reminds us, turning back to the negative affect of older queer texts can reshape our politics of the present in powerful and productive ways. Revisiting *I'll Get There* with an eye to its many queernesses exposes how the novel simultaneously establishes and undermines conventions of the post-Stonewall gay young adult problem novel. The novel also upends the boy-and-his-dog story that typically purchases, in Tribunella's words, "potential heterosexuality ... at the expense of great trauma" (31), while also spurning those conventions of feral and Bad Boy tales that would otherwise have Davy outgrow and relinquish his "primitive" attachment to the stuffed coyote. Through his refusal to come out, straighten up, or even fully acknowledge that his trip might have a "there," Davy defies critical imperatives to reflect any coherent sexual identity, choosing instead to dwell in the pleasurable perversions of queer childhood. The novel further invites its readers to linger in its "bestial relationship"—a kind of "social sodomy," according to Tribunella—and, like other boy-and-dog stories, take pleasure in "all that it offers as an exemplar of a secure, successful, and pleasurable attachment in contrast to the typically more embattled attachments of life" (46). Davy begins and ends the novel "at" queerness; queerness permeates the novel; queerness bleeds outside the time and place of the novel, which dwells perpetually in its own incompleteness, invisibilities, murky middle, and never-ending trip.

As something of a queer YA urtext, Donovan's novel has twice established for better or worse critical understandings of the genre's conventions—first in 1969, and again with its rerelease in 2009. Through its (in)visibilities, temporalities, and representations of reading, however, *I'll Get There. It Better Be Worth the Trip.* also functions to shape the affective contours of queer YA and, as a result, many of the themes discussed throughout this book. Over the next chapter in particular, I will return to the role of elliptical queer sex, queer reading, and modes of sexual being in excess of gay identity as represented in queer YA and its anxious criticism. And as queer theories of childhood and children's literature grow richer by the moment and we approach the next anniversary of Donovan's novel, the queer trip taken by Altschuler, *Julius Caesar*, a stuffed coyote, Davy, and his phallic dog warrants retreading, again and again.

CHAPTER 2

Risk: The Queer Pedagogy of
The Man Without a Face[1]

In his 2005 study *The New Gay Teenager*, Ritch Savin-Williams traces the "invention" of gay youth in the 1970s and 80s, and the subsequent emergence of what he calls the "suicidal script" of gay youth identity through the 80s and 90s (58). When medical and sociological researchers first began documenting the issues confronting gay teens, Savin-Williams explains, the subjects of their studies were mostly homeless, hustlers, delinquents, and other "at-risk" adolescents (62). As a result, gay youth came to signify as "martyr-target-victims," a trope insisting that when young people live openly as queer, they are incontrovertibly risking a barrage of homo/transphobic violence and laundry list of harmful pathological conditions (Rofes 42). When the *It Gets Better* project was launched in 2010, these narratives began circulating with increased intensity and reach. In his 2012 study, Rob Cover confirms that researchers frame discussions of queer youth suicide "through a risk discourse, which is often derived from assumptions which drive quantitative research and statistics that have formed a significant part of the methodological work of suicidologists" (1). In order to obtain funding for necessary public services, researchers emphasize vulnerability and risk, and the martyr-target-victim narrative endures in discourse about young queers.

In this chapter, I illustrate how queer YA might provide richer—and potentially more productive—versions of risk than the limited yet pervasive narrative of "at-risk." Like Cover, I want to challenge the idea that "risk," when associated with queer youth, necessarily entails harm and violence. Whereas Cover argues that "we should avoid indulging the view that . . . risk is produced simply by the existence of queer persons," I want to consider the pleasurable risks offered by queerness (4). A goal of this chapter is to rethink the assumed constitution of risk by asking: at-risk of what? What does it mean for queer youth to actively "risk" (as a verb) versus being labeled as "at-risk"? In some studies on queer youth, we are provided with little beyond tautology. Linda Goldman, for example, lists "risk-taking behavior" as one of the "signs of at-risk youth": in other words, to be at-risk is to risk taking risks (97). Such literature takes for granted the meaning of risk, and instead of offering a more nuanced articulation of the concept, presents solutions for managing risk while preventing and overcoming presumed victimization. Recall, too, how children's and YA literature is often anxiously imagined as a "risk-management strategy" for containing undesirable behavior (Hurley, "Discontents" 9).

Furthermore, while acknowledging that queer youth experience sexual violence at a higher rate than their straight peers, I want to rethink the assumption that sex inevitably risks harm. As Judith Levine points out, "Commonly in the professional literature, sex among young people is referred to as a 'risk factor,' along with binge drinking and and gun play, and the loss of virginity as the 'onset' of intercourse, as if it were a disease." (xxvi–vii). The alternate vision of risk I propose emerges from Isabelle Holland's *The Man Without a Face* (1972). Much like John Donovan's *I'll Get There. It Better Be Worth the Trip*, Holland's novel is often censured by contemporary critics for its ostensibly outdated and problematic content, including an intimate teacher/student relationship. This relationship, I argue, offers a model of queer pedagogy that illuminates the productive and pleasurable aspects of risk, including risk's potential for altering our approaches to sexuality and relationality. First, however, I will offer an overview of scholarship that relies on an "at-risk" model of queer youth. Against this archive I will posit Adam Phillips's work on risk and Deborah Britzman's theorization of risk's relationship to queer pedagogy, and I will demonstrate how the temporality of anxiety permeates scenes of education—often carrying, as in Holland's novel, an erotic charge. In conversation with *The Man Without a Face*, Britzman and Phillips allow us to think through risk with greater complexity, resisting the impulse to reduce queer youth to martyr-target-victims and dodging a teleological narrative of sexual identity.

Queer Youth and Risk: An Overview

One need not look far for evidence of queer youth being at-risk of numerous perils, and indeed, this demographic continues to confront a plethora of systemic violences—a reality I do not wish to minimize. Many studies seek to tackle these issues. Hong et al, for example, describe suicide as "a major public health concern. A number of studies have reported high rates of suicide attempts among sexual minority youth; and these youth were significantly more likely to be at risk of suicidal behavior than youth in the general population" (885). In "Risk and Protective Factors for Homophobic Bullying in Schools," Hong and Garbarino illustrate how and why "students who frequently experience homophobic bullying are at an elevated risk of several negative outcomes, including depression, anxiety, hostility, mental health symptoms, health problems, poor school functioning, school absenteeism, substance use, risky sexual behaviors, post-traumatic stress disorder, self-harm, and suicidal behavior" (272). Moreover, the Centers for Disease Control and Prevention (CDC) Youth Risk Behavior Surveillance System "monitors six types of health-risk behaviors that contribute to the leading causes of death and disability among youth and adults," and regularly releases data on LGB youth ("YRBSS"). Noting that "most lesbian, gay, bisexual (LGB) youth are happy and thrive during their adolescent years,"[2] the site also flags that "some LGB youth are more likely than their heterosexual peers to experience negative health and life outcomes," the primary risk being forms of violence including "bullying, teasing, harassment, and physical assault" ("LGBT Youth"). The 2015 national YRBS survey found that 34 percent of LGB students "were bullied on school property," 10 percent "were injured or threatened with a weapon," also at school, 18 percent had experienced physical violence when dating, and 18 percent had been sexually assaulted ("LGBT Youth"). This is to say nothing of the compounded alienation and violence, both symbolic and physical, that is experienced by Black and Indigenous queers and queers of color, homeless queer youth, and the trans community.

Troubled by the notion that queer youth seem defined by their potential victimization, Eric Rofes suggests that we must continue to address the harsh material realities of queer youth while expanding our analyses to examine "the role of pleasure and sex in young people's lives" (57).[3] According to Susan Talburt, resistance to the trope of martyr-target-victim has put another narrative into circulation, resulting in a dichotomous pair of adult-created stories working to define queer youth, both of which circulate in queer YA: "(1) narratives of risk and danger and (2) narratives of the well-adjusted, out, and proud gay youth" (18). According to Talburt, these stories function to "make youth intelligible—to others and themselves in narrowly defined ways," and severely limit the creativity and imagination with which we understand sexuality (18). It follows, then, that some scholars eschew discourses of risk entirely and instead deploy a resilience-based model for thinking about youth. In *Children and Families 'at Promise': Deconstructing the Discourse of Risk*, Christine E. Sleeter rightly points out that the "at-risk" label "deflects attention away from injustices perpetrated and institutionalized by the dominant society and again frames oppressed communities and homes as lacking the cultural and moral resources for advancement" (x). Similarly, Cover indicates that we must move away from imagining "queerness as a risk itself," adopting instead "a lens that focuses on youth resilience, agency, changing cultural forms, and new or alternative understandings of sexuality" (4). Sleeter proposes to "reframe oppressed groups in terms of '[at]-promise,' presenting portraits of children, parents, and teachers who refused to accept definitions based on deficiency and mobilized local cultural and personal resources to achieve with excellence" (x). "Promise," however, might function as another kind of limiting teleology; it asks queer youth to follow a particular narrative and reach a specific destination, similar to the trajectory espoused by Savage and Miller's *It Gets Better* anti-bullying YouTube project. Although *It Gets Better* has enabled many queer adults to share their personal stories with young people, its overarching narrative relies on the assumption that queer adolescence is plagued by a storm and stress of the most vicious variety, and that growth into adulthood promises a refuge from anti-queer bullying and violence (more on this in chapter six). Further, the project fails to account for those youth who may *not* fulfill that which they ostensibly "promise." Instead of pursuing this avenue, I will consider what alternatives the concept of risk—which offers a less teleological temporality—can yield in discussions of youth, pedagogy, and anxiety.

Rethinking Risk

At-risk discourse elides the fact that risk can have a relationship to pleasure in addition to harm. Phillips explains:

> We create risk when we endanger something we value, whenever we test the relationship between thrills and virtues. So to understand, or make conscious, what constitutes a risk for us—our own personal repertoire of risks—is an important clue about what it is that we do value; and it also enjoins us to consider the pleasures of carelessness. (33)

Phillips examines "the ordinary risks of adolescence that extend into adult life," risks that are necessary to determining our relationship to objects beyond our control, outside ourselves (30). He explains vis-à-vis one of his patients, a ten-year-old who, although terrified of water, was learning to swim:

> For the boy the risk of learning to swim was the risk of discovering that he, or rather his body, would float. The heart of swimming is that you can float. Standing within his depth, apparently in control, was the omnipotence born of anxiety;

the opposite of omnipotence here was not impotence, as he had feared, but his
being able to entrust himself to the water. The defense of vigilant self-holding
precluded his ability to swim. He needed a "generous kind of negligence" with
himself. It is possible to be too concerned about oneself. (30)

Phillips's swimming metaphor illustrates not only the pleasurable and productive stakes of risk, but also the role of anxiety in risk. Here, anxiety is at the
root of a sense of control and power that Phillips suggests is only "apparent";
relinquishing this power is a kind of risk—a necessary, "generous kind of negligence"—that leads to discovery. This link is key: anxiety produces the illusion
of a coherent, stable self, but is simultaneously indicative of the unstable and
precarious ground upon which subjectivity rests. Anxiety, then, speaks to the
twin gestures of pinning down and undoing.

Phillips's metaphor is useful for interpreting scenes of reading in queer
YA, the likes of which we've already seen in Donovan's novel (recall Davy and
Altschuler's "murky middle" version of *Julius Caesar*) and will continue to see
in *The Man Without a Face*. Reading is a kind of risk with stakes that vary from
the standard pathologies. Rarely mentioned in conversations about risk are
possibilities for new forms of kinship, community, and pleasure, all of which
could be said to have buoyant properties, to continue with Phillips's metaphor.
What the swimming boy and readers alike risk is a false sense of omnipotence
and control in favor of entrusting their bodies to an outside object. Insofar as
the reader risks one, potentially safe space, another stands to be gained: a new
world that justifies and motivates the initial risk, one that presents potentially
transformative and pleasurable relational possibilities. In "Queer Pedagogy
and Its Strange Techniques," Britzman imagines

> a theorization of reading as being always about risking the self, about confronting
> one's own theory of reading, and about engaging one's own alterity and desire.
> Thinking itself, in classroom spaces, might take the risk of refusing to secure
> thought and of exposing the danger in the curious insistence on positing founda-
> tional claims at all costs. (94)

Here, Britzman highlights how queer pedagogy involves reading practices that
are inevitably and productively "at-risk," but at-risk of forgoing the security and
stability of sedimented categories of sexuality and gender in favor of queerness's open waters. Britzman points to how risk, pedagogically speaking, should
not be taken for granted as something to be managed or minimized. Instead
of leading us to danger, Britzman's queer pedagogical risk underscores the
precariousness of an initial, supposedly stable subject position while allowing

for a proliferation of new ways of thinking about identification (including a resistance to the idea of identity) and relationality.

Following Britzman, I want to imagine two shifts in our current pedagogical paradigm of queer YA. First, instead of privileging the representation of "resolved" LGBT identities to help shield queer youth from victimization and risk (recall Brent Hartinger's approach to Donovan's novel, as outlined in my previous chapter), I want to explore how queer YA may invite a more sustained consideration of risk as something pleasurable and productive. This involves a queer pedagogy where the notion of a coherent, transparent, "resolved" self is risked in favor of a queer uncertainty and the anxiety that attends scenes of risky reading.

Pedagogy and Anxiety

Throughout her work, Britzman explores the relationship between education, pedagogy, and anxiety.[4] A primary goal of *After-Education* (2003), for example, is to insist that anxiety perpetually attends the scene of education.[5] Further, in "The Very Thought" (2009), Britzman argues that the affective register of education stems from primal psychoanalytic scenes that are inherently anxious and produce resistance to thinking about the limits of knowledge: "Education begins with the anxiety of dependency, helplessness, and fears of separation," Britzman explains; "This can mean that our defenses against thinking the thought of education . . . somehow anticipate our educational dangers: dependency and the anxieties of having to relive the profound helplessness of one's infancy" (7). Later, in "Between Psychoanalysis and Pedagogy" (2013), Britzman draws on Arthur Jersild's 1955 volume *When Teachers Face Themselves* to explore the close ties between the history of educational theory and anxiety, asserting that "Jersild saw the history of educational theory as a history of anxiety, defense and alienation" (107). Britzman uses these links to consider how "the field of education" can benefit from "a psychoanalytic style," which invites "the desire to learn more from otherness," confrontations with "the difficult knowledge that is already there," and "an interest in working within the uncertainty in our own learning, of narrating the conditions of education with a difference, itself an emotional situation difficult to know" (115).

For Britzman, psychoanalysis opens the door to thinking education's unconscious. She describes an "unthought" of education, through which we can "call into question . . . the subject-presumed-to-know, the capacity of the subject's response to be unencumbered by that which it cannot tolerate, and the subject's own 'passion for ignorance'" ("Queer Pedagogy" 80). Further, psychoanalysis returns Britzman to those primal drives and affective forms—including phantasy, loss, love, desire, and anxiety—that fuel our impulses to teach and learn ("The Very Thought" 17).[6] For Britzman, then, anxiety both partially describes the scene of education and enables new approaches to thinking about teaching and learning. Fundamental to these new approaches is a rethinking of reading practices in light of anxious affect and the possibilities for identification this affect produces. "That is," Britzman explains, "pedagogy might provoke the strange study of where feelings break down, take a detour, reverse their content, betray understanding, and hence study where affective meanings become anxious, ambivalent, and aggressive" ("Queer Pedagogy" 84). Britzman sees anxiety and ambivalence as generative affects, since they can challenge our "investment in pinning down meanings, in getting identities 'straight.'" ("Queer Pedagogy" 85). She asks:

> What if one thought about reading practices as problems of opening identifications, of working the capacity to imagine oneself differently precisely in one's encounters with another and in one's encounters with the self? What if how one reads the world turned upon the interest in thinking against one's thoughts, in creating a queer space where old certainties made no sense? ("Queer Pedagogy" 85)

Following Britzman, I see anxiety as an affect that attends scenes of reading, one that shapes and is shaped by reading practices. Anxiety has the potential to produce a kind of resistance to the teleology and fixedness of many critical approaches to queer YA, while "possibly unhinging the normal from the self" and "multiplying alternative forms of identifications and pleasures" (Britzman, "Queer Pedagogy" 85). The pervasiveness of anxiety in education—the way anxiety circulates in discourse and gives form to pedagogical and reading practices—is in part why theorizing an affective economy of anxiety provides such an appropriate and useful approach to queer YA.

An anxious temporality also permeates Kevin Kumashiro's work on pedagogy and crisis. Like Britzman, he argues that learning can often be emotionally disturbing for students since it involves "unlearning" previous lessons. For Kumashiro, this creates a scenario where students "are both unstuck (i.e., distanced from the ways they have always thought, no longer so complicit with oppression) and stuck (i.e., intellectually paralyzed and needing to work through their emotions and thoughts before moving on with the more academic part of the lesson)" (63). Recall Phillips's description of worrying as simultaneously implying "a future, a way of looking forward to things" (56) and "an unproductive mental process that got [his patient] nowhere. . . . It was among other things an attempt to arrest the passage of time" (47–48). We see a similar relationship to temporality in Kumashiro's scenario, which involves students being both "unstuck" and "stuck"—even "paralyzed," which echoes Lacan's use of "halting" to describe the temporal symptoms of anxiety. I want to pick up on this "stuck-ness," this paradoxical temporality, of both anxiety and pedagogy.

Thus far, I have been relatively unconcerned with fine distinctions between "worry" and "anxiety," focusing instead on how the two terms seem to share a temporality that is simultaneously stalled and future-oriented. Here, however, I am compelled to make a sharper differentiation between the two terms. Recall Phillips's suggestion that the "distinction we tend to make is that worry always has an object, that worrying is beyond displacement, whereas one can feel anxious without knowing what the anxiety is about" (52).[7] As a result of worry's object-orientation, Phillips argues,

> Worries . . . show a coherent subject in an intelligible, if unsettling, narrative; they assume a pragmatic self bent on problem-solving, not an incurably desiring subject in the disarray of not knowing what he wants. We use worries to focus and are prone to use them to simulate purpose (just as when we are intimidated by possibility). (57)

"Worrying," he continues, "tacitly constitutes a self—or, at least, a narrator—by assuming the existence of one; for how could there be a worry without a worrier?" (57). For Britzman, however, anxiety in education asks us to avoid stabilizing meaning ("Queer Pedagogy" 85).[8] If worrying, then, produces a temporarily coherent subject, anxiety differentiates itself through its undoing, halting, and impeding selves, even if this undoing results from a subject's attempts to pin itself down and/or render itself coherent.[9] This, as I discussed earlier in this chapter, is the apparent omnipotence of Phillips's swimming boy, whose sense of power and stability emerges from the very anxiety that gestures simultaneously to his instability and precariousness. By keeping alive a kind of vital and transformative anxiety, pedagogy—which has been theorized elsewhere in terms of futurity and hope[10]—becomes attuned to delay, risk, stalls and starts, and subjective ambiguity. "Learning," as Kumashiro writes, "is about disruption and opening up to further learning, not closure and satisfaction" (43).

In what follows, in conversation with Holland's *The Man Without a Face*, I will continue to illustrate the potential that emerges from the risks, anxious occlusions, lateral relations, and ambiguities of queer YA. Holland's novel depicts the relationship between teacher and student as an interval in tension with the future and forward-oriented movement. My objective is to illustrate the productive and creative relations that occur inside delay and through risk.

The Man Without a Face and the Boy in the Golden Cocoon

Holland's novel is told from the perspective of fatherless fourteen-year-old Charles "Chuck" Norstadt, who is desperate to attend boarding school in order to flee his verbally abusive, serial divorcée mother and tyrannical older sister Gloria. Like *I'll Get There. It Better Be Worth the Trip*'s Davy, Chuck's only friend is an animal: in this case, a mangy stray cat named Moxie. In order to pass the entrance exam for the school that will guarantee his escape, Chuck approaches the mysterious loner and former teacher Justin McLeod—our titular faceless man—who lives in isolation in the hills near the Norstadts's summer cottage. Eventually, McLeod takes pity on Chuck and agrees to tutor him. While Chuck is at first resistant to McLeod's gruff demeanor and severe teacherly methods, the two eventually warm to one another. McLeod, initially aloof, ultimately reveals to Chuck the story behind his disfigurement: he was drunk driving with a teenage boy in the car, they crashed, and the boy was killed. As the summer passes with student and teacher spending every day together, Chuck's affection for and attraction to McLeod deepens. One night toward summer's end, Chuck returns home to discover that his beloved Moxie has been kicked to death by Gloria's boyfriend, and Gloria has vindictively left Chuck a stack of newspaper clippings about his missing father, who "died of chronic alcoholism in Sydney, Australia, where he had been living on skid row for some years" (145). Overwhelmed and traumatized, Chuck runs to McLeod, collapses into bed with him, and narrates, "I didn't know what was happening to me until it had happened" (147). The next morning, ashamed and confused, Chuck rebuffs McLeod's attempt to talk things through. Chuck returns to the city, passes his exam, and begins school. Later, overcome with guilt and "sick with shame for—again—having run away," Chuck decides he must apologize to McLeod and confess "how much [he] loved him" (152). He arrives to find McLeod's house empty, however, and receives the news that McLeod died of a sudden heart attack a month prior and bequeathed his entire estate to Chuck. The novel concludes with Chuck returning to school and reflecting on McLeod's "talent for salvaging flawed and fallen creatures" (157).

As cited in chapter one of this book, Kirk Fuoss critiques *The Man Without a Face* for "grant[ing] physical expressions of homosexual love all the presence of an ellipsis" (164). What Fuoss describes as *The Man Without a Face*'s sexual ellipsis is not the only aspect of Holland's story that has drawn criticism, however. As with other early queer YA titles, like Donovan's, critics tend to focus on stereotypes and ambiguities. Hanckel and Cunningham, for example, write that "Holland's novel contains one of the most destructive and fallacious stereotypes—the homosexual as child molester. . . . In light of such limited coverage of the gay experience in YA fiction, the possible identification of such a major character as a corrupter of children is grossly unfair" (534). A *Kirkus Review* even goes so far as to call Holland's two protagonists "emotional cripples" ("The Man Without a Face"). Cart and Jenkins, who acknowledge that Holland was writing at a time when gay relationships were taboo, maintain that "the author nevertheless equates homosexuality with disfigurement, despair, and death, and her novel, along with Donovan's, reinforced some of the stereotypical thinking about homosexuality that became a fixture of LGBTQ literature" (22). Like Fuoss, Corinne Hirsch takes issue with the novel's occlusions, arguing at length for the importance of clarity and resolution in YA:

> Having introduced themes rich with ambiguity, the exigencies of the novel demand that they be worked out more fully. How might Charles deal with the complicated emotional and sexual feelings he has developed? What would be a realistic outcome of his relationship with McLeod? Adolescents, no less than adults, deserve a fully developed fictional experience. If Holland wishes to consider the difficult problems she does, she has a responsibility to explore their implications.... In *The Man Without a Face* ... Holland perceptively raises and partially explores complex questions; but in the end she evades them. (33–34)

Aside from Hanckel and Cunningham's labelling of McLeod a "child molester," which I find extreme, I do not disagree with much of the above criticism. Holland's novel is filled with stereotypes. The stale pathology of the fatherless gay is in full effect (on page 99, Chuck has a dream where one faceless man—his missing father—literally morphs into another, i.e. McLeod), and McLeod's tragic and isolated existence is not exactly an appealing representation of queer life. What interests me, however, is what these critiques assume and overlook. Hanckel and Cunningham and Cart and Jenkins's supposition is that *The Man Without a Face* (and, by extension, other early queer YA titles like Donovan's novel) can only be read in terms of the potential harm caused by their many outmoded stereotypes. As a result, these texts are viewed as having little to no pedagogical value, are of interest only as historical documents, and are rife with the wrong kinds of visibility or, as Hirsch argues, incomplete visibilities. What these critics overlook is how *The Man Without a Face*'s occlusions, ambiguities, and seemingly harmful representations also speak to sideways teacher/student relations, pedagogy's queerness and riskiness, and the desire to resist "coming out."[11] Hirsch's critique in particular privileges a notion of "resolved" sexuality, foreclosing the productive potential of incompleteness. Chuck's risks, however, align with what Britzman calls "risking the self," as he launches himself into the indefinite postponement of identity instead of assuming a complete, resolved self ("Queer Pedagogy" 94). Holland's novel queers pedagogy, not only by eroticizing it as space of desire between teacher and student, but also by representing it as a site of anxious temporality, where delay and forward movement are constantly in tension.

In *The Queer Child*, Stockton explores ideas surrounding delay, pleasure, and pain vis-à-vis Henry James's 1891 novella *The Pupil*, which bears a number of thematic similarities to *The Man Without a Face*.[12] To introduce her analysis, Stockton poses the following questions:

> To what extent has man/boy love, at least for a century, in some contexts, func-tioned as a substitute lateral relation for men and boys?—especially if each of them has been publicly trapped in delays, with the dictates of arrested develop-ment and ghostly gayness thrust upon them. Or to meld these questions: has what is called man/boy love found surprising outlets in mutual pain, giving men and boys ways to meet inside delay? (62)

Like James's tutor and pupil, Chuck and McLeod form a sideways relation premised on pain and what Stockton calls "the dictates of arrested develop-ment"—that is, queerness, which Freud and others have pathologized as a developmental delay. Stockton's approach, however, is to consider the teacher/student relationship in *The Pupil* through the lens of masochism, which she describes (drawing on Deleuze) as "a special way of pursuing a pleasure that comes on delay" (*Queer Child* 78). For Stockton, this masochism emerges from the verbal play between teacher and student: "Talking, of course, can be a delay, even itself a sexy delay," she writes; "It's a delay since it often isn't sex (it's talking, after all), but it can be greatly suffused with pleasure, even a highly sexualized pleasure, even if the topic of the talking is pain. . . . Talking can even be a kind of whipping: a verbal (and imaginative) painful enjoy-ment" (*Queer Child* 63). Again, there are a number of links here between Stockton's analysis of *The Pupil* and Holland's novel. To a degree, we could read Chuck and McLeod's relationship as masochistic, since delay is integral to their interaction, and Chuck derives a kind of flirtatious pleasure from the way McLeod treats him strictly and harshly. See, for example, the exchange on page 69 of Holland's novel, when Chuck provokes McLeod by critiquing his sentence structure. Chuck narrates:

> I decided to live dangerously. "I thought you were never supposed to end a sen-tence with a preposition."
>
> "I, too, can quote," [McLeod] said deadpan. "There is a certain type of insubor-dination going on around here up with which I will not put."

I couldn't help but grinning. "You're not serious about be having to do that Latin word bit, are you, Mr. McLeod?"

. . . "Oh, yes." . . . I sighed loudly. It really is against my principles to give in to an adult. But somehow, of the two of us, I had a strong feeling he wasn't going to do the yielding.

This excerpt also foreshadows the fact that McLeod resists Chuck's physical advances until he finally presumably "yields" to Chuck in the novel's ambiguous sexual climax.

Holland's novel emphasizes the anxious affect that structures the relationship between tutor and pupil and circulates with these notions of delay, pleasure, and risk. In lieu of following Stockton and making the case that Chuck is a masochistic child, I examine instead the sideways relations and occlusions that take place in the pedagogical space of Holland's novel, or what Chuck calls his "golden cocoon" (Holland 121).

Holland's narrative is built around a series of risks that Chuck takes as he enters into and fulfills his pedagogical contract with McLeod. Chuck's story has much in common with Phillips's metaphor of the swimming boy: *The Man Without a Face* is essentially the story of a boy who learns to entrust his body and self to open waters—in this case, the risky, free-floating space of queerness. Chuck "risks his self" through a pedagogy that culminates not in the resolution of a transparent and stable sexual identity, but rather in the incompleteness of his sense of self. This incompleteness manifests itself in Chuck's desire for delay, which is in constant tension with the futurity of pedagogy, and also demonstrates how queerness, quite productively and transformatively, can take shapes and form relations that defy critical calls for sexual resolution.

As Chuck makes his first trek to McLeod's house, the main risk he perceives is an attack from McLeod's "man-hating dog" and a fear of being rejected as a pupil by the former schoolteacher: "The butterflies in my stomach were threatening to become bats," narrates Chuck as he approaches the house (26). Although he is shunned by McLeod, Chuck shares details about his uncomfortable situation at home, and McLeod reluctantly agrees to tutor him: "I'll coach you. But you'll have to do it my way, and that means the hard way," McLeod tells Chuck; "It will be tough. But if I ever find you haven't done the work I've assigned you, you won't come back. Are you sure it's worth it?" (35). Together, Chuck and McLeod enter an interval of pedagogy: "three hours every morning five days a week" (35). Chuck emphasizes his desire to prolong their time together when, later in the novel, he begins referring to his time with McLeod as feeling "like I was in a sort of golden cocoon and I didn't want to break out of it" (121). This desire, however, is in tension with the forward momentum and future-orientation of their pedagogical arrangement, a tension embodied by the trope Chuck selects to capture his feelings: a cocoon, which must inevitably break open, regardless of its inhabitant's desire to stay within. The metaphor of the cocoon, then, provides an anxious sense of power and stability for Chuck. It is a temporary means of pinning himself down while simultaneously recognizing the vulnerability of the metaphor that lends him momentary safety.

As the novel progresses, many of Chuck's risks involve "approaching" McLeod with increasing degrees of physical closeness, while the stakes remain rejection at the hands of his stern tutor. Chuck's intimacy with McLeod deepens significantly after McLeod reveals the story behind his disfigurement to Chuck, and Chuck describes an involuntary desire to make physical contact with McLeod: "Without my volition, my hand reached towards his arm and I grasped it. He didn't move or say anything. The good half of his face was as white as paper. Then he jerked my hand off and walked out" (93). McLeod later apologizes and renews their friendship, Chuck confesses that he shared McLeod's secret with some local boys, McLeod forgives him, and the next time they make contact it occurs—appropriately, given Phillips's metaphor—while the two are swimming:

> I forgot he was an adult and a teacher and forty-seven years old. I even forgot what I had done to him. I forgot everything but the water and being in it and chasing and being chased, far from the shore with nothing around or moving except us. It was like flying. I thought suddenly, I'm free. And the thought was so great I poked him again on the way up. We swam some more, this time parallel with the shore, then played some more, then back to where we'd been. (117)

Like Phillips's swimming boy, Chuck risks entrusting his body to a previously unknown object. In Chuck's case, however, this object is not the water, but McLeod. Further, the form of this passage makes clear the pleasure Chuck derives from delay. His desire to linger in the golden cocoon with McLeod is reflected most strikingly in the repetition of the word "forgot" and the circular construction of "chasing and being chased" in addition to the final sentence, where "some more" repeats and also rhymes with "the shore," producing a repetition-like effect. The final sentence also ends with "back to where we'd been," suggesting that Chuck and McLeod's playful romp is repeated ad infinitum (or, rather, Chuck wishes it could be repeated ad infinitum). We might also be reminded of Davy's repetitive and stagnant dream about the beach, in *I'll Get There. It Better Be Worth the Trip*, as described in my previous chapter.

For Chuck, touching McLeod is a pleasurable kind of risk, the consequences of which he seems to be partially unaware. McLeod, in his resistance to Chuck's touch, anticipates Chuck's shameful and tormented response to their elliptical intimacy at the novel's end. McLeod, in other words, is aware that Chuck is taking a series of risks through this touch. Chuck is risking the safety of his golden cocoon, his sense of self, and the pleasure he receives from attempting to linger in a space of delay with McLeod. In another instance following the arm-grabbing incident, McLeod recoils from Chuck: "'I like you a lot,' I [Chuck] said . . . I wanted to touch him . . . I reached over and touched his side. The hot skin was tight over his ribs. I knew then that I'd never been close to anyone in my life, not like that. And I wanted to get closer. But at that moment McLeod sat up and then stood up" (120). McLeod's response prompts Chuck to ask him, "Do you think I'm a queer?" to which McLeod answers, "No, I do not think you're a queer . . . Everybody wants and needs affection and you don't get much. Also you're a boy who badly needs a father" (120–121). Chuck, however, dismisses McLeod's suggestion, insisting that "I didn't want to think about home at all. I felt like I was in a sort of golden cocoon and I didn't want to break out of it" (121). In other words, on one level, Chuck anxiously senses the risk he is taking: disrupting the safety of his cocoon (an inevitable disruption) and actively recognizing the straight "world" he is risking through his desire for contact with McLeod. On another level, he takes great pleasure in cocoon-dwelling with his teacher. In order to preserve this stasis, on another occasion, Chuck postpones the level of physical contact that would ultimately prove too risky for him: "The sun was hot. I was still on my side, one arm under my head. Just as I was dropping off I put the other across his chest, feeling the skin and hair under my hand. A sort of an electric feeling went through me. I half sat up" (139). Here, sensing the potential for his cocoon to rupture, Chuck withdraws his touch and retreats to the comfort and pleasure of immobility. Chuck's physical back-and-forth with McLeod is a series of calculated, anxious, and pleasurable risks that put into play Chuck's desire for delay with his desire for a level of physical intimacy with McLeod that would, in a sense, impel him forward and away from what he perceives to be safety.

Interestingly, Chuck's feeling that his desire to touch McLeod is "queer" and the electricity sparked by their contact recall an earlier passage in Holland's novel, which depicts a risk suggestive of Britzman's theory of reading as "risking the self . . . about engaging one's own alterity and desire" ("Queer Pedagogy" 94). In this moment, following a lesson, Chuck expresses his distaste for poetry. McLeod responds by appealing to Chuck's fascination with airplanes, reading aloud John Gillespie Magee Jr.'s "High Flight." Chuck reacts physically to the poem: "It was queer, what it did to me. There were little explosions in my head and stomach and a tingling down my back. My throat was dry. McLeod was looking at me. 'Here,' he said, holding out the book. 'Take it'" (70). Notable in this passage is Chuck's use of the word "queer" to describe his response to the poem, the same word he later uses about his desire to touch McLeod. Although we could interpret "queer" as "strange/unusual" in the context of his bodily response to the poem and "queer" in conversation with McLeod to mean "non-heterosexual/gay," the two "queers" nonetheless signify in excess of these definitions. If Chuck's desire to touch McLeod is a queer erotic longing, his response to the poem might also be erotic, where the scene of pedagogy arouses a similar bodily response—"little explosions in my head and stomach and a tingling down my back" (70)—that is brought about by physical contact with McLeod, i.e. "a sort of an electric feeling" (139).

The "High Flight" scene depicts a risk through which Chuck engages his "alterity and desire" (in Britzman's words) and discovers, by reading, a new site of erotic contact, a queer aspect of his self that emerges in a moment that fuses pedagogy with poetry and a student's desire for his teacher ("Queer Pedagogy" 94).[13] Crucial, too, is how the temporality of anxiety underwrites Chuck's response to the poem, which establishes the scene of pedagogy as one that lingers in the present despite its orientation towards the future. Chuck does not respond to the poem with an efficient phrase like, "What it [the poem] did to me was queer," but instead he narrates, "It was queer, what it did to me," which invites the reader to dwell in the multiple clauses and contemplate the ambiguous referent of "it." Does the first "it" refer to the poem (i.e. the poem was queer) or Chuck's response to the poem? Does the second "it" refer to the poem, McLeod's performance of the poem, or a combination of the two? Like Chuck, the reader sits momentarily in an interpretive space, invited to dwell alongside an ambiguous, erotic response to poetry while considering the significance and implications of such a response. Here, Chuck's queerness emerges through pedagogy and reading, but crucially, the reading does not provide an "identity" per se. Instead, the erotics of reading mingle with Chuck's queerness more broadly: his desire for physical contact with McLeod, the pleasure he finds in delay, and the series of risks that cause him to question his sense of self.

The ambiguous "it" returns in the novel's much-scrutinized moment of elliptical sexual contact between Chuck and McLeod. Collapsing into McLeod's arms, Chuck narrates:

> I could feel his heart pounding, and then I realized it was mine. I couldn't stop shaking; in fact, I started to tremble violently. It was like everything—the water, the sun, the hours, the play, the work, the whole summer—came together. The golden cocoon had broken open and was spilling in a shower of gold. Even so, I didn't know what was happening to me until it had happened. (147)

Chuck's retrospective narration brings the tension between stasis and futurity "together" in a single moment, breaking open and spilling the golden contents of Chuck's secure cocoon, and the ambiguous "it" returns to signify whatever happens between Chuck and McLeod. Cart and Jenkins interpret the "it" as "a spontaneous ejaculation" (21), but I prefer to consider the multiple possibilities suggested by the ambiguity of "it." The next morning, Chuck realizes for the first time that his desire for delay was in tension with the series of risks he was taking: "Somewhere, for a long time," he narrates, "I had known—not that this would happen, but that something would happen, and then everything would be over" (148). Despite this epiphany, ambiguity continues to loom large: Chuck had the knowledge "somewhere" (where?) that "something" (what?) would take place, ending "everything" (which includes what?). This ambiguity—again in the form of "it"—endures in the morning-after conversation between Chuck and McLeod:

> There is nothing in that morning's conversation that I am not bitterly ashamed of. But of all the things I said I am most ashamed of . . . what I said next.
> "What does it make you?"
> "I've known what I was for a long time."
> And so had I. Without knowing I knew it, I had known. What did that make me? I stared at him. (149)

Here, the "it" again refers to something and nothing in particular: "it" is something that "makes" McLeod, and also something that Chuck "knew" and "had known," but "without knowing."[14] The multiple, contradictory conjugations of "to know" (continuous, preterite, past perfect) contribute to the occlusions of Holland's novel (what, exactly, does Chuck know and not know?) while reinforcing Chuck's sense of temporal collapse. The end of delay—and, perhaps, McLeod's final "lesson" to Chuck—marks an anxious orientation to past, present, and future.

This is the moment in Holland's novel that some critics take issue with. We're never told what lies on the other side of Chuck's cocoon; or to grow this now banal metaphor, we're never shown the butterfly. It remains unclear—or, at least, unspoken—what McLeod "is," how Chuck understands himself or what he has become by the novel's end, and how Chuck's sexuality will presumably play out after the story's conclusion. While Fuoss reads this as a negative and potentially harmful lack of resolution (164), I see this as an appropriate culmination of the anxious pedagogy that has been taking place between teacher and pupil. Chuck risks his self and his world, trusts his body to the unknown, and emerges with an ambiguous and unstable relationship to sexuality. In

Britzman's words, Chuck is "refusing to secure thought," denying the reader an easy resolution or way of understanding his sexuality and desire (94). Instead, we are left with the impression that queer desire is in excess of sexual identity. Desire in Holland's novel emerges through a combination of pedagogy and the erotics of reading, sideways relations between teacher and student, and an anxious longing to dwell in a golden cocoon that constantly, through touch, risks eruption. Although it fails to provide resolution, *The Man Without a Face* succeeds, by virtue of this failure, in providing a model of queerness that speaks to the risky but productive "open waters" of sexuality, or what Kristeva would call the pleasurable "incompleteness" of the adolescent psychic structure (139). And, crucially, it is pedagogy that lends shape and temporality to Chuck and his relationship with McLeod.

Like *I'll Get There. It Better Be Worth the Trip, The Man Without a Face* offers us a series of stereotypical problem novel conventions and the potential to produce a reading that opposes these conventions. And as in Donovan's novel, remnants of the psychoanalytic feral tale persist in Holland's story. In particular, Holland provides a paternal character (a teacher, as opposed to an "analyst or therapist"), who "assumes an Oedipal relation to the boy subject, serving as a foster father and often countering the influence of the feral or den mother" (Kidd, *Making* 10). Indeed, like Davy, Chuck has a toxic mother whom he must ostensibly grow away from in order to grow up. This Oedipal dynamic, more pronounced in Holland, still does not offer us the feral tale's typical trajectory as described by Kidd: "the white, middle-class male's perilous passage from nature to culture, from bestiality to humanity, from homosocial pack life to individual self-reliance and heterosexual prowess—that is, from boyhood to manhood" (*Making* 7). We do, however, see the same attachment to nature that we get in Donovan. In addition to Chuck's close relationship to (poor, murdered) Moxie the cat, McLeod is a trainer of horses. Much remains to be said about the role of these animals in the story: as Lydia Kokkola indicates, "the assumption that equestrian energy is a masculine force is used to make literary stables such a fascinating space for investigating gender identity, sexual orientation, and desire" (142). In particular, the horses seem to buttress Holland's depiction of McLeod as a stern but sensitive pedagogue with an attachment to animals that parallels many quintessential lonely and isolated queer protagonists. Interesting, too, is that Chuck's final meditation involves comparisons to the horses, specifically McLeod's "'talent . . . for salvaging flawed and fallen creatures. Himself included.' *And me*, I thought" (157). Setting aside the problematic figuration of the novel's two queer characters as damaged "creatures," it is compelling that Chuck, like Donovan's Davy, concludes the novel by reinforcing his connection to "nature" instead of abandoning it. Chuck is "salvaged," maybe, and he acquires the material markers of adulthood by inheriting McLeod's estate, but he also remains somewhat static, "caught between . . . modes of life," as Kidd writes about the feral tale's protagonist (*Making* 191), instead of resolutely growing into the heterosexual, "paternal role" (*Making* 10).

Perhaps the pedagogy of queer YA isn't necessarily about demonstrating how to grow up into a nonheterosexual identity. Perhaps this pedagogy is more along the lines of what Chuck experiences when McLeod reads the poem: a feeling of ambiguous queerness, but also the desire to dwell in this queerness, in the anxious space between delay and movement, to take pleasure in anxiety and ambiguity without fashioning them into something that means in any straightforward manner. It is possible, too, that this queer pedagogy extends to the reader, who may learn something from the relationship represented in the novel. I might also add that Holland's novel remains radical for its unapologetic representation of a consensual sexual intergenerational relationship that is not, in my opinion, readily reducible to pedophilia or molestation. As Kokkola points out in a section of her study dedicated to "Cross-generational carnal capers" (which does not, intriguingly, include a discussion of *The Man Without a Face*), "Blanket assumptions that teenagers cannot make informed consent about sex affects adolescents' autonomy in ways that may have far reaching consequences" (117). This dimension of Chuck and McLeod's bond remains controversial; unsurprisingly, Mel Gibson omitted the more intimate parts of their relationship from his 1993 film adaptation.

In "Precocious Education," Britzman writes,

> Our sexuality gives us the instability of curiosity, the desire to learn, and the passion to ignore all that stands in the way of learning. Without sexuality there is no curiosity. The question of sexuality is central to . . . crafting a self who can invent, over and over again, the courage to stand up for the self, to feel passionately for the conditions of others, to create a life from the experiments of learning to love and making from this learning to love a love of learning . . . We must also note that . . . sexuality is also the place where injustices, anxieties, and modes of aggression attach and become enacted. (39)

Holland's novel demonstrates how anxious calls for resolved, transparent LGBT visibilities in queer YA not only flatten the queer potential of early novels like *The Man Without a Face*, but also ignore the critical and transformative capacity of pedagogy and reading, which enable us to learn about those anxious yet pleasurable intervals, risky moments, and spaces of delay where identification is indefinitely postponed. Queer YA, then, does not necessarily do the pedagogical work that some critics claim it does and/or want it to do. Instead of sitting comfortably in its sexually resolved adulthood, queer YA circulates within an affective economy of anxiety, remaining invested in the dwellings and delays of its youth, in occlusions and ambivalences, its passionate attachments, desires, and fears. "When education is reduced to its most literal time," Britzman asserts, "it collapses into phantasy and idealization to foreclose our capacity to think the thought of education. Lost as well is the question of why any education is an encounter with what is not yet, an experience with what is most incomplete in us" ("The Very Thought" 6). Here, in conversation with *The Man Without a Face*, Britzman helps us realize how queer pedagogy and an alternative perspective on risk might bring to light those productive incompletenesses and tense temporalities that many queer YA critics tend to overlook.

it's not just a game....

.... it's a Gayme!

(Click anywhere to go on)

About Game..

CAPER in the CASTRO
Version 1.0

© 1989 C.M. Ralph All Rights Reserved

A Gay and Lesbian Based
Adventure Mystery Game with Sound, Text & Graphics.

Caution: This game includes scenes of violence and other material which may
be inappropriate for persons under the age of 18. Please use discretion.

Disclaimer: This game is a work of fiction. Any resemblance to actual places,
incidents or people (be they alive or dead) is entirely coincidental.

Figure 3.1. *Caper in the Castro* title screen. Copyright C. M. Ralph, 1989. Retrieved from https://archive.org/details/hypercard_caper-in-the-castro. Reproduced with permission.

CHAPTER 3

HIV/AIDS: Playing with Failure in
Caper in the Castro and *Two Boys Kissing*

On December 20, 2017, a *Vice* headline announced that "You Can Now Play the First LGBTQ Computer Game, For the First Time." Indeed, the long-lost *Caper in the Castro*, a "Gay and Lesbian Based Adventure Mystery Game with Sound, Text & Graphics," released by C. M. Ralph in May 1989, had been recovered by its creator and restored with the assistance of the LGBTQ Game Archive (see Pearson and figure 3.1). *Castro* invites players to assume the role of Private Detective Tracker McDyke and solve a series of puzzles: "Who kidnapped Tessy LaFemme, renowned drag queen" and "What is Dullagan Straightman (notorious villain) really up to?" Following its initial release, Ralph described *Castro* as "CharityWare," and requested that players "make a donation to any AIDS Charity of your choice in any amount." Ralph has explained that she "wanted to do something for the LGBT community that had embraced her and her partner while also honoring the nearly 90 percent of their Southern California friends who had died from AIDS related illnesses" (Shaw, "Caper").

Castro's plot is compelling. As the gamer (playing as Tracker McDyke) investigates Tessy LaFemme's disappearance, a larger conspiracy unfolds: notorious villain Dullagan Straightman is plotting to poison gay bar drinks with a lethal bacteria. The game's goal gradually becomes twofold as players discover that, in addition to rescuing Tessy from her captor, they must neutralize the bacteria that is intended to eliminate the Castro's queer community. Although AIDS itself is never named in the game, except on the title screen under the "CharityWare" call for donations, the thematic resonances with HIV/AIDS are undeniable. At one point, should players choose to consume the wine available in a venue called Club 102, *Castro* delivers the message (as seen in figure 3.2): "The House Wine has been tainted with a deadly, fast-acting bacterial virus. You are about

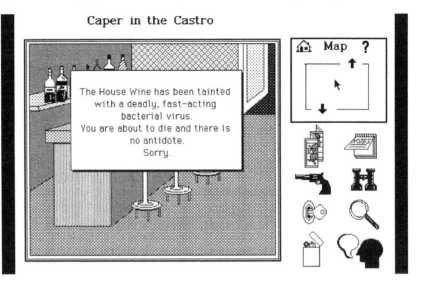

Figure 3.2. Death message delivered in Club 102. From *Caper in the Castro,* copyright
C. M. Ralph, 1989. Retrieved from https://archive.org/details/hypercard_caper-in-the-castro.
Reproduced with permission.

to die and there is no antidote. Sorry." Despite *Castro*'s tongue-in-cheek humor
and playful tone, it is challenging to not feel the affective weight of HIV/AIDS
in this game, which was created in the midst of a health crisis that was being
disavowed by the Reagan and Bush administrations, and which asks players
to uncover the conspiracy of "Straightman" to murder vast numbers of queers
by unleashing a "bacterial virus."[1]

In *Playing with Feelings*, Aubrey Anable argues that "video games are affective systems" (xii). "When we open a video game program," Anable continues,

> we are opening up a 'form of relation' to the game's aesthetic and narrative prop-
> erties, the computational operations of the software, the mechanical and material
> properties of the hardware on which we play the game, ideas of leisure and play,
> ideas of labor, our bodies, other players, and the whole host of fraught cultural
> meanings and implications that circulate around video games. (xii)

In this chapter, I think through the way that playing *Castro* today might make
us feel about the past and present of HIV/AIDS. *Castro* invites us into an affective system in which we feel the entanglements of dated gaming technology,
specifically, a point-and-click HyperCard interface and low-resolution black
and white graphics; a queer mystery involving a deadly threat that is not HIV

yet strongly recalls HIV; the history of HIV/AIDS and the ghosts of those lost to the epidemic; and our embodied present-day selves, playing and failing to play a glitchy thirty-year-old game through a web-browser-based emulator. Games like *Castro* draw us into a "circuit of feeling between their computational systems and the broader systems with which they interface: ideology, narrative, aesthetics, and flesh" (Anable xii). Notably, I argue, *Castro* allows us to play with and feel some of the anxieties that circulate around and within YA literature about HIV/AIDS. YA tends to represent HIV/AIDS as simultaneously everywhere and nowhere, a looming threat that nonetheless typically leaves young protagonists untouched. HIV/AIDS is a ghostly presence that is disavowed and ubiquitous, one from which YA attempts to distance its young characters in order to preserve their innocence. Typically, YA characters affected by HIV/AIDS are parents, uncles, or strangers—not the young protagonists themselves. HIV/AIDS is also often portrayed as a historical issue that has little to no bearing on present-day life. Similar to much popular discourse about HIV/AIDS, YA generally does not represent HIV/AIDS as an ongoing part of young people's lives.

A novel released during the queer YA boom, David Levithan's *Two Boys Kissing* (2013), illustrates this temporal chasm with noteworthy clarity. The book, set in the present day, is narrated by a ghostly chorus of men who died during the worst of the HIV/AIDS crisis in the 1980s and 1990s. This chorus struggles, and continually fails, to intervene in the lives of the book's young protagonists. The past, in other words, fails to assert itself in the present in large part because the present refuses to acknowledge the past. Failure is crucial to both *Two Boys Kissing* and *Caper in the Castro*, and it has also emerged as a key concept in video game studies and queer theory. Jesper Juul argues, for instance, that video games are unique because they let players experience and experiment with failure in ways that other forms do not, and Jack Halberstam has explored how failure allows queers to dodge coercive normative structures and "poke holes in the toxic positivity of contemporary life" (*Queer Art* 3). As I will explain, *Castro* sets players up to feel, repeatedly, negative affect typically associated with failure: powerlessness, frustration, and the sensation of loss. These affective forms clarify some of the critical anxieties about HIV/AIDS in YA, and they might also help us reconcile the history of HIV/AIDS with its persistence in the present.

Anable argues that video games "are uniquely suited to giving expression to ways of being in the world and ways of feeling in the present that can tell us something about contemporary digitally mediated and distributed subjectivity" (xii). The ways we can fail at playing *Castro* open us to new pathways for feeling our way through what Alexandra Juhasz and Ted Kerr call the "media ecologies" of HIV/AIDS, which include the "interlocked uses, systems, technologies, and appropriations of past AIDS signification." If YA generally fails to accurately and effectively represent HIV/AIDS, and if *Castro* allows us to feel YA's failures at an embodied level, then perhaps these feelings might orient us toward more fertile and nuanced ways of reading and writing about the relationship between young people and HIV/AIDS. Dwelling with failure, that is, might help us feel the need for an enhanced network of HIV/AIDS—one that recognizes that HIV/AIDS is an ongoing crisis in the lives of young people. *Castro*, moreover, challenges us to find pathways that avoid those anxious rehearsals of innocence that tend to pervade children's and YA literature about HIV/AIDS.

HIV/AIDS in YA: An Overview

The first YA book to deal with HIV/AIDS was M. E. Kerr's *Night Kites*. Published in 1986, the novel features a teenage protagonist whose older brother is sick with AIDS-related illnesses. As Christine Jenkins and Michael Cart point out, however, this novel did not inspire a trend: HIV/AIDS "would receive major thematic or topical treatment in only three other YA novels in the eighties" (39). In addition to the four novels published in the 1980s, only thirteen texts "that included any character who was HIV positive or had AIDS appeared in the nineties" (Jenkins and Cart 67). Moreover, just one of the affected characters in these thirteen books is a young person; the rest are adults, "usually uncles or teachers" (Jenkins and Cart 67). Lydia Kokkola concludes that, during this time period, HIV/AIDS functions mostly as a "punishment" for sexually active and/or queer characters (48).

In addition to underrepresenting HIV/AIDS, YA novels tend to inaccurately portray the transmission of HIV/AIDS and the lived realities of HIV+ people. Melissa Gross (1998), along with Annette Y. Goldsmith and Debi Carruth (2008; 2009), conducted several studies of HIV/AIDS representation in YA, which culminate in an annotated bibliography published in 2010. As of 2008, they counted ninety-three YA novels that are "written for young adults aged eleven to nineteen, contain a protagonist in this age range, are written in or translated into English, are fiction, and contain at least one character who is HIV positive or who has AIDS" (*HIV/AIDS* x). These authors conclude their detailed content analysis with an overall negative assessment: the characters with HIV/AIDS overwhelmingly "have little to no relationship to the protagonist" (106); although the American blood supply has been safe since 1985, novels published as late as 1995 used blood transfusion as "the primary explanation for the transmission of HIV" (109); "unreasonable fears" such as casual contact, kissing, and transmission through tears or sweat "dominate the reasons why protagonists fear HIV/AIDS" (110); despite advances in HIV/AIDS treatment, most characters with HIV/AIDS "die or are dying by the end of the book" (112); and books tend to make a "mystery" out of "how the largest single group of characters acquire HIV/AIDS"—these are "marginal characters who the protagonist knows only slightly, if at all" (40). Gross, Goldsmith, and Carruth report that "the message being overwhelmingly sent by this set of books is that HIV/AIDS does not happen to people about whom the protagonist cares" (36).

Gross et al.'s research demonstrates how YA has consistently kept HIV/AIDS at a substantial remove from youth themselves. Novels that feature HIV+ young people are often "set outside of the developed world," primarily in Africa and Papua New Guinea (*HIV/AIDS* 112). The anxiety, here, seems to stem from adult desires that (White, "Western") young people remain untouched by HIV/AIDS, or if they are affected, that they remain somehow "innocent": thus, the blood transfusion plot. Gross et al. offer Alex Flinn's *Fade to Black* (2005) as a rare example of a YA novel that exposes the inaccuracies and critiques the unreasonable fears present in so many other books. The novel's HIV+ teenage protagonist, Alex, has a mother who insists on telling others that he was infected through a blood transfusion. To her chagrin, Alex eventually reveals the truth: he was infected through heterosexual sex. The book "does an excellent job of depicting the consequences of superstitious thinking, bigotry, and illogical panic," Gross et al. write, yet *Fade to Black* remains an "outlier" in the genre ("What Do Young Adult Novels Say" 410).

Sarah Brophy argues that "Stories of HIV infection and AIDS in the mainstream media are invested in managing and containing anxiety," and this is equally true of how children's and YA literature handles the relationship between young people and HIV/AIDS (5). In Megan Blumenreich and Marjorie Seigel's 2006 study of books about HIV/AIDS written for children in kindergarten through grade 5, for example, the authors conclude: "In all of the books in which children are the people with HIV/AIDS and in those in which a heterosexual person has HIV/AIDS, the idea of an 'innocent victim' is invoked" (100). Robert McRuer's "Reading and Writing 'Immunity': Children and the Anti-Body" exposes a similar attachment to the "innocent" narrative. Children's literature about AIDS from the late 1980s and early 1990s, McRuer argues, reflects liberal notions of AIDS as "everyone's disease," evacuating the gay male body while individualizing and desexualizing the context of the epidemic (184). He posits a binary of "immunity/implication" at the core of these texts: by virtue of their innocence, children are "immune" to the virus while the heterosexualized carriers are represented as requiring nothing more than compassion from the stories' young protagonists (187). Crucially absent,

McRuer writes, are a sense that HIV/AIDS is a collective, political issue and not an individual one; representations of sex-positive education as opposed to abstinence-based curricula; and the notion that HIV+ people (in addition to doctors and HIV- protagonists) have the right to be centered in these stories. Like Gross et al., McRuer makes it clear that the misrepresentation of HIV/AIDS in children's and YA literature can be potentially harmful to its young audiences. Together, these critics illustrate how adult authors and publishers seem more interested in anxiously rehearsing the imagined innocence of young people—keeping them at arm's length from HIV/AIDS—than engaging with the realities of how young people navigate their relationship to the virus.[2]

To this day, Jenkins and Cart indicate, "AIDS-related literature remains a very modest subgenre of LGBTQ+ literature" (67). There has been no significant study conducted on the topic since Gross et al. published their annotated bibliography, which is now a decade old. Moreover, an informal *Goodreads* search that I conducted with a research assistant yielded only eight YA titles published in the last five years (2015–2019) that deal directly with HIV/AIDS.[3] Of these titles, six are set in the 1980s or 90s; of the two titles that feature a contemporary setting, only one (Christopher Koehler's *Poz*) is about a young HIV+ protagonist (the other is about a protagonist with an HIV+ father). YA seems determined to represent HIV/AIDS as a historical issue that is largely detached from young people themselves. Yet Centers for Disease Control and Prevention (CDC) statistics indicate that in 2017, "youth aged 13 to 24 made up 21% (8,164) of the 38,739 new HIV diagnoses in the United States and dependent areas." Moreover, HIV+ youth "are the least likely of any age group to be linked to care in a timely manner and have a suppressed viral load" ("HIV and Youth"). Despite what YA suggests, HIV/AIDS continues to be a very real part of the lived experience of many young people in contemporary America.

Failures of the Shadow Uncles: *Two Boys Kissing*

Levithan's *Two Boys Kissing*, which initially seems to defy the trend of displacing or eliding HIV/AIDS, has garnered critical attention for the uniqueness of its narrative voice. Levithan's book is set in the present and focuses on the lives of seven queer teens: Craig and Harry, ex-boyfriends who are trying to set a world record for the longest kiss in support of their friend Tariq, who was gay bashed; Neil and Peter, whose relationship is affected by Neil's reluctance to come out to his family; Avery and Ryan, who are beginning to date after meeting at a queer prom; and Cooper, who is accidentally outed to his homophobic father. The story is narrated by a chorus of "shadow uncles," the ghosts of gay men who died during the height of the AIDS epidemic. "We are . . . your angel godfathers," they explain, "your mother's or your grandmother's best friend from college, the author of that book you found in the gay section of the library. We are characters in a Tony Kushner play, or names on a quilt that rarely gets taken out anymore. We are the ghosts of the remaining older generation" (Levithan 3).

Generally speaking, critics praised Levithan's use of this chorus, commenting on its innovativeness and affective force. Readers "can't shake the dead souls to which Levithan has given such eloquent voice," writes Louis Bayard in the *Los Angeles Times*, arguing that the chorus "enlarg[es]" the story's themes and "tease[s] out cross-generational epiphanies." In the *School Library Journal*, Karyn Silverman calls the chorus "a magnificent construct," "the true emotional core" of the novel and "a serious contender for best voice of 2013" that communicates a "palpable and powerful" "sorrow for the lives left behind, the lives unlived." s.e. smith's blog review argues that the chorus preserves voices that "played such an important role in queer history, in the history of radical health activism, in social history." Although she is ambivalent about the narrative authority evoked by the shadow uncles, Jackie C. Horne concedes that "the first person plural narrator clearly gives the book much of its power." And in the *Lambda Literary Review*, Lydia Harris calls *Two Boys Kissing* "a powerfully explosive work of literary art" due in large part to the chorus, which "gives [Levithan's] words a resonance, melding history with the present and projecting into the future."

A handful of scholarly articles has also been written on *Two Boys Kissing*.[4] Of particular interest is Angel Daniel Matos's essay, which argues that Levithan's chorus defies temporality to cultivate a "trans-generational" and "trans-historical" queer community (62). Matos convincingly makes a case for the novel's "reparative agenda," which aims to historicize contemporary queer struggles in the context of a collective that includes the shadow uncles, Levithan's coterie of young present-day protagonists, and, presumably, the reader, who "can potentially become intimately familiar with [their] place in history" (64). For Matos, this collision of past and present enables a hopeful political agenda uncommon in other queer YA novels. He maintains: "*Two Boys Kissing* breaks away from the conventions of YA novels with queer content and unsettles many of the generic expectations of YA fiction" (60). Indeed, as all of the novel's critics flag, Levithan's story offers a powerful reminder of the entire generation that was lost to HIV/AIDS. The ghostly chorus certainly makes *Two Boys Kissing* stand out amongst other YA novels on similar themes, which tend to—as McRuer points out—focus on individuals instead of the collective. This communal impulse, as Matos highlights, is a compelling rarity. *Two Boys Kissing* does not, however, depart from how YA anxiously keeps HIV/AIDS at a "safe" distance from its young protagonists.

In her moving memoir of the AIDS crisis, Susan Schulman writes:

> We still have to work every day to assert the obvious, that in fact, there are two distinctly different kinds of AIDS that are not over.
> 1. There is AIDS of the past.
> 2. There is ongoing AIDS.
> Neither is over, although they are treated quite differently in the present moment. (42)

Two Boys Kissing primarily represents "AIDS of the past" while neglecting "ongoing AIDS."[5] Despite the centrality of the chorus, AIDS is explicitly named only a handful of times in the novel, first on its eighth page, when the shadow uncles proclaim that "some of us swear we died of heartbreak, not AIDS." Prior to that, the uncles use coded language to describe their relationship to AIDS: they are "characters in a Tony Kushner play" and "names on a quilt," references that would elude readers without the relevant intertextual knowledge. Otherwise, the virus remains absent from the present-day setting, aside from one incident when a homophobic radio caller expresses his hope that Craig and Harry, the two boys kissing, are "giving each other AIDS" (129). None of the novel's young protagonists are affected by HIV/AIDS, and only one secondary character—a teacher, Mr. Bellamy—is explicitly connected to the virus. HIV remains a fundamentally historical issue, and the record-breaking public kiss becomes the locus of contemporary queer activism—as opposed to, for example, the kinds of collective political action that McRuer calls for, those that would center sex-positive education and the voices of people living with HIV.

The fissure between past and present takes shape early in the novel, when the shadow uncles narrate how Neil, en route to his boyfriend's house, "is struck by a feeling of deep, unnamed gratitude. He realizes that part of his good fortune is his place in history, and he thinks fleetingly of us, the ones who came before. We are not names or faces to him; we are an abstraction, a force" (2). Certainly, as the chorus points out, Neil is lucky to have been born following the worst of the AIDS epidemic. However, Neil's thoughts are "fleeting" and the shadow uncles remain an "abstraction": HIV/AIDS is relegated to the past, to a "place in history." Matos acknowledges that HIV/AIDS causes a "spatial and temporal divide" between the shadow uncles and the novel's contemporary protagonists, but he highlights how the latter "inhabit a time in which they are not only aware of AIDS, but ultimately able to control it with relative success thanks to the existence of protease inhibitors and increased awareness of safe sex" (62). If Levithan's present-day characters are indeed aware of HIV/AIDS as something that exists beyond a historical "abstraction" or recourse for homophobic slurs, they give no indication.

HIV is also something of an abstraction in *Castro*. The game's "bacterial virus" is not HIV—it is not called HIV, nor is it transmitted like HIV—yet its role in this game (which was, again, designed to raise funds for AIDS charities) links it to HIV. *Castro*'s "circuit of feeling" is powered in large part by hyperbolized anxieties about HIV/AIDS that also circulate in YA and popular discourse about HIV/AIDS. Recall Gross et al.'s observation that "unreasonable fears" like "casual contact" (i.e. kissing, sharing drinks) are pervasive in YA about HIV; *Castro* gives us a "fast acting" virus that spreads though alcohol consumption and, like HIV, has "no antidote." The origin of *Castro*'s virus is at the center of the game's mystery, just as YA often makes a "mystery" out of how characters acquire HIV (*HIV/AIDS* 40). Furthermore, *Castro*'s virus is the result of a conspiracy targeted specifically at the queer community, who felt and continues to feel the impact of HIV/AIDS in a profound way. Schulman notes that US governments have been "pretending away the deaths of 540,436 adults and 5,369 children from AIDS in the United States of America (as of 2008)," that they disregarded "AIDS as it was happening" and continue to imagine "that past AIDS has no impact on survivors," and "that ongoing AIDS is inevitable, sad, and impossible to change" (50–51). Placing a villain named "Straightman" at the center of a plot to murder queers, in *Castro*'s case, is an apt reflection of how many queers may feel about the deficient government responses to the AIDS crisis in America.

Castro also invites us to feel these anxieties through its aesthetic. The Castro neighborhood, as represented in the game, is something of an apocalyptic wasteland. Although the bacteria has yet to be released when the game begins, Castro's landscape—rendered in crude, black and white graphics—is a haunting one. The game unfolds at 3:30am, and the Castro is all but abandoned. If the player clicks on the night sky outside "The Gayme Room," the game's opening setting (see figure 3.3), a text box appears containing the first stanza of Henry Wadsworth Longfellow's melancholy poem "The Day is Done": "The day is done, and the darkness / Falls from the wings of Night, / As a feather is wafted downward / From an eagle in his flight." The only non-player characters Tracker McDyke can encounter are the Gayme Room's unconscious bartender, a dead body in the trunk of a car, a naked woman who can be spied upon through the window above Straightman's office, the bouncer of Club 102 (who will murder you unless you correctly answer his question), a handful of couples in the aptly named "Red Herring Cafe," and Tessy, the kidnapped drag queen whom you ultimately discover chained to the wall of a secret room. East of the Gayme Room is a boarded-up, scorched building: the "Gay Apparel Clothing store," which "burned down last week under mysterious circumstances" in a fire that also killed its proprietor. Every time McDyke passes the bank, "You hear gun

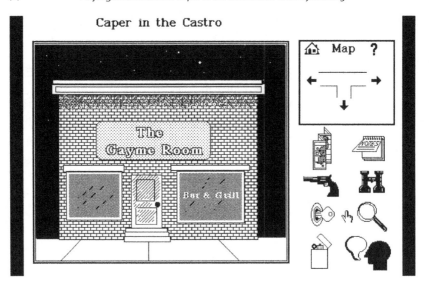

Figure 3.3. Opening setting of *Caper in the Castro*. Copyright C. M. Ralph, 1989. Retrieved from https://archive.org/details/hypercard_caper-in-the-castro. Reproduced with permission.

fire and feel 2 bullets whizzing just over your head" (if you try to enter, you are arrested and lose the game). Dying in the game returns players, again and again, to the image of a tombstone that reads, "Here Lies a Mediocre & Unsuccessful Private Detective." The affect evoked by this digital world is one of dread and impending doom. It is a place that has already been harmed by Straightman and is under threat of further, more significant harm—unless McDyke can put a stop to it. This further threat is, of course, the virus that both is and is not HIV.

Castro exemplifies what Anable calls "the aesthetics of failure" in video games (123). She emphasizes the close relationship between affect and aesthetics, given that the latter "is derived from the Greek word *aesthesis*, meaning 'sensation' or 'feeling'" (120). Anable theorizes the aesthetics of failure vis-a-vis contemporary games that deploy "simple graphics and low-resolution imagery"—akin to what *Castro* offers—to mislead the player into believing that victory will be easily achieved (123). Ultimately, through challenging controls and frustrating gameplay mechanics, these games deny the player such satisfaction. Anable considers this to be an intentional game design strategy, a "preferred aesthetic and an ideological tactic" (123), which has the potential to "shift our attention away from perceived personal failings and back to failures of a larger ideological system"—capitalism, for example, which relies heavily on glitch-free relationships between machines and their operators (129). In *Castro*'s case, the story of Straightman's conspiracy—as told through the game's stark landscape; rudimentary, monochromatic graphics; and looming threat of queer genocide—might return us to the government's failure to see queer lives as worthy of recognition, protection, and mourning. In terms of the gameplay failures it causes, however, *Castro* is something of a different case. When players such as I fail at *Castro*, it is not always as a result of intentional pathways built into the gameplay, despite the game's many avenues to character death. *Castro* invites the question: how does a video game make us feel when it *unintentionally* denies us the chance to succeed, when repeated failures are the result of a glitch?

How to Fail at *Caper in the Castro*

The first time I booted *Caper in the Castro*, I was excited to start playing. I found the plot synopsis to be witty and captivating, and the screenshots I viewed online filled me with fuzzy nostalgia for the blocky, low-resolution graphics and Chicago font endemic to 1980–1990s Macintosh software. It was thrilling to see overt queer themes and characters housed in such a retro digital environment. The game itself, however, is glitchy and often deeply frustrating to play. Launching *Castro* through the Internet Archive emulator was its own challenge: before starting the game, players have to configure the simulated Macintosh desktop to properly produce sound. On several occasions, I was somehow booted from the game into a HyperCard home screen (which required a restart of the emulator). Dialogue boxes often contain spelling errors. Players have to type in commands to progress, and the game is unforgiving where the specificity of these (occasionally misspelled) prompts is concerned—at one critical juncture, for example, the player must misspell "shackles" as "shakles" to achieve the appropriate effect. Typing often produces a "sticky key" effect, where the same letter is unintentionally reproduced multiple times. Yet the game's most agonizing glitch is that every keystroke produces the correct result except for the hyphen (-). Whenever I tried to input a hyphen, nothing would happen.

Hyphen-free gameplay would typically seem to be a minor issue, except at one point the player must dial a phone number (922–5489) and unlock a safe (combination: 64–69–102; see figure 3.6) in order to receive valuable clues, and the game will not accept these entries without hyphens in the appropriate place. I tried playing on my personal Apple laptop, my Apple office computer, and Apple tablet; I conferred with my research assistant, a PC user; I attempted cutting and pasting hyphens from various word processing applications; I experimented with a near-infinite number of keyboard shortcuts: all efforts were in vain. In case my technological aptitude is in doubt, I am not the only gamer to experience this

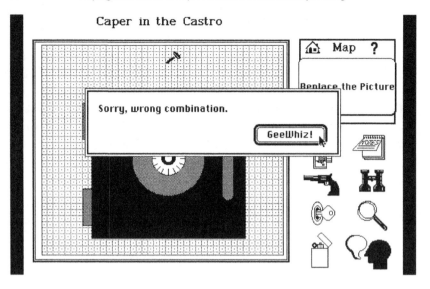

Figure 3.4. Failing repeatedly to crack the safe due to lack of hyphen access. From *Caper in the Castro,* copyright C. M. Ralph, 1989. Retrieved from https://archive.org/details/hypercard_caper-in-the-castro. Reproduced with permission.

glitch. The game's sole Internet Archive review (as of May 2019) reads, "honestly the only problem is i cant finish the game because i cant use the space bar, '-', and the bottom keys on my keyboard are off one letter in game." (I did not experience the first or third issues).[6] I lost my patience; I felt like I was wasting my time. My annoyance was such that I walked away from the game for several weeks. If I couldn't play this game properly, I didn't want to play it at all.

Eventually, out of desperation, I cheated. A complete play-through of *Castro* is available on YouTube, created by a gamer, Puck, who somehow had access to the elusive hyphen (Puck Was Here). I watched the video until Puck made the phone call, unlocked the safe, and received the clues. I played again, clicking my way through the game. I made some headway. I uncovered a dead body, discovered a few more clues, and shot my way through the window into Club 102. There, I encountered another annoyingly specific prompt that I couldn't crack.[7] I abandoned the game again for a while, and eventually returned to Puck's YouTube video. At this point, I had essentially given up on solving the game myself, so I watched Puck play their way through *Castro*, liberate Tessy, and destroy the toxic bacteria. I "passed" the game, just to have the experience, but it was deeply unsatisfying. I felt like I didn't earn it—rather, I was frustrated because the glitchy game hadn't permitted me the gratification of completing it on my own. It denied me the pleasure of a fair victory.

In *The Art of Failure*, Juul suggests that video games' uniqueness lies in how they allow us to play with the sensation of failing, "to experience and experiment with failure" (30). Whereas we tend to avoid failure in real life, Juul argues, we often pursue failure when playing a video game, because through failure we learn, adapt, and approach success. In fact, Juul claims, the more we fail at a game, the more satisfying will be our eventual victory. Good video games, therefore, set us up for repeated failure but also "promise us a fair chance of redeeming ourselves" (7). What Juul describes, however, is a kind of deliberate, intentionally programmed failure unlike what I experienced while playing *Castro*. I certainly fell into a number of traps purposefully set up by the game (I drank the lethal house wine, I was killed by the Club 102 bouncer, I was arrested by the police for attempting to break into the bank), but my most substantial and frustrating pathways to failure were through the game's glitches. "While we dislike feeling responsible for failure," Juul writes, "we dislike even more strongly games in which we do not feel responsible for failure" (20). This is precisely why I was so annoyed by *Castro* the first few times I played it: it refused me the agency to overcome my failures and complete the game on my own terms. In fact, it denied me the opportunity to pass the game at all without what I understood to be cheating. Technically I succeeded, but I still felt like I had failed.

Castro's compelled failures illuminate anxieties surrounding agency and failure that are present in *Two Boys Kissing*. In Levithan's novel, these anxieties emerge through the temporal gap that divides the novel's ghostly chorus from its contemporary protagonists, the specters of the AIDS crisis from a present that resists remembering. The passage that illustrates this dynamic most clearly occurs towards the end of the novel. Cooper, outcast by his homophobic father, drives to a bridge with the intent of committing suicide. The shadow uncles watch in horror, despairing at their inability to intervene, at their lack of agency: "We want to close our eyes. Why can't we close our eyes?" (189). They proceed to describe a series of queer youth deaths using this same rhetorical structure: "Why must we watch as a twelve-year-old puts a gun to his head and pulls the trigger? Why must we watch as a fourteen-year-old hangs himself in the garage, to be found by his grandmother two hours later?" (189). This continues for three additional sentences. Then, the shadow uncles ask:

> Why must we die over and over again?
>   Cooper lifts himself into the air. Here we are, thousands of us, shouting no, shouting at him to stop, crying out and making a net of our bodies, trying to come between him and the water, even though we know—we always know— that no matter how tight a net we make, no matter how hard we try, he will still fall through.

We die over and over again.
Over and over again. (189)

On the one hand, in its failure to account for the ongoing impact of HIV/AIDS on young people's lives, *Two Boys Kissing* perpetuates an unfortunate, longstanding YA trend. On the other hand, however, we could read the novel as illustrating this precise failure: the failure of the past to intervene meaningfully in the present, because the present will not recognize the past in any consequential way. Levithan's chorus opens an affective circuit where past collides with present, but the two temporal zones remain unreconciled—the ghosts of the past rail against the present, for the present continually fails to fully acknowledge the past. Due to this lack of control, the ghostly chorus's efforts are doomed to fail. "Listen to us," the shadow uncles insist: "We fruitlessly demand that you listen to us" (188). Yet the present refuses to listen, the "net" of bodies will fail to catch the falling boy, and the uncles are destined to die "over and over again," a point emphasized by the threefold repetition of this phrase.

Although Matos acknowledges the limited influence of the shadow uncles—"current queer generations rarely think about them anymore," he notes (64)—he insists that the ghostly chorus "bonds the narratives of distinct queer communities that have been fractured by the hammers of time, illness, and progress" (61), and argues that "different queer generations" are "connected . . . through political convictions" (67). In my view, however, the past and present in *Two Boys Kissing* remain unreconciled and irreconcilable. But this might be the novel's most powerful point: the present continually refuses to address the history of the AIDS crisis and recognize its ongoingness. Like Schulman, Brophy points to the ways in which public discourse figures the AIDS crisis as being "over": "'over' through indifference or inaction, through a refusal to grieve, through its 'Africanization,' which includes the sense of its being 'over' here, in North America" (8). Nonetheless, Brophy notes, "the epidemic's ghosts" endure, protesting

> against their being exorcized, rendered untroublesome by a public rhetoric of AIDS that would fast-forward public consciousness to a sometime future world, one purified of the scourge and its 'victims,' a world, in other words, purified of grief and mourning. (8)

This is the very dynamic that *Two Boys Kissing* illustrates so forcefully. The shadow uncles lament their lack of impact in the present, a world in which the legacy of HIV/AIDS is not acknowledged, a world in which they remain a mere "abstraction." This is also a world where the weight of their deaths have not had an appropriate effect on the temporal orientations of queer youth: "It galls us, we with such a limited future," the shadow uncles narrate, "to see someone brush it aside as meaningless, when it has an endless capacity for meaning, and an endless number of meanings that can be found within it" (155). *Two Boys Kissing* enacts a version of the queer double-take discussed in this book's introduction: Levithan shows us how looking back and then looking forward can be a futile gesture, one that only leads to a failure of the present to acknowledge the pedagogical value of the backwards look.

In *Playing with Feelings*, Anable asks, "How can a video game affectively reorient us toward history?" (2). *Castro* offers its version of HIV/AIDS, Straightman's "bacterial virus," as a "mystery" to be solved by the player—but the resolution of this mystery is severely impeded by a series of glitches. When I attempted to "win" *Castro*, but instead died and failed "over and over again" because the game unfairly refused me the chance to succeed, I felt the embodied, affective effects of failure. Of course, the simulated deaths and failures I encountered in *Castro* are far from equivalent to the countless real lives lost to AIDS. Yet by repeatedly compelling players to fail, *Castro* opens us into an affective circuit where we as players might feel the present-day endurance of historical failures, and feel these failures embodied as our own. As Halberstam suggests in *The Queer Art of Failure*, the negative affect associated with failure "disturbs the supposedly clean boundaries between . . . winners and losers" (3). Such feelings reframe "success" in the context of the game and ask us to consider what "winning" might even look or feel like, if "winning" is even possible or desirable. In *Two Boys Kissing*, the shadow uncles evince similar feelings. They lack the agency to intervene in the present, failing "over and over again" to prevent ongoing violence and suicide amongst queer youth, who themselves die "over and over again." Playing *Castro* today, this equation is flipped, as we present-day players fail "over and over again" to successfully engage with this historical object and handily solve its mystery. *Castro* obliges us to feel the affective weight—the frustration, the hopelessness—of those failures represented in *Two Boys Kissing*: the failure of the present to properly mourn the past and recognize the ongoingness of HIV/AIDS, and the consequential failure of the past to have any authority over the present.

Networking Failure

In her final chapter, Anable invites us to consider the social possibilities that might emerge from failing at video games. She asks, "What if, through video games, the feelings associated with failure were put to different ends? Might that experience have some affective and socio-technological significance that extends beyond the context of our play?" (104). Anable argues that games offering an aesthetic of failure "ask us to *feel failure differently*—not quite sit and accept failure, but more to *flail with failure*" (116). She looks specifically at games that require unconventional and difficult bodily movements—phone apps that require unusual manipulations of the device, for instance. Such ostensibly nonproductive gestures, "in relation to machines designed for the more orderly and smooth operations of immaterial labor," Anable suggests, might "reverse the individualization of failure and deflect it back onto the failings of larger systems" (116). *Castro* only requires standard use of a mouse and a keyboard to navigate its point-and-click-based environment: nothing too atypical. Yet the frustrating failures it nonetheless compels return us to the broader socio-political failures I outline above. Following Anable, I ask: where else might these fails and flails take us?

In order to "pass" *Castro* and at least partially overcome my many failures, I naturally turned to the Internet, something that would have been much more difficult when *Castro* was initially circulating. I could not solve the game in isolation. I had to move from HyperCard, the Macintosh software Ralph used to build *Castro*, to the World Wide Web, which HyperCard paved the way for. As Jim Boulton explains, "HyperCard was the first hypermedia program, directly influencing the Web, the browser, and countless websites"; the software was "a direct inspiration for Enquire, the hypertext program that evolved into the Web." In other words, I had to become part of a network of texts and people brought together by *Castro*: Puck the online gamer, the *LGBTQ Video Game Archive*, and various articles about and interviews with C. M. Ralph (one of which provides the "shakles" tip). As does Wreck-It-Ralph in Halberstam's reading of the video-game-inspired Disney film, I found "an alternative path" through the game "by virtue of a glitch" ("Queer Gaming" 196). *Castro* denied me a hyphen, the character used to join words and numbers, but it asked me to join and connect myself elsewhere and through other means. This aligns with (C. M., not Wreck-It) Ralph's original motivation for designing the game: to pay homage to her queer family, and to raise money in support of people living with and dying from HIV/AIDS. At its core, *Castro* is a game for and about community.

My research into *Castro* led me to a particularly striking fact. *Castro's* opening screen contains a caution: "This game includes scenes of violence and other material which may be inappropriate for persons under the age of 18." Yet as an article in the *Washington Blade* about *Castro* indicates, as of late 1989 only two people had successfully solved the game: the article's author (who admits to having cheated by hacking HyperCard) and a 14-year-old boy, "an avid computer gamer [who] was therefore aided by his understanding of the typical conventions of role-playing games" (Yockey). Young people were and likely still are playing this game, are part of its network of players, even if they do not belong to its intended audience. What the *Washington Blade* and Gross et al's research demonstrate is that young people are often silent participants when it comes to the various media ecologies of HIV/AIDS: they are denied a visibility and presence that reflects their actual level of engagement and participation. These ecologies—or networks, to slide from an organic metaphor to one more appropriate given this chapter's digital focus—occlude the involvement of young people, keeping them at an anxious distance despite their material realities.

Two Boys Kissing also makes clear this temporal and generational network failure. At one point, the shadow uncles meditate on the absence of phone cords in the contemporary world. "Reading this today," they suggest, directly addressing the reader, "you might not even know what a phone cord is" (28–29). They insist that "once upon a time," however, "a telephone cord seemed like nothing less than a lifeline" (29). They continue:

> It was your attachment to the outside world and, even more than that, your attachment to the people you loved, or wanted to love, or tried to love. . . . It kept us tethered to each other, tethered to all the questions and some of the answers, tethered to the idea that we could be somewhere other than our rooms, our homes, our towns. We couldn't escape, but our voices could travel. (29)

The phone cord is a paradox. It is limiting and liberating, "tethering" the uncles to a place from which they cannot escape, while simultaneously allowing them access to an outside world. Matos picks up on this moment and argues that it nourishes the novel's communal impulse, allowing "the narrators to create networks between their world and the world of contemporary queer youth" (63). By comparing the "'anachronistic' phone cord . . . to the cordless cellular phone," Matos explains, "the shadow uncles demonstrate how differences of technology mediate a way of uniting different queer generations" (63–64). These generations are far from united, however, and consistent with the failures compelled by the rift between past and present established throughout the novel, any attempts at networking fail. While the shadow uncles fetishize the phone cord, they remain vociferously anti-digital. In their view, the analog unites while the digital divides. "All of these men and boys with their computers," they lament, "all of these men and boys with their phones. . . . All of these men and boys fragmenting themselves, hoping the fragments are pieced together on the other end. . . . All of these men and boys still lonely when the rush is over, and the devices are off, and they are alone with themselves again" (65). Unlike the analog cord, which serves to liberate through physical attachment, digital technology—despite being tetherless and therefore ostensibly more free-ing—results only in further alienation. Indeed, Cooper, the novel's unhappiest character and its sole uncoupled protagonist, is the figure most closely associated with digital technology. Cooper's homophobic expulsion is the result of his father discovering porn on his computer; his unhappy sexual encounters and futile search for connection are mediated by digital apps.[8] Instead of seeking to bridge this technological divide, the shadow uncles insist on the superiority of their network while perceiving the younger queer generation as fragmented by technology, not "united" by it, as Matos suggests. According to the ghostly chorus, contemporary youth are simultaneously hypernetworked and alone, tethered to the wrong kind of technology, trapped in the wrong circuit.

Ironically, the novel's central plot subverts the shadow uncles' anxious and somewhat patronizing view of contemporary technology. It is thanks to the Internet, after all, that Craig and Harry are able to disseminate their record-breaking kiss and anti-homophobia protest. As the kiss reaches its conclu-sion, Tariq's broadcast has gone viral (the only real "viral" component of the contemporary plot): "Tariq sees that there are almost half a million people, around the world, who are watching this" (194). The novel's ambivalence about technology requires a final gesture on Tariq's part, however: "Then he stops looking at the computer and looks straight at life" (194). Despite this and despite the chorus's insistence that contemporary technology is more alienating than community-building, the Internet brings the novel's protagonists into a queer collective that crystallizes around the kiss. Neil and Peter, observing the kiss's final countdown, "call out the numbers along with everyone else. They hold hands, feel like they are witnessing something monumental, something that could change things. It won't, but that feeling, that spirit will live on in everyone here, everyone who sees. The spirit will change things" (194). This is perhaps the one moment in the novel where its two networks briefly unite in a circuit of "feeling," which is also described as a "spirit"—the spirit, that is, of the ghostly chorus. The characters are tethered to one another both materially and digitally; the spirit is transmitted to those physically present ("everyone here") and, through the web, to those watching online ("everyone who sees"). Consistent with the generational dichotomy elsewhere in the novel, however, the narrative remains ambivalent. The kiss "won't" change things, but "the spirit will"; on the following page, the shadow uncles remind us: "We watch you, but we can't intervene" (195). The novel nonetheless hopes, however, that the uncles have somehow intervened. Albeit briefly, the story provides a moment where analog joins with digital to allow contemporary youth a moment of networked, affective union—a fleeting instance of reconciliation between the past of HIV/ AIDS and a present that denies this past while refusing to recognize its contemporary connections to young people.

Young people themselves have forcefully critiqued such anxious desires to render historical HIV/AIDS and ignore its ongoingness. An online art project entitled "Your Nostalgia is Killing Me" offers "a digital rendering of a (queer) child's bedroom circa the late 1990s, outfitted with the greatest hits from AIDS culture," as "a battle cry for the present" (Juhasz and Kerr). The creators, Vincent Chevalier and Ian Bradley-Perrin—both young men living with HIV—have expressed how "they meet people their own age who have a better sense of AIDS of the past than they do of AIDS now" (Juhasz and Kerr). Juhasz and Kerr explain: "All of the cultural fetishization of the past of AIDS . . . makes it almost impossible for people to conceive of HIV in the now. That in turn makes it harder for people to consider what needs to be done now in response to the ongoing crisis." In their artists' statement, Chevalier and Bradley-Perrin use language also found in *Two Boys Kissing* to emphasize the importance of building a network that includes a fuller sense of the past *and* present of HIV/AIDS:

> Do not let the dregs of our history be your horse blinders as you move through today's world because things are different now as they were different then. Allow the history to be real and *tethered* to a time and place and reason such that the output is responding to today and is ready for tomorrow. Let the past sleep some such that it can be more present in the choices you make on reality, not the reality itself. (Emphasis added.)

Here, Chevalier and Bradley-Perrin argue for an enhanced network of HIV/ AIDS, one that tethers past to present in such a way that the present must recognize the past, "responding" to it meaningfully and allowing it to be "present" without becoming "the reality itself." This passage echoes Christopher Castiglia and Christopher Reed's critique of queer temporal theory in *If Memory Serves*, in which they argue that certain theorists disconnect "theory from history by ignoring the relationship of its concerns to the social specificities of the present, particularly the temporal warps brought about by AIDS, or to the theoretical and social insights of the past that might help us respond to cultural reactions to the epidemic" (24).[9] Castiglia and Reed look specifically at memory and its ability to transform us in the present, arguing that the past is "worth recalling as a realm of possibility in the present and, by extension, the future" (7) Following Anable, we might consider why *Caper in the Castro* is worth playing today. What can this game, resurrected as a ghost from the past, tell us about ourselves in the present and our relationship to HIV/AIDS?

Both *Castro* and *Two Boys Kissing* open us into the possibility of a network, even if this network often fails to effectively join the past of HIV/AIDS to its present. These texts simultaneously represent and elide HIV/AIDS while foregrounding the discursive failures that surround the virus. As Kerr and Juhasz explain, "AIDS is an assemblage: a constellation of things, processes, and experiences (including those of the past and present) having to live alongside and in connection with each other." Together, *Castro* and *Two Boys Kissing* ask us as players and readers to consider our accountability to this assemblage. How do we reconcile the past of HIV/AIDS with its present and the future, why and where do we fail to do so, what does it feel like to fail, and what are the consequences of this failure? Through these texts we also see anxieties emerge surrounding the relationship of young people to HIV/AIDS, and how "child/youth" as category is often represented as irreconcilable with the virus. As "Your Nostalgia is Killing Me" demonstrates, however, youth are very much affected by and engaged with discourse about HIV/AIDS.

Anable reminds us of the relational qualities of affect, which grants us "the embodied capacity to feel—that which simultaneously opens us up to the world as relational beings and reminds us that our own sense of individuation and connection is always partial and extremely limited" (xix). Recall, too, Brian Massumi's suggestion, as quoted in the introduction to this book, that "intensified affect" brings "a stronger sense of embeddedness in a larger field of life—a heightened sense of belonging, with other people and to other places" (214). Dying and failing "over and over again," much like Levithan's shadow uncles, *Castro*'s players feel the affective weight of cumulative loss—of loss and failure in the game, and the losses and failures associated with the HIV/AIDS crisis—while being plunged into a larger network through which such feelings circulate readily. Yet as Kathryn Bond Stockton points out, "Sometimes in the long arc of the accumulation of loss something builds . . . that you then retrospectively understand as this tremendous benefit and generative aspect of failure" (Ruberg 208). Here, Stockton argues not for a recuperation of failure, for turning failure into productivity, but she invites us instead to think about the alternative paths down which failure might lead us. Indeed, by making players feel and endure failure "over and over again," *Castro* points us to new networks and connections while challenging us to reexamine how we feel about and understand "winning" and "losing" in the context of broader social and cultural structures.

As Halberstam suggests, "Maybe we can think of some more complex reasons to design games where the only outcome is losing" (Ruberg 209). Like *Castro*, such games might invite us to dwell and "flail" with failure instead of racing forwards to ostensible victory. Such nonlinear lingerings—which we have seen elsewhere in this book, particularly in the sideways motions of queer YA protagonists Davy and Chuck—might recall the temporality of anxiety that permeates queer YA's affective economy. Like the other queer YA texts explored thus far, *Castro* opposes teleology through the many failures it induces. *Castro*'s playability, however, adds a new dimension to this nebulous body of queer YA texts—it presents the stall-and-start, sideways temporality of anxiety as a ludological structure. It offers us, that is, the opportunity to play with and feel the temporality of anxiety as it emerges through failure. It also renders more explicit the texts and readers/players to which queer YA is connected—including those young people who are not necessarily imagined to be participants in these networks. Moreover, it challenges us to consider our role, as readers and critics of queer YA, in potentially shoring up structures that privilege narrative and sexual teleology, while potentially eliding the lived realities of young queers—especially when it comes to representations of HIV/AIDS. As Levithan's shadow uncles narrate, "We have already done our part. Just as you are doing your part, whether you know it or not, whether you mean to or not, whether you want to or not. Choose your actions wisely" (195).

CHAPTER 4

Dystopia: Queer Sex and the Unbearable in *Grasshopper Jungle*

On History and Shit

Austin Szerba, the sixteen-year-old narrator of Andrew Smith's 2014 novel *Grasshopper Jungle*, is obsessed with history. With compulsive attention to detail, Austin catalogues the minutiae of the world's destruction by mutant mantises with voracious appetites for sex and human flesh—a catastrophe that begins with the accidental release of an experimental virus in Austin's stiflingly small, recession-ravaged hometown of Ealing, Iowa. No detail appears too insignificant or inappropriate for Austin's thorough documentation of the apocalypse: the bowel movements and masturbatory habits of the novel's supporting players; his recurring sexual fantasies that involve a three-way in Sweden with his girlfriend and male best friend, both of whom he admits to loving; the lurid particulars of every blood-soaked death at the mandibles of those pesky rampaging mutant bugs. "History never tells about people taking shits," Austin protests. "I can't for a moment believe that guys like Theodore Roosevelt or Winston Churchill never took a shit. History always abbreviates out the shit-taking" (69). If you've read Smith's book, *you know what I mean.* "*You know what I mean*" is, in fact, the refrain that often accompanies Austin's account of events—a refrain that invites us to doubt, in the grand tradition of unreliable narrators, Austin's self-described "unimpeachable," "historical" account of the end of the world (86). Austin's insistent, italicized repetition of "*You know what I mean*" implies that we don't actually know what he means, otherwise, why would he have to continually assert that we do?

"This is how history works: It is omniscient," Austin explains:

> Everyone trusts history. Think about it—when we read history books—nobody
> ever asks, *How did you find this out if it happened before you were born?* History
> is unimpeachable, sublime. It is my job. I can tell you things that nobody could
> possibly know because I am the *recorder*. I found out everything in time, but I'm
> abbreviating. Cutting out the shit. (86)

This is, of course, loaded with irony, because Austin has already told us how
integral shit is to his narrative. He continues, "You have to trust me. This is history. *You know what I mean.* Why wouldn't you trust me? I admitted everything.
Think of how embarrassing these truths are to me" (87). And it does indeed
appear that Austin admits and describes everything, including events he couldn't
possibly know anything about, although he does gesture to the paradoxes and
impossibilities of recording an exhaustive history. "You could never get *everything* in a book," Austin narrates; "Good books are always about everything"
(76). In the context of a story where Austin's impulse is to overdescribe and
repeatedly ask for the reader's trust, his abbreviations and silences become
all the more apparent and audible. It is this relationship between excess and
abbreviation that interests me in this chapter.

I argue that Austin's silences mark moments of the unbearable—as theorized
in Lauren Berlant and Lee Edelman's *Sex, or the Unbearable* (2014)—and that
Austin's narration enables us to think, in broader terms, about queer negativity in relation to children's literature. In recent years, as dystopian novels like
Grasshopper Jungle explode in popularity, critics have expressed intense anxieties
about trends in "dark" children's literature and the potential for these books
to harm, traumatize, or, conversely, nourish their young readers.[1] Given their
perception that a vulnerable young audience lies on the other end of these
texts, many critics seem affectively overwhelmed when responding to children's
literature with dark themes. For some critics, literary dystopias beget dystopian childhoods: dark themes risk stripping young readers of their supposed
innocence. For others, literary dystopia is an appropriate mirror for the social,
emotional, and physical dystopia—the storm and stress—that characterizes
many adolescent experiences, sexual and otherwise.

Grasshopper Jungle, I argue, responds to contemporary dystopian children's
literature and its anxious criticism in two ways. First, Smith's novel satirizes G.
Stanley Hall's *Sturm und Drang* model of adolescence by toying with and hyper-
bolizing the generic conventions of the YA problem novel.[2] Next, *Grasshopper
Jungle* speaks back, tongue-in-cheek, to those critics who view dystopian YA as
a potentially damaging force in the lives of young readers: Smith's novel forcefully assumes this destructive, negative position with delirious excess. This plays
itself out on terrain I'm calling the unbearable of children's literature, which,

in *Grasshopper Jungle*, emerges specifically through queer sex and sexuality.[3] Austin graphically describes violence and sexuality without being able to fully bear the affective burden of such representations; *Grasshopper Jungle*'s excessive rendering of the violent, sexual darknesses of children's literature makes hypervisible through contrast Austin's inability, and more generally, the frequent inability of children's literature criticism, to bear such darkness. Queer sex, in *Grasshopper Jungle*, occupies the novel's negative space. Queer sex exists only in the margins of Austin's otherwise vividly sketched narrative, which simultaneously literalizes and amplifies to satirical effect the self-shattering and world-destroying impulses of queer negativity. Before elaborating, however, in tribute to Austin, I'll begin with a little bit of recent history.

Dystopia and the "Dark Side" of YA

Lately, hugely popular dystopian children's and YA franchises like (among many others) Suzanne Collins's *The Hunger Games* (2008–2010), James Dashner's *The Maze Runner* (2009–2016), and Veronica Roth's *Divergent* (2011–2013) have attracted the anxious attention of the popular imagination, including numerous critics who ruminate on the dangers and pleasures these texts present to young audiences.[4] In December 2010, as dialogue about queer YA and queer youth swelled, the *New York Times* offered a debate on "The Dark Side of Young Adult Fiction" in which seven authors, scholars, and critics were invited to answer the following questions: "Why do bestselling young adult novels seem darker in theme now than in past years? What's behind this dystopian trend, and why is there so much demand for it?" These critics seem to agree that while dystopian YA might indeed be a recent trend, "the dark side" of children's literature isn't anything new; as Michelle Ann Abate points out, "children's literature has long engaged with weighty cultural issues, complex sociopolitical concerns, and even graphic violence." This debate also illustrates how popular conceptions of adolescence have not substantially shifted since Hall, at the turn of the twentieth century, first proposed *Sturm und Drang* as one of this life stage's fundamental qualities. As Kent Baxter explains, Hall positions "volatility" as adolescence's "most characteristic trait" (15); indeed, many of the *Times* respondents see adolescence as a dystopian time unfolding in surroundings that are often experienced as dystopian. Dystopian YA, for the *Times* critics, presents a useful mirror for adolescents who, as Paolo Bacigalupi writes, "are uneasily aware that their world is falling apart." This subgenre offers a source of "hope for humankind," in the words of Lisa Rowe Fraustino, "even if . . . it turns out that the society is beyond repair."

Multiple *Times* contributors propose that forms of discipline enabled by institutionalized education and technological surveillance engender in part the dystopian dimensions of adolescence. Scott Westerfeld, author of the *Uglies* series (2005–2007), suggests that "schools are places where teens are subject to dress codes, have few free speech rights, and are constantly surveilled. . . . Is it any wonder that dystopian novels speak to them?" Poet and novelist Jay Parini writes that school "may even be more brutal these days, with an excess of testing and the watchfulness not only of parents and teachers but the big eyeball of the system itself, its vision intensified by video surveillance cameras, Facebook and the omnipresent Web, which tracks everyone down . . . forever." As a result, Parini continues, young people "feel trapped, forced into a world of tests that humiliate and unnerve them." Deviating somewhat from these arguments in her claim that dystopian novels provide an escape for young readers, Maggie Stiefvater remains nonetheless invested in the idea that these texts enable adolescents to negotiate their relationship to an "increasingly complex" world: "In a culture defined by shades of gray," she writes, "I think the absolutely black and white choices in dark young adult novels are incredibly satisfying for readers."

The similarly affirmative responses that emerged in the wake of the *Times* debate concur that the darkness of dystopian novels reflects something inherent to the adolescent experience. Many authors refer to their own teenage reading memories and/or provide anecdotes about their students and/or children as evidence of this connection.[5] Gayle Forman, in a *Time* essay entitled "Teens Crave Young Adult Books on Really Dark Topics (and That's OK)," turns to science, citing "new brain mapping research" that finds "that adolescence is a time when teens are capable of engaging deeply with material, on both an intellectual level as well as an emotional one" and "the parts of the brain that processes [sic] emotion are even more online with teens than with adults." These perspectives recall Baxter's investigation of the adult "invention" of adolescence at the turn of the century, which saw the

> rise [of] two distinct and interrelated conceptions of this age category: the squeaky-clean "ideal" adolescent, who is controlled, controllable, and will enable the human race to attain a type of moral perfection; and . . . the "real" adolescent (as much a construction as the ideal), who represents a kind of cultural anxiety of the physical and sexual threat the adolescent can become if left to his or her own devices (12).

To put it somewhat crudely, many contemporary responses to YA understand dystopian YA as an important pedagogical component of the "real" adolescent's transition into something approaching the "ideal" adolescent—reading about dystopia helps young people both translate and manage their experience of *Sturm und Drang*. As Basu et al. point out, the "didacticism" of dystopian YA is often "reminiscent of that of Victorian novels for children," yet "the unequivocal clarity of their message" is "perhaps one of the strongest sources of appeal for young adult dystopias" (5).[6]

The counterpoint to the above—dystopia begets dystopia—is perhaps best represented by a viral 2011 *Wall Street Journal* essay entitled "Darkness too Visible," in which Meghan Cox Gurdon bemoans the disturbing themes, profanity, and "hideously distorted portrayals of . . . life" present in contemporary literature for young people.[7] "How dark is contemporary fiction for teens?" Gurdon asks, rhetorically; "Darker than when you were a child, my dear: So dark that kidnapping and pederasty and incest and brutal beatings are now just part of the run of things in novels directed, broadly speaking, at children from the ages of 12 to 18." Gurdon spends most of her word count detailing the "lurid" images and themes she finds repellent, pausing only briefly to reflect on why she would have us reject these texts: because the disturbing behavior YA represents may transmit itself, virus-like, to young readers. Parents should keep watchful eyes on their children's reading material, Gurdon concludes, and push back against publishers who "use the vehicle of fundamental free-expression principles to try to bulldoze coarseness or misery into their children's lives."

Gurdon's essay did not go unchallenged. Sherman Alexie, author of *The Absolutely True Diary of a Part-Time Indian*, wrote a response entitled "Why the Best Kids Books Are Written in Blood" defending the relevance and importance of dark themes in children's literature, and the ensuing conversation spawned NPR radio and print pieces.[8] "Adolescence is a dark time for a lot of people," writes Linda Holmes in an NPR essay, "not a fake-dark time, because they got a pimple, but a real dark time, because they have a friend who drinks too much or is abused at home or has a mental illness and wants to kill himself." The responses to Gurdon's initial piece were so multitudinous that she published a defensive follow-up, also in the *Wall Street Journal*, two weeks after her first piece appeared. In this essay, entitled "My 'Reprehensible' Take on Teen Literature," Gurdon rebukes her critics for exaggerating the perils of adolescence: "Adolescence, I've been instructed," she writes, "is a prolonged period of racism, homophobia, bullying, eating disorders, abusive sexual episodes, and every other manner of unpleasantness." Gurdon's take is that adolescence "feels more dramatic at the time than it will in retrospect," and that adult authors "do young people a disservice by seeming to endorse the worst that life has to offer." And Gurdon is not alone in this anxiety. We might also recall this book's introduction, in which I highlight Maria Tatar's October 2011 *New*

York Times essay "No More Adventures in Wonderland." Like Gurdon, Tatar fears for the safety of young audiences who are exposed to the "darkness" of contemporary children's literature, and she eulogizes a Golden Age literary tradition. While the dystopia-affirmative critics argue that loss and other dark experiences are natural parts of adolescence, Tatar and Gurdon suggest that dystopian childhoods can be catalyzed by children's literature that represents a loss of innocence without enough redemption.

These critics might disagree on the ultimate effects of dystopian children's literature, but taken together, they illustrate how the ostensibly "dark" and "adult" themes of sex, loss, and death exist in anxious, contentious, and affec-tively charged relation to children's literature, and, crucially, how childhood and adolescence remain ready vessels for adult projection and invention. It is worthwhile mentioning that none of the critiques of dark children's literature that I could locate in mainstream publications, online and otherwise—includ-ing the *Times* debate, which would seemingly be most invested in presenting a range of opinions—offers the unfiltered perspective of an actual child or adolescent reader.[9] Adults, in other words, remain the primary participants in the conversation about what young people should or should not read and the potential effects of reading. This is most likely because, as adults, we have deep and long-standing investments in the categories of childhood and adolescence. As Baxter explains, "we continue to invent adolescence because it satisfies a cultural need to define ourselves in relation to this liminal space that is close enough to share our hard-won values and distant enough to accommodate our deepest fears. The invention of adolescence is the invention of ourselves" (20). I'm also reminded of Kathryn Bond Stockton's persuasive critique, in *The Queer Child*, of the retrospective innocence model for understanding childhood. "The child is the specter of who we were when there was nothing yet behind us," Stockton writes; "From the standpoint of adults, innocence is alien, since it is 'lost' to the very adults who assign it to children. Adults retrospect it through the gauzy lens of what they attribute to the child" (30).

My contention is that anxious critiques of dystopian YA that struggle with this loss of innocence—especially sexual innocence—flag the fraught terrain of children's literature's unbearable. In *Sex, or the Unbearable*, Berlant and Edel-man provide "an analysis of relations that both overwhelm and anchor us—an affective paradox that often shapes the experience of sex" (vii). Crucially, for these authors—and for my purposes here—these relations are about sex but not limited to sex.[10] Relationality, for Berlant and Edelman, often entails an encounter with negativity that troubles our sense of coherence and sovereignty. Although sex "holds out the prospect of discovering new ways of being and of being in the world," they write, "it also raises the possibility of confronting our limit in ourselves or in another, of being inundated psychically or emotionally" (vii). Sex is a form of relationality, they continue, that "is invested with hopes, expectations, and anxieties that are often *experienced* as unbearable" (vii).

Berlant and Edelman understand the unbearable as emerging through relationality, through "an encounter with the estrangement and intimacy of being in relation" (viii). In reading children's literature, we as adult readers are in frequent relation with an imaginary child; yet, this a child from which we are always estranged, because, as Stockton and Baxter point out, children and adolescents possesses characteristics that we as adults have "lost" and/or continue to fetishize. In this sense children's literature also brings us in relation to ourselves as imaginary child readers, and to each other as adults who may engage with real child readers through texts that risk producing these unbearable feelings. These are often relations and encounters, as Berlant and Edelman write, "that both overwhelm and anchor us" (vii). What are all the critics I cite above if not simultaneously anchored and overwhelmed by their relation to the audience they imagine on the other end of children's literature? Loss, death, sex, and violence in children's literature bring these critics into affective relation with an imagined audience that breaches any sense of readerly sovereignty. The critics who affirm dystopian themes see them as crucial to managing the dysfunction often inherent to the adolescent experience, while Tatar and Gurdon's overwhelm manifests itself as the anxious desire to impose limits on the violence and sex to which young readers are exposed. This relationship to an imaginary audience prompts us as critics to articulate anxieties about how we conceive of the powers, limits, potential, and dangers of texts for young people.

So, back to *Grasshopper Jungle*, and our meticulous narrator, Austin. Smith's novel illustrates what I've outlined above: that (1) critics fetishize dystopia as an ideal manifestation of the adolescent experience, though this is but a recent permutation of Hall's century-old *Sturm und Drang* argument; and (2) critics of children's literature have a powerful affective relationship to particular forms of sex, loss, and darkness that are graphically represented within the genre. My contention is that in Smith's novel the unbearable—what Berlant and Edelman describe as the feeling of psychic or emotional inundation—manifests itself through rare silences in and abbreviations of Austin's narrative. *Grasshopper Jungle*, as I will explain, depicts graphic violence and sex in such detail and with such regularity and hyperbole that it satirizes the equation of dystopia with adolescence. As Gurdon writes, "the young-adult category seems guided by a kind of grotesque fun-house sensibility, in which teenage turbulence is distorted, magnified and reflected back at young readers" ("My 'Reprehensible' Take"). And this is precisely what *Grasshopper Jungle* delivers as it revels in its own excess, thumbing its nose at the likes of Gurdon. Yet Austin's narration is simultaneously unable to bear the full weight of the queer sex he experiences. Queerness, the novel's locus of dystopia, functions as a shattering negativity that literally brings about the end of the while disrupting Austin's otherwise comprehensive narration.

The "Unstoppable" Adolescent as Horny Mutant Bug

Grasshopper Jungle is subtitled *A History*, and documenting history is indeed Austin's preoccupation throughout the novel. But Austin's narrative also plays with other conventions—including those belonging to dystopian literature, the YA problem novel, and the confession. Providing an adequate and concise summary of the multiple narrative threads woven by Austin feels like a Herculean task. In addition to narrating a history of how he and his best friend Robby accidentally release the highly contagious "Contained MI Plague Strain 412E," which transforms humans into flesh-eating, ravenous, horny insects that bring about the end of the world, Austin is also concerned with navigating his sexual desire for and intrusive fantasies about his girlfriend, Shann, and Robby, who self-identifies as gay. Additionally, Austin gives us insight into McKeon Industries, who created the plague during the Cold War in hopes of producing "Unstoppable Soldiers." He furthermore traces the history of his own immigrant Polish family—the lives, loves, and deaths of his ancestors—including a queer great-grandfather and a great-great grandfather who invented a urinal that ends up in Eden, the underground refuge built by McKeon and discovered by Austin, Shann, and Robby, which enables them (along with Robby's mother, Austin's dog Ingrid, and Ah Wong Sing, a cook) to survive the mutant plague.

As detailed in Austin's voice, the viral spread functions to parallel Austin's sexual hunger and frustration with the frenzied copulation and ravenousness of the mutant grasshoppers, reiterating hyperbolically the notion that dystopia is intrinsic to the experience of adolescence. Joseph Campbell explains this connection between dystopia and YA: "These texts show the various power discourses at work on the adolescent as he or she moves from metaphoric childhood 'utopia' to metaphoric adolescent 'dystopia,'" he explains; "The usefulness of this genre is that . . . it shows more clearly the ways that society constructs the adolescent subject" (178). In *Grasshopper Jungle*, Smith constructs the dystopian adolescent subject as the equivalent of a rampaging mutant insect. "Bugs do two things," Austin explains. "They eat and they fuck. . . . Ealing, Iowa, was just like . . . a new planet of horny soliders" (135). Moreover, the novel carries to parodic extremes the adult anxieties surrounding adolescence—as described by Baxter and others—to the point that adolescents are not only dystopian figures themselves, but literally responsible for bringing about the end of the world. "Everything was a mess," narrates Austin, summarizing the chaos created by both the plague and his sexuality: "I was in love with my two best friends, and I was making them both miserable at the same time. And there were horny bugs up above us that were eating the whole planet" (329).

Notably, the release and dispersal of 412E hinges on and is paralleled with key moments in Austin's journey of sexual confusion. The plague is initially unleashed following Austin and Robby's first kiss on the roof of the Grasshopper Jungle strip mall—Shann, asleep in Robby's van outside, remains oblivious. Following the kiss, the boys descend through a trap door into the *Buyer and Cellar* thrift shop, where the plague is contained in a glass globe. Austin and Robby accidentally leave the door open, and the bullies who hours earlier assaulted Robby and Austin enter the thrift store, steal the globe, and smash it on the pavement outside, where it mixes with Robby's blood (spilled during the bullying incident) and frees the virus moments after Austin's kiss with Robby intensifies his sexual confusion. The kiss and the virus soon merge in Austin's mind as "experiments." "But I don't think things called *Plague* are the subject of the kinds of experiments we do in the lab at [school]," says Robby as the boys wonder what they've uncovered. Austin thinks to himself: "That's what it was—what Robby and I had done up there on the roof at Grasshopper Jungle . . . An experiment. It's perfectly normal for boys to *experiment*" (62). Shortly thereafter, Austin instructs Robby: "Don't say anything to Shann." Robby replies: "You mean about what we saw in her stepdad's office, or what we did up on the roof?" Austin can only muster a "Shit" before imagining that he "had two arguing and confused heads sprouting up from [his] shoulders" (63).

Here, feverish adolescent sexuality—queer sexuality, specifically—is figured in *Grasshopper Jungle* as the cause of the apocalypse. It is remarkable that this virus is unleashed during a gay kiss and activated through contact with the blood of a gay-identified adolescent. Like the virus in *Caper in the Castro*, as discussed in this book's previous chapter, this virus is not HIV but is quite strikingly linked, semiotically, to HIV. Here, Smith's novel opens up two contradictory interpretive possibilities: a critique of homophobic panic that places gay men at the center of HIV transmission, and/or the homophobic reiteration of this very panic. Regardless, the circumstances surrounding the virus's release cement its enduring association with queerness—just as the kiss and the virus both become "experiments" to Austin.

In addition to conflating catastrophic scientific and confusing sexual experiments, Austin's narrative evinces his gradual transformation into something of an "unstoppable soldier" himself; eating and fucking, the mutant bugs' priorities, become Austin's as well. Throughout the novel, Austin often describes objects of sexual desire in terms of food. Early in the novel, for example, he imagines Krzys Szczerba's wife, Eva Nightingale, as having "breasts like frosted cupcakes and skin the color of homemade peach ice cream. Her body was a soft and generous pillow of endless desserts" (69). Toward the end of the novel, when the plague is running rampant, the main characters have escaped to Eden, and Austin has recently had sex with Shann for the first time, nearly every character is described in edible terms. These descriptions are often mere pages apart, intensifying the force of Austin's sexual hunger. "Robby Brees's voice sounded the way soft vanilla ice cream feels and tastes inside your mouth on a blistering summer day," Austin narrates on 359; on page 360, Austin describes Connie Brees, Robby's mother, as having "skin . . . the color of perfectly prepared, soft and warm buttered toast. . . . Her hair, which fell softly over her bare shoulders, was the color of apple spice cake. . . . Robby's mother made me very horny"; on the following page, Austin notes that "Robby's skin reminds me of the warm insides of a late-summer white peach. . . . Robby's hair is the color of graham cracker piecrust"; and one page later, on 362, Austin "can almost smell the ginger and orange blossom lotion [Shann] smooths on her skin. Her hair is summer wheat and her skin is the color of a perfect October butternut squash." Austin concludes this section with a direct comparison between himself and the mutant mantises: "I love Shann Collins so much I am afraid it is killing me. I love Robby Brees the same way. I am an unstoppable train wreck to their lives" (362).

Austin possesses many of the traits of typical problem novel protagonists who are "often configured by their adult authors as awkward, rebellious, unhappy, presenting loci of suffering, injustice, or unfulfilled longings and deviant sexualities" (Hilton and Nikolajeva 1). This characterization is taken to an extreme, however, as Austin's thirst for sex and food renders him an avatar of what Baxter describes as the "real," anxiety- and threat- producing adolescent whose sexuality brings about not only (inter)personal dystopia, but through his metaphorical transformation into an unstoppable horny soldier himself, the apparent end of most life on Earth. It is worth noting, too, that the first mutant bug "hatches" from its victim outside a gay bar, the *Tally-Ho!*, after Robby convinces Austin to accompany him "just so [Robby] could see what the future is like" (115). Again, Austin's narrative links the spread of the virus with a moment of queer sexual intensity: "Robby Brees and I stood there in the parking lot of the *Tally-Ho!*, which was Waterloo, Iowa's one and only gay bar. I thought about fucking things. And while I thought about fucking things . . . we witnessed firsthand what happens to a person who swallowed a mouthful of *Stanpreme* pizza that had been contaminated by *Contained MI Plague Strain 412E*" (124).

Austin most clearly crystallizes as an "unstoppable" dystopian force toward the end of the novel when it becomes clear that he and Robby have the means to prevent the apocalypse, but—like horny teenage Bartlebys—they seem to prefer not to. Robby's blood, which created the plague, is kryptonite to the mutant bugs. The novel sets the stage for an epic, victorious battle as the boys, armed with paintball guns loaded with Robby's blood, emerge from Eden to confront the mantises. Yet *Grasshopper Jungle*'s penultimate chapter concludes as follows:

> This is what the end of the world looks like.
>
> Leaping and skittering over the strands of barbwire that lined the highway out toward the old McKeon House came dozens and dozens—hundreds and hundreds—of little, hungry and horny Unstoppable Soldiers.
>
> "Holy shit," Rob said.
>
> "Holy shit," I agreed.
>
> We drove.
>
> I lit another cigarette. (379–80)

In *Grasshopper Jungle*, adolescents who are also unstoppable forces of destruction catalyze dystopia and do not prevent the apocalypse in spite of their abilities. The adolescent body is adult anxiety incarnate and hyperbolized. These bodies are unbearable, organizing the world and our understanding of ourselves as adults, while simultaneously undoing and destroying this same world.

Although Smith's novel contains elements of the *Bildungsroman*, or "coming-of-age" story—Austin does "grow up" to become a father in the epilogue, after all—it simultaneously delivers something of a reverse feral tale. Instead of illustrating, as Kidd describes, "the white, middle-class male's perilous passage from nature to culture, from bestiality to humanity, from homosocial pack life to individual self-reliance and heterosexual prowess," *Grasshopper Jungle* depicts the adolescent's descent into an animality represented by torrid, irrepressible, catastrophic queer sexuality (*Making* 7). Citing a Swedish-language study by Maria Lassén-Seger, Lydia Kokkola notes that "metamorphosis into animal form is commonly used as a trope for expressing the adolescent characters' ambivalence about the changes puberty begets on their bodies and, by extension, their ambivalent feelings about their sexuality" (144). We can interpret this trope, she continues, as a symptom of adult authors' anxieties and ambivalences about teenage sexual desire and maturation. In *Grasshopper Jungle*, however, Austin's transformation (which is not physical, i.e., Austin does not actually become a mantis) operates satirically, illustrating those adult anxieties and ambivalences about adolescent sexuality that are typically responsible for perpetuating this trope. Also significant is the praying mantis form itself, which according to

Elizabeth Grosz embodies "an intimate and persistent link between sex and death, between pleasure and punishment, desire and revenge which may prove significant in understanding key details of male sexuality and desire" (278). Drawing on Grosz' analysis, Kokkola comments that a bestial incarnation of human sexuality "expresses something which is fearful, a fear which may or may not be overtly recognized" (163). Smith's mutant mantises, then—created by humans and reliant on them as both food and host—is a fitting embodiment of Austin's sexual anxieties and the anxieties of those adult critics who fear the propagation of storm and stress through dystopian YA. Here, compellingly, we see a number of genres and their conventions colliding in Austin's account of queer sexual chaos: YA, dystopia, science fiction, the problem novel, the *Bildungsroman*, and—as I will now explain—history and the confession.

History, Confession, and Manipulation

As I hinted at the beginning of this chapter, Austin's impossibly comprehensive history includes mundane details about simultaneous events that realistically he could never know, causing us to continually doubt his reliability and inviting us to question what, ultimately, Austin omits and why. Take, for example, Austin's jumpy narrative inserted at the conclusion of a story about Krzys Szczerba, inventor of the Nightingale urinal:

> It was hard for me, at times, to separate out the connections that crisscrossed like intersecting highways through and around my life in Ealing.
> It was the truth, and I had to get it down.
> *And that was our day. You know what I mean.*
> I took off my boxers and went to bed.
> It was 6:01 a.m.
> The end of the world was about four hours old. Just a baby.
> Johnny McKeon was picking up two dozen donuts at that moment.
> Ollie Jungfrau was waking up, trying to decide if he should masturbate or not.
> It was just after three in the afternoon in Afghanistan.
> Louis, the Chinese cook at *The Pancake House*, whose real name was Ah Wong Sing, was taking a shit in the public restroom at the *Ealing Coin Wash Launderette*. (69)

Austin's narrative has the simultaneous effect of dislocating the reader in time and space and then cohering these multiple strands—the "intersecting highways"—into an omniscient perspective (from multiple events in 1905 to disparate events unfolding in the present day at 6:01 a.m.) that performs authority ("It was the truth").

On one hand, Austin's narrative is a confession. The novel's second page concludes as Austin discloses an "erotic plan" that he "fantasizes over": that Robby would drive Shann and him into the "cornfields surrounding Ealing, and Robby wouldn't say anything at all as I climbed on top of Shann and had sex with her right there on the piles of Robby's laundry that always seemed to lie scattered and unwashed in the dirty old Ford Explorer" (9). Austin's account often recalls Foucault's theory of confession as a "ritual that unfolds within a power relationship" (61), one that provides "pleasure in the truth of pleasure, the pleasure of knowing that truth, of discovering and exposing it, the fascination of seeing and telling it, of captivating and capturing others by it, of confiding it in secret, of luring it out into the open" (71). Austin's ostensibly truthful and complete confession seems to provide us, as readers, with power and pleasure through the intimate access he grants to the details of his and others' lives. However, he also makes a number of critical omissions.

These omissions position Austin as both the recuperator and manipulative mediator of history. As Raffaella Baccolini argues, "Dystopia depends on and denies history . . . dystopias show a profound interest in history and, more precisely, in its control, which often implies its revision and even erasure" (115). She moreover indicates that "History, its knowledge, and memory" are often "dangerous elements" that provide citizens of a dystopia with tools for resistance; "in the critical dystopia," Baccolini writes, "the recovery of history is an important element for the survival of hope" (115). However, dystopian fiction also typically relies on antagonists—generally, oppressive states and their apparatuses—who "strictly control[] and manipulate[]" "information about the past and present" (Baccolini 115). Austin, as dystopian locus, functions as both—he recovers and records the history of McKeon industries while simultaneously manipulating this history by offering it in the guise of a confession. Crucial, however, is what remains unconfessed.

Strikingly, Austin's elliptical description of his intimate night with Robby remains the only undocumented event in his otherwise painstakingly—and often painfully—thorough account. Here is his description of this evening:

> We finally could forget about everything. Robby played a crackling vinyl recording of *Exile on Main Street*, and we got drunk on screw-top wine and smoked cigarettes and took off our T-shirts. I opened my notebook and drew sketches of Robby as he reclined, bare chested, on the floor in the slate-colored streetlight that came through the apartment's open window. It was warm, and outside the sound of insects in the night was electric. The music sounded better than

anything I'd ever heard. I had never been so happy in my life. I played with the little silver medal against my bare chest. I wrote poetry while we sat there like that in the dark and talked about our favorite poems and books and laughed and smoked. And Mick Jagger sang to us: *Tryin' to stop the waves behind your eyeballs, Drop your reds, drop your greens and blues.* (145–46)

Here, Austin claims an ability to "forget about everything," but this assertion is immediately followed by a characteristically detailed—if uncharacteristically affective and seemingly subjective—account of the moment. The chapter ends and the next begins the following morning, as Austin awakens, hungover and remorseful, his limbs entangled with Robby's. We aren't told exactly what unfolded, but whatever happened momentarily disrupts Austin's claims to truth-telling. After arriving at school, Austin narrates:

I prayed with the other students in the classroom, but I only thought about Robby Brees. . . . I did not talk to Robby for days after that. I needed to talk to my father. I did not have any idea what I would say. I told Shann I was sick. She thought it was from drinking wine with Robby the night before. That may have been true. I had no way of figuring out if anything was true or not true on that Tuesday after I spent the night with Robby. (150)

Eventually, Shann confronts Austin about the reality of his relationship with Robby. "Have you ever kissed Robby?" Shann asks. Austin narrates: "I had to tell her. I loved Shann, and I do not lie. 'Um, yes,' I said." "Have you and Robby ever had sex with each other?" is Shann's next question. Austin replies, "Uh. Um, no," and then maintains, "I did not lie to her" (249). However, pages earlier, Austin provides us with evidence that he may, in fact, have lied to Shann. He omnisciently narrates another scene involving Robby's bedroom, in which "Connie Brees was making certain her son, Robert Brees Jr., was not at home. She went through Robby's room, looking for a box of condoms she found on the floor of Robby's bedroom on Tuesday afternoon when Robby was at school [the night after Austin slept over]" (178). Pages later, Austin tells us that Connie and Ah Wong Sing had "used up the last of the condoms Connie Brees had found on the floor of Robby's bedroom" (189). The details of Austin's intimacy with Robby remain the most "abbreviated" (to use Austin's word) part of his history; he can only provide us with traces and allusions as opposed to his regular, thorough, graphic, "historical" narrative. This, I suggest, is because sex with Robby is an unbearable encounter for Austin.

Compare Austin's unusually elliptical account of his night with Robby to his description of sex with Shann, which takes place later in the novel:

Shann Collins helped me put my penis inside her vagina, and we had sexual intercourse right there on the floor of Eden's bowling alley, below a pair of shoes and a pink ball that had *Wanda Mae* embossed in gold on it. Our sex was noisy and urgent and wet. I rubbed my kneecaps raw, scraping them on the rough carpeting at the shoe-changing station. I pushed Shann along on her butt until her head and mine bumped against the rattling rack of bowling shoes. (317)

A mere four pages later, Austin reminds us not only of the encounter itself, but of his propensity for and skill at recalling and recording detail, a sharp contrast with his admitted inability to decipher truths following his encounter with Robby: "Moments earlier, Shann Collins and I had sexual intercourse below Wanda Mae Rutkowski's pink bowling ball and tricolor bowling shoes. Wanda Mae Rutkowski had feet like Godzilla. While my penis was inside Shann Collins' vagina, I noticed that Wanda Mae Rutkowski's shoes were women's size 11. It is my job to notice accurate details, no matter what is going on" (321–22).

So, what to make of the curious omissions and attention to affect that attend Austin's night with Robby, and the surfeit of detail delivered in staccato, scientific prose—consistent with Austin's voice throughout the novel—used in his description of sex with Shann? It's tempting, I'll admit, to accuse Smith or his publishers of omitting the gay encounter in favor of the straight one, a move that wouldn't be at odds with children literature's lengthy history of censoring queer characters, themes, and sex, a tendency that I discuss in the first two chapters of this book. In line with my approach to John Donovan and Isabelle Holland's novels, however, I want to unpack the effects of silence and ambiguity instead of simply dismissing such omissions as the products of homophobia (which, I'll add, they might well be).[11] I ask: what is the effect of this moment of silence in relation to the volume of Austin's other descriptions? The "darkness" of queer sex in Smith's text is something that is particularly unbearable for Austin, something that affectively overwhelms him—with desire, guilt, love, and so on—while reorienting his approach to relationality and violently reshaping the outside world. These effects are not entirely unlike those I discuss in chapter two, which emerge from risk and queer pedagogy in Holland's *The Man Without a Face*. Austin's queer encounter, in this case, comes to inhabit the novel's negative space.

Queer Sex and Negative Space

I intend "negative" to signify vis-à-vis both art and queer theory. In terms of the former, Austin's encounter with Robby exists only in sharp relief against its thoroughly detailed surroundings. Queer sex is "an area" of *Grasshopper Jungle*, to deploy the *OED* definition of "negative space," that contains "no contrasting shapes, figures, or colors itself," but is "framed by solid or positive forms." Negative space, the *OED* continues, often "constitutes a particularly powerful or significant part of the whole composition." For Berlant and Edelman, negativity "signifies a resistance to or undoing of the stabilizing frameworks of coherence imposed on thought and lived experience" (xii). On one level, Austin's encounters with Robby, which begin with the rooftop kiss, function to actually annihilate Ealing, Iowa (and, presumably, the world outside Eden) by prompting the release of the plague. Austin's is a destructive queerness that literalizes the negative, antisocial queer stance that Edelman adopts elsewhere in *No Future: Queer Theory and the Death Drive* (2004). On another, personal level, queer sex undoes the otherwise "coherent," "stable framework" of Austin's grand, masterfully controlled, "unimpeachable" narrative. As Leo Bersani suggests in his foundational work on queer negativity, "Is the Rectum a Grave?", we can "think of the sexual as, precisely, moving between a hyperbolic sense of self and a loss of all consciousness of self" (218). This is the trajectory we see Austin follow in *Grasshopper Jungle*, as his omniscient narrative collapses into negative space at the moment of his queer sexual encounter.

Just as Austin is both liberator and manipulator of history, he is also the paradoxical site of both queer negativity and what Edelman in *No Future* calls "reproductive futurism" (2)—the monolithic logic that centers heterosexual reproduction as the normative model for social and political relations. Austin's hetero sex, vividly described, is procreative—Shann eventually gives birth to a son, Arek, and the novel's epilogue positions the aptly named Eden as the sole bastion of humanity amidst the mantis plague that has presumably spread catastrophically. Yet Austin's sexual confusion remains unresolved in the epilogue: "I continue to be torn between my love for Shann Collins and Robby Brees," he narrates, concluding that "Sometimes it is perfectly acceptable to decide not to decide, to remain confused and wide-eyed about the next thing that will pop up in the road you build" (383). He rooms alone, declining to sleep with either Shann or with Robby, although "Shann does not like it" (383).[12] As in Donovan and Holland's novels, Austin refuses the "coming out" narrative that many critics demand from queer YA. The adolescent, as it has been since its invention at the turn of the twentieth century, is one of society's greatest promises and among its greatest threats. Austin recuperates and records history, yet manipulates and distorts it. His queerness is self- and world-destroying, while his reproductive straight sex preserves a final link to futurity. To exaggerated effect, Austin embodies the hopes, fears, fantasies, and anxieties of those critics so deeply invested in theorizing the potential real-life effects of queer and dystopian YA, critics who see this genre as having the capacity to improve the lives of adolescents (and thus, given the logic of reproductive futurism and its symbolic investment in the figural child, pave the way for a better future for us all), or poison the lives of young readers through the viral contagion of dystopia and its dark themes.

My use of the language of infection, here, is most obviously because a virus is at the core of *Grasshopper Jungle*'s dystopia,[13] but also because Gurdon herself describes the spread of "dark" themes from reader to text as an act of viral transmission. It is "likely," she writes, "that books focusing on pathologies help normalize them and, in the case of self-harm, may even spread their plausibility and likelihood to young people who might otherwise never have imagined such extreme measures." "Self-destructive adolescent behaviors," Gurdon concludes, "are observably infectious and have periods of vogue" ("Darkness"). Indeed, as Kokkola notes, "there seems to be a wide-spread fear that teenage readers will automatically wish to emulate the characters" in YA (12). With tongue firmly in-cheek, *Grasshopper Jungle* seems to speak directly to critics like Gurdon and Tatar who fear the consequences of dark children's literature on young readers. Early in the novel, Austin recalls being suspended for writing a book report on Robert Cormier's *The Chocolate War*, a famously controversial YA novel by the author of *I Am the Cheese* (the latter is described as a "bleak classic" by Williams in her article on dark YA). Summoned to the office of Pastor Roland Duff, headmaster of Curtis Crane Lutheran Academy, Austin is "counseled . . . about masturbation and Catholicism" (34). "My fear is that when boys read books such as this," Duff explains to Austin, "they will assume there is nothing at all wrong with masturbation, and may, out of curiosity, attempt to masturbate." Duff continues, with increasing hyperbole: "In history, entire armies have been defeated because their soldiers masturbated too frequently. It happened to the Italians in Ethiopia" (34).

Here, *Grasshopper Jungle*, a book that contains numerous masturbation references, references another book that deals with masturbation in a parody of how adults imagine the consequences of such texts on young readers. My intention is not to conflate the representation of self-harm with the representation of masturbation; clearly, these are two distinct behaviors with radically different stakes and implications. However, I think it worthwhile to flag as troublesome the logic of contagion that underlies Gurdon's assumptions about the effects of representation. This is, after all, the same logic that *Grasshopper Jungle* satirizes: the absurd hyperbole of Pastor Duff's argument about the Italians' defeat in Ethiopia (they were destroyed because of excessive masturbation) is the same hyperbole that structures *Grasshopper Jungle*, wherein humanity is annihilated by avatars of "unstoppable" adolescent sexuality.

We might again return to my first two chapters to consider how queer sexuality functions as negative space, in its dual sense, elsewhere in queer YA and its criticism. As in *Grasshopper Jungle*, the elliptical queer sexual moments in both *I'll Get There. It Better Be Worth the Trip* and *The Man Without a Face* constitute the negative space of these novels, their omission a sharp contrast with the narrative that surrounds them. These moments also have a particular disruptive force: they disturb both narrative and the protagonist's sense of self, reorienting Davy and Chuck's view of relationality. And as I illustrated through the related criticism, these moments also disturb critics by forcing them to encounter the imaginary young audiences on the other ends of these texts, which often leads to assumptions about the potential readerly effects of the negative space of queer sex. Critics, it seems, are often unwilling to encounter this negative space in ways that avoid fetishizing a certain iteration of the adolescent reader. Like *Big Mouth*, discussed in this book's next chapter, *Grasshopper Jungle* offers us a satirical approach to coming-of-age conventions and criticism through its hyperbolic approach to generic tropes and the anxieties they tend to evoke. Unlike *Big Mouth*, which delivers its satire through horror and camp, *Grasshopper Jungle* turns to dystopia and science fiction to offer us a vision of the apocalypse brought about by an adolescent with an acutely anxious relationship to his queer, sexual self.

As a potent source of anxiety, the unbearable darkness of children's and YA literature is a rich site for exploring the affective contours of the genre. For if one of children's literature's fascinating particularities is how it is so heavily laden with adult desires and anxieties, then it strikes me that children's literature also possesses a unique affective force: a power to invoke desire and anxiety with such potency that they risk becoming unbearable. Yet these are affects that simultaneously remind us of our relations to one another, the books we love and hate, and the children we imagine at the other end of children's literature.

I want to say more, but you can't get everything in a book chapter. Good book chapters are always about everything. You know what I mean.

CHAPTER 5

Horror and Camp: Monsters and Wizards and Ghosts (Oh My!) in *Big Mouth*

Parental Advisory: Explicit Content

Beware: you are about to encounter a haunted house, unruly children, ghosts, evil wizards, and an array of depraved monsters. The subject of this chapter, believe it or not given such content, is an animated comedy about puberty: Netflix's *Big Mouth* (2017–). Horror and camp are both integral to this series, which, like Andrew Smith's *Grasshopper Jungle* (the focus of this book's previous chapter), responds to anxieties about adolescent sexuality with a satirical edge. *Big Mouth*, however, does not relegate queerness to negative space as does Smith's novel. Instead, the show offers childhood queerness and polymorphous perversity as universal, that is, not limited to those characters who self-identify as queer. It does so, as I will illustrate, by uniting horror with camp to represent and deflate anxieties that circulate around and within queer YA literature and culture.

Big Mouth, a critically praised yet controversial show, invites adult viewers to voyeuristically and vicariously re-experience the pleasures and horrors of adolescence. The show's staging and subsequent campy, reassuring upheaval of pubescent anxiety and terror might also appeal to its younger fans. *Big Mouth* deploys conventions and tropes from a variety of traditions: children's animation, Gothic horror, and the feral tale, among others, in order to send up the more terrific aspects of pubescent *Sturm und Drang*—in particular, the loss of bodily control and its associated shame. *Big Mouth*'s approach to monsters is particularly compelling. Unlike those monsters that function as avatars of abject queerness and are typically eradicated from traditional horror films, *Big Mouth*'s Hormone Monsters align themselves with children's animation through their narrative endurance. Distinct from monsters in children's films, however, *Big Mouth*'s monsters remain incarnations of unbridled, polymorphous perversity; they have little attachment to any particular sexual orientation and no regard for bourgeois respectability.[1] Horror and its monsters, in *Big Mouth*, become a tool for critique, for raising the lurid, queer specter of pubescent sexuality while demonstrating the communal impulses and shared nature of shame. Before elaborating, however, I'll offer a brief genealogy of camp, which is central to *Big Mouth*'s horror show.

Camp, as Harry Benshoff and Sean Griffin explain, "is an often confused and confusing term. It has been called a sensibility, a taste, and an aesthetic, and it shares similarities with literary devices such as parody, irony, and satire. Camp can be both a reception strategy as well as a mode of cultural production" (*Queer Cinema* 119). The term has a robust critical legacy and risks overdetermination through its rabid (over)theorization. Like "queer," which is closely associated with "camp," its fungibility can be both strength and weakness, and its meaning, usefulness, and politics have been feverishly contested over the years. Indeed, as Kenneth B. Kidd and I write in our introduction to *Queer as Camp*, "The place of Camp in queer culture and queer studies is complicated" (13).

Although camp's theoretical origins are often traced to Susan Sontag's widely cited 1964 essay "Notes on 'Camp,'" Dennis Denisoff indicates that the "first English definition of camp as a conscious act of artifice appears in J. Redding Ware's 1909 dictionary *Passing English of the Victorian Era*, where he defines it in full as 'Actions and gestures of exaggerated emphasis. Probably from the French. Used chiefly by persons of exceptional want of character'" (100). Sontag preserves camp's roots in "artifice and exaggeration," noting that "the essence of Camp is its love of the unnatural" (53). Moreover, the moral stance in this initial definition endures, albeit ironically, in camp's function as a tool for cultural subversion deployed by marginalized communities. As both reception strategy and aesthetic technique, camp embraces those aspects of "low" culture often eschewed by the mainstream. Typically, camp is affiliated with (White) gay men. Sontag, for example, writes that "homosexuals, by and large, constitute the vanguard—and the most articulate audience—of Camp" (64), although she has been criticized for stripping camp of its critical, political edge. Moe Meyer, for one, explains that camp has been "considered frivolous, aestheticized, and apolitical," and he claims it as "the vehicle for an already existent—though obscured—cultural critique" (145). Camp consists of "an ensemble of strategies," as Steven Cohan writes, for enacting "a queer recognition of the incongruities arising from the cultural recognition of gender and sexuality" (1). Similarly, Corey Creekmur and Alexander Doty point to camp's usage as a subversive reception strategy:

> For some time (at least since the model embodied by Oscar Wilde), [the] queerly 'different' experience of mass culture was most evident, if coded, in the ironic, scandalous sensibility known as camp—perhaps gay culture's crucial contribution to modernism. An attitude at once casual and severe, affectionate and ironic, camp served to deflate the pretensions of mainstream culture while elevating what that same culture devalued or repressed, thus providing a strategy for rewriting and questioning the meanings and values of mainstream representations. (2)

As critics including Noah Fields point out, however, and as I will discuss later in this chapter, communities of color have been integral to shaping the contours of camp.

I do not intend to settle on a coherent definition for camp in this chapter, as doing so would contradict the confounding qualities of the term itself. As Fabio Cleto explains, "camp hasn't lost its relentless power to frustrate all efforts to pinpoint it down to stability, and all the 'old' questions remain to some extent unsettled" (2). I will, however, focus on those elements of camp that are crucial to how *Big Mouth* represents and "deflates," in Creekmur and Doty's words, anxieties about adolescent sexuality that circulate in queer YA's affective economy. Integral to *Big Mouth*'s campiness is how the series depicts adolescent sexuality as horrific, yet it refuses to permit the anxiety and shame emerging from these horrors to be taken too seriously. As Sontag notes, "The whole point of Camp is to dethrone the serious. Camp is playful, anti-serious. More precisely, Camp involves a new, more complex relation to 'the serious.' One can be serious about the frivolous, frivolous about the serious" (62). *Big Mouth*, as I will explain, combines a variety of campy elements and genres—including children's animation, horror, and the musical—with what Kathryn Bond Stockton calls "dark camp" to highlight the sociality of shame while simultaneously allowing viewers to laugh at it.

Notes on *Big Mouth*

Big Mouth, which premiered on Netflix in September 2017, is an animated comedy co-created by Nick Kroll, Andrew Goldberg, Mark Levin, and Jennifer Flackett.[2] The show is based on Kroll and Goldberg's experiences growing up together in Westchester County, New York. *Big Mouth* has been almost universally praised

Figure 5.1. Maurice the Hormone Monster greets Andrew in *Big Mouth* episode 1.1, "Ejaculation." Copyright Netflix Inc., 2017. Retrieved from Netflix.com.

by critics for masterfully balancing shockingly lewd humor with a sympathetic, nuanced, and sensitive portrayal of its young protagonists (as of July 2019, it boasts a rare and coveted score of 100 percent on critical aggregator *Rotten Tomatoes*). Truly, *Big Mouth* knows little restraint. The show's pilot introduces the Hormone Monster (voiced by Kroll), a furry, phallic beast aptly described by Troy Patterson as "one of Maurice Sendak's Wild Things redrafted as a satyr." The Hormone Monster (who happens, perhaps uncoincidentally, to be named Maurice) bursts forth from protagonist Andrew (John Mulaney)'s desk in the middle of a sex-ed lesson, urging him to flee class to masturbate in the school bathroom and "climax into that thin toilet paper" (see figure 5.1). "Go away, you're not real," Andrew protests. Maurice retorts, "If I'm not real, then how come I'm sending blood to your sweet penis right now?" This initial episode (entitled "Ejaculation") proceeds to explore two humiliating experiences: Andrew's best friend Nick (Kroll, again) accidentally spies Andrew naked and feels ashamed at his own comparatively small penis; Andrew ejaculates in his pants while slow-dancing at a school function. The episode concludes with the two boys bonding over their shared shame: "Everything's embarrassing," Nick says. "Everything is *so* embarrassing," Andrew agrees. In this first episode, acknowledging the universality of puberty's horrors and humiliations emerges as one of *Big Mouth*'s primary objectives.

In subsequent episodes, *Big Mouth* explores topics like menstruation ("Everybody Bleeds"), sexual confusion ("Am I Gay?"), female sexuality and masturbation ("Girls Are Horny Too") and pornography addiction ("The PornScape"). The cast is racially diverse, gender-balanced, and features an openly gay character (Matthew, voiced by Andrew Rannells), an adult lesbian romance, an initially toxic character who later comes out as bisexual (Jay, voiced by Jason Mantzoukas), and a debauched ghost (of Duke Ellington, voiced by Jordan Peele) who serves as a clumsy mentor to the show's young protagonists. *Big Mouth* often develops its themes through spontaneous and irreverent musical numbers. The titles of episodes two and three, for example, are also the names of their featured songs: respectively, an REM parody sung by a tampon who resembles Michael Stipe, the band's frontman; and a campy cabaret number performed by Andrew, who is accompanied by the ghosts of gay icons Socrates, Freddie Mercury, and former Supreme Court Justice Antonin Scalia (ha!). In "Everybody Bleeds," a Hormone Monstress (Maya Rudolph) joins the cast to mediate protagonist Jessi (Jessi Klein)'s adolescence; the show's second season adds the Shame Wizard (David Thewlis) and the Depression Kitty (Jean Smart) to the array of ghastly avatars who embody the more fearful aspects of the teenage experience. Throughout, the show invokes a clever and subtle didacticism while plumbing puberty's raunchiest depths. In one moment, *Big Mouth* offers up an entertaining yet informative overview of Planned Parenthood's various services ("The Planned Parenthood Show"); in another, the Shame Wizard puts Andrew on trial for excessive masturbation and unbridled horniness, eliciting salacious witness testimonies from an absurd array of jerk-off aids (a sock, a webcam model, the illustration from a margarine tub, a tomato), and emphatically accusing the boy of seeking "to drench this entire planet in [his] rotten jizz" ("The Shame Wizard").

Located somewhere at the frenetic interchange of adult gross-out comedy, teen sex romp, teen sex-ed, camp horror/musical, and cartoony nostalgia, *Big Mouth* resists classification and—despite Netflix's "Mature Audiences" rating—does not have an obvious audience.[3] As Kerry Mallan and Roderick McGillis point out in their study of camp and children's culture, such ambiguity is one of camp's fundamental characteristics. Many campy children's texts, they explain, "work to confuse not only such things as gender, time and place, but also age of reader/viewer" (7). *Big Mouth* also toys with the three genres Benshoff and Griffin identify as fundamental to camp cinema: "musicals, horror films, and cartoons," all of which "flaunt their lack of realism and their disdain for the 'normal'" (*Queer Images* 71).[4] *Big Mouth* combines vibrantly primary-colored drawings—the kind we might associate with child-friendly favorites like *SpongeBob Squarepants* and *Dora the Explorer*—with young protagonists and themes relevant to adolescence, but also explicit content.[5] Indeed, the show exemplifies many of the qualities of camp as delineated by Mallan and McGillis. *Big Mouth* reeks of "bad taste" (3) and "abject excess" (13); it is a "mocking" (3), "guilty pleasure" (10) that "delights in impertinence," trades in "nostalgia," and prefers on occasion "to challenge rather than satisfy" (3).[6] Writing in the *New Yorker*, Patterson describes the show in appropriately paradoxical terms, indicating that *Big Mouth*'s young protagonists "exhibit levels of behavioral cluelessness, emotional ignorance, and psychological confusion wholly appropriate to that age," yet "verbally, the kids seem much older." Ultimately, he writes, the show "feels at times like a Larry David take on Judy Blume, as played by the Muppet Babies. At other times, it's more like 'What's Happening to Me?' as done by R. Crumb." These incongruities are reinforced by the show's heroes: childlike in appearance, but in possession of definitively adult-sounding voices.

As a result of these representational torsions, critics are generally uncertain how to characterize the show's audience, often evincing anxiety about its content while admitting (sometimes reluctantly) that it might be pedagogically useful to (some) young viewers. In her *Common Sense Media* review of the series, Joyce Slaton points out that "teens could do worse than watching a show that talks frankly about feeling weird about your body, normalizing these complex topics in a surprisingly sweet way." Jen Chaney describes the show as "a hilarious and vital portrait of puberty" that "deserves a spot in the Coming of Sexual Age Hall of Fame," although "most parents would probably deem it way, way too explicit to show to an actual 12-year-old." KT Hawbaker claims that, in the span of one season, the show covers "more than most U.S. high school sex ed classes would ever embark on." Patterson, however, admits that he finds *Big Mouth* "a great prod to getting serious about the parental controls on my television."

Predictably, the series also generated the usual hyperbolic conservative reactions, which included a petition for *Big Mouth*'s cancellation that accused the show of normalizing child pornography, promiscuity, and abortion (Shugerman).[7] The series addresses and sends up anxieties surrounding its own content on a number of occasions, all of which involve breaking the fourth wall. In the final episode of season one, "The PornScape," Andrew's porn addiction culminates in an *Apocalypse Now* parody. Nick and Maurice must enter Andrew's laptop to rescue him from a hellish nightmarescape filled with monstrous pornographic creatures, including a giant purple dildo that attempts to bludgeon our heroes to death. Once escaped, Maurice remarks: "I know this seems embarrassing now, boys, but maybe one day you'll look back on this time fondly and perhaps even make something beautiful about it." "What, like a show about a bunch of kids masturbating?" Andrew suggests. Nick observes, "Isn't that basically just like child pornography?" "Holy shit, I hope not," Maurice replies.

"I mean, maybe if it's animated we can get away with it." Then, immediately before the credits roll and the season concludes, Maurice gives us viewers a knowing look and asks: "Right?" In camp cinema, according to Jack Babuscio, humor "results from an identification of a strong incongruity between an object, person, or situation in its context," and *Big Mouth* relies a great deal on this strategy (127). *Big Mouth* piles on the incongruities—we see children in what appears, aesthetically, to be a children's animated show, speaking in adult voices about porn and masturbation with a monstrous companion—and then the episode pointedly invites audiences to consider just how incongruous *Big Mouth* really is. Is the show for young people or adults, both or neither? Are animated kids masturbating "something beautiful" or "basically just like child pornography"? How can these possibilities even co-exist in the same text?

In addition to campily fusing children's animation, comedy, and horror, *Big Mouth* offers up a surprisingly rich number of other intertexual switchpoints. The series contains traces of feral tales; the Romantic child and its monstrous counterpoint, the revolting child (Scahill); children's and YA literature; horror and the Gothic. The show also invites us to think about queerness, the polymorphously perverse child, and the relationship between shame and camp. As I will explain, the show adopts a universalizing approach to queerness and the queer child—similar to what we see in Stockton's work—but this queerness involves centralizing, deflating, and also occasionally eroticizing anxiety and shame.

Hormonal Horrors: Revolting Children and the Gothic

Critics often use the language of horror to describe *Big Mouth*. Kathryn Shattuck writes that the show recounts "tales of teenage terror" from which "no one escapes unscathed." Ben Travers calls the series "a horror show—a funny horror show, but a horror show nonetheless." Tyrone Barnes entitles his article "Big Mouth: The Terror of Adolescence." Mark Healy explains that *Big Mouth* is interested in examining "puberty's dark forces." And using appropriately embellished language, Glen Weldon distills *Big Mouth*'s primary message: "Your body, like mine, like everyone's, is a surreal and frequently terrifying Lewis-Carroll hellscape where everything exists in a state of constant flux, where rules of logic and intellect get trammeled by whim and caprice, and where the governing authority is casually malicious and heedlessly cruel." The series "visit[s] horrors and humiliations on its characters," Weldon continues, concluding that *Big Mouth*'s singular power is that it "hasn't forgotten the abject hell of adolescence—and it's not about to let you forget it, either."

Beyond describing the show in such terms, critics have yet to assess the specific horror conventions that the show deploys in service of meaning-making. Babuscio explains the connection between camp and horror:

> The horror genre, in particular, is susceptible to a camp interpretation. Not all horror films are camp, of course; only those which make the most of stylish conventions for expressing instant feeling, thrills, sharply defined personality, outrageous and "unacceptable" sentiments, and so on. In addition, the psychological issues stated or implied, along with the sources of horror, must relate to some significant aspect of our situation and experience; e.g. the inner drives which threaten an individual's well-being and way of life, . . . coping with pressures to conform and adapt, . . . the masking of 'abnormality' behind a façade of 'normality' . . . personal rebellion against enforced restrictions. (124)

Big Mouth is undoubtedly "outrageous," interested in "thrills" and "instant feeling," and contains many "sharply defined" personalities. Many of Babuscio's criteria for campy horror also align themselves with coming-of-age themes: the show explores the adolescent "inner drives" of sex, the "pressures to conform" faced by teenagers, and the feeling of being "abnormal" when confronted with a host of bodily and emotional changes. Three features of horror, I argue, are of particular importance to *Big Mouth*: the horror film's revolting child, the Gothic, and monsters. Together they offer commentary on shame, queerness, and childhood perversity, yet *Big Mouth* ultimately aligns itself with the qualities of children's horror in order to universalize queer childhood.

In "Nightmare on Sesame Street," Steven Bruhm indicates that "North American and British culture has become obsessed," following the Second World War, "with the representation of children, and especially children in the context of horror and Gothic violence" (100). This obsession has produced what Andrew Scahill calls the "cinema of revolting childhood," which offers up alien, demonic, monstrous, possessed, all-knowing, murderous, and otherwise horrific children for our terror and delight (2).[8] Revolting children, Scahill explains, "evoke an ambivalent response—one marked by horror at the child's 'unchildlikeness' and indeed pleasure at that very transgression" (2). This balance between repugnance and attraction is central to the function of horror more generally. As Jessica R. McCort argues, audiences "must be emotionally invested in the situation at hand, must experience a physical response to the text that is rooted in fear, disgust, and repulsion," yet must also "feel excited by the horrifying experience that he or she has willingly engaged in as the reader or viewer of the text" (10). As I have already illustrated, *Big Mouth*'s campy pleasures rely heavily on the incongruity the show generates through its representations

Figure 5.2. Maurice's shadow looms over Andrew and Nick in the *Big Mouth* opening credits. Copyright Netflix Inc., 2017. Retrieved from Netflix.com.

of animated children talking frankly and graphically about sex. And certainly, the critical responses to the show evince the kind of "ambivalence" Scahill flags. There is tremendous pleasure to be found in the show, but also no small degree of "horror at the child's 'unchildlikeness'" in addition to "disgust" and/ or "fear" that real-life children might succumb to the show's ribald pleasures.

Big Mouth's children build on a legacy that can be traced back to the Romantic "Child of Nature" and the child of the feral tale, as discussed elsewhere in this book. As Scahill explains, the Romantic "Child of Nature" becomes the horror film's "Feral Child when it turns on the notion of bodily control" (17). *The Exorcist*'s possessed Regan McNeil, for example, "is feral and frightening because she cannot (or will not) control herself. Besides becoming wildly animated, she also loses control of her bodily functions" (Scahill 17). As a number of critics argue, Regan (and similar revolting girls) can be read as manifestations of anxieties about female sexuality and puberty. Their "budding sexuality is hyperbolized as an outwardly directed violent rage and made monstrous through its articulation in the visual spectacle of bodily fluids," Scahill writes, and such characters "are deemed dangerous in their liminality—on the cusp of womanhood, knowledge, and sexuality" (63). *Big Mouth*'s opening credits establish the loss of bodily control as a primary theme. Set to Charles Bradley's cover of the Black Sabbath song "Changes," the credits deliver a series of images that speaks to this central motif: a tree emerges suddenly from the ground (a nod, perhaps, to the Child of Nature); Nick's eyes widen as he grows upwards uncontrollably; Jessi's silhouette, rendered as an hourglass, sprouts breasts as sand seeps from her head into her torso; the Hormone Monstress's clawed hand flicks an illustrated uterus, causing blood to ooze onto and stain a padded white surface; a drawing of Andrew in a school notebook grows long armpit hair that undulates, tentacle-like; and finally (as seen in figure 5.2) Andrew and Nick gaze upward, eyes full of terror, as the Hormone Monster casts a looming shadow over their supine bodies.

Many episodes of the show deal explicitly with the losses of bodily control inherent to puberty, and *Big Mouth* supplies the Hormone Monsters as embodiments of these frightening sensations. Characters frequently express anxiety at feeling out of control, in the throes of the Monsters that transform their bodies and shape their urges. In "Am I Gay?" Andrew gets repeatedly and uncontrollably erect at the sight of a movie trailer starring The Rock. "The PornScape" deals entirely with Andrew's inability to control his porn consumption. In "Am I Normal?" Nick agonizes over the late onset of his puberty, represented by the infirm and incompetent Hormone Monster, Rick. "Mom, I'm telling you," Nick asserts, "there's this, like, disgusting thing inside me." In "Everybody Bleeds," we see allusions to those films (*Carrie*, *The Exorcist*) that associate abjection with the idiosyncratically cisgender female experience of puberty. Jessi gets her first period, unexpectedly, on a class trip to the Statue of Liberty and while wearing white shorts. What's worse: she is forced to use a 9/11 memorial towel as an improvised pad. "This is a nightmare," says her friend Missy (Jenny Slate) forebodingly, "this is what we're all afraid of." Later, the Hormone Monstress makes her first appearance in a scene that recalls any number of child possession films, including *The Exorcist*. As Jessi stands alone in her room gazing out the window, sinister music plays, the wind whistles, and geese honk eerily as they fly towards the quarter moon. In a sudden explosion of thunder and lightning Connie appears, tendrils of her long red hair snaking across the room to ensnare Jessi (see figure 5.3). "You want to shoplift lipstick, you want to listen to Lana Del Rey on repeat while you cut up all your t-shirts," Connie commands Jessi. "You want to scream at your mother and then laugh at her tears!" Jessi transforms: her face glows with an eerie light; she projects a sinister shadow on the wall behind her. Her mother enters the room, and Jessi yells, "Get the hell out, Shannon!" Her mother stammers: "Your hair looks nice . . ." But Jessi interrupts, screaming: "I said GET OUTTTTT!" The episode concludes with Jessi sobbing on her bed while Connie cackles maniacally, thunder crashing in the background.

In *The Gothic in Children's Literature: Haunting the Borders*, Anna Jackson, Karen Coats, and Roderick McGillis describe how

Figure 5.3. Jessi under the demonic influence of Connie, the Hormone Monstress, in *Big Mouth* episode 1.2, "Everybody Bleeds." Copyright Netflix Inc., 2017. Retrieved from Netflix.com.

> Key moments of feminine transition—menarche, marriage, childbirth, etc.,
> marked as they are by blood, submission, loss of a firm sense of one's former
> identity, and loss of control—are potentially moments that are best represented
> with Gothic motifs. That is, they are moments when symbols of dark labyrinthine
> tunnels, monstrous trolls, ghosts, wayward fluids, murder, etc. are the best sym-
> bols we have for the bodily and social changes wrought by menstruation and the
> possibilities it closes and opens for women's subjectivity. (5)

In addition to the "wayward fluids" and monsters of "Everybody Bleeds," *Big Mouth* also uses the horror convention of the doppelgänger (recently resurrected in Jordan Peele's *Us* [2019]) to explore body shaming through the character of Missy, who is teased about her flat chest and begins feeling deeply self-conscious. In "What Is It about Boobs?" Missy's mirror image comes to life and torments her throughout the episode with various demeaning comments: "Take a hard look in the mirror, lady," Evil Missy heckles, "you look like an understuffed scarecrow in that Baby Gap sweatshirt." The episode that unites a series of Gothic conventions most clearly, however, is "Sleepover: A Harrowing Ordeal of Emotional Brutality," in which haunted houses, abject fluids, and violence (both physical and emotional) combine to tell the stories of two sleepovers-gone-awry. In one, Andrew and Nick arrive at Jay's massive, maze-like, and eerie house ("this place looks like the Holocaust Museum," Andrew remarks) and receive a tour. "This is our percussion room, this is the armory, and this is the door we never open," Jay explains, as a shadow moves spookily across the light seeping through the door's cracks (turns out it's Jay's mother's craft room). Later, in the basement (drawn such that it nods to *Fight Club*), Andrew, Jay, and Nick are tormented by Jay's older brothers, who force the boys into a bloody fist fight before they are permitted to watch porn, and then attempt to coerce the group into a game of "jizzcuit" (google it, should you feel so inclined). Nick and Andrew plan an escape, and the episode becomes a video game parody: they collect stray coins as they make their way through the house, Andrew uses his anti-acne medication and exfoliating brush as weapons to fight Jay's brothers, and the boys eventually make it out.

Meanwhile, at Jessi's house, mean girls Devin (June Diane Raphael) and Lola (Kroll, again) are tormenting Missy, who is riding a delirious sugar high after consuming too many Cokes. Missy hallucinates and starts kissing the family dog; Devin and Lola photograph the kiss and threaten to post the pictures online. Jessi, defending Missy, physically attacks Lola to retrieve her phone. Missy cries and vomits uncontrollably. Lola and Devin end up fighting, and to repair the group, Jessi tells Lola, "I want to help you make up with Devin." Replies Lola, in a *Silence of the Lambs*-themed non sequitur, "Wait, are you saying we should kill Devin, take her skin and wear it, and then blame the whole thing on Missy, or what?" "This is going to be my harrowing middle-school story that I tell on [storytelling podcast] *The Moth*," concludes Missy. "The Feral Child is a reminder that nature is wild and untamed, violent and survivalist," Scahill tells us, and *Big Mouth* often says the same about its young protagonists (17).

For all the abject excess it represents, however, *Big Mouth*'s overall effects are pleasure and reassurance. Recall the introduction to this book, wherein I outline Kristeva's argument that the adolescent novel, "as a permanent witness to our adolescence . . . would enable us to rediscover the state of incompleteness (which is as depressive as it is joyful) that leads in some respects to what we call aesthetic pleasure" (139). The adult spectator's nostalgic identification with *Big Mouth*'s revolting pubescent child is, in part, what permits pleasurable consumption of the show while simultaneously undoing the anxieties attached to the show's more horrific and abject representations. Scahill writes that the revolting child provides similarly narcissistic pleasures for its queer viewers: "I recognize the revolting child as not-me and yet me-as-I-once-was. As the revolting child navigates those experiences of secrecy, rejection, alienation, and rage, so too does the queer spectator" (3). *Big Mouth* takes a Stockton-esque, universal approach to queerness, however, where the queer feelings and abjection of puberty are monsters we as adults all once knew, queer-identified or otherwise. "If you scratch a child, you will find a queer, in the sense of someone 'gay' or just plain strange," Stockton explains in *The Queer Child* (1). For Stockton, children are queer in their "pain, closets, emotional labors, sexual motives, and sideways movements" (3). All children, that is, tend to resist—if only temporarily—the linear narrative of growth into heterosexual adulthood through nonnormative desires, erotic attachments, and Freudian polymorphous perversity. What *Big Mouth* offers adults is a chance to revisit this space of queer "incompleteness," and, per horror convention, be simultaneously revolted and delighted by the experience.

Big Mouth's queer temporal trajectories and their attendant affects are reinforced by the form of animation itself. Benshoff and Griffin remark that "cartoons embody a sort of 'polymorphous perversity'—the ability to transform being and desire in multiple and constantly shifting ways" (*Queer Images* 74). In *The Queer Art of Failure*, Jack Halberstam notes the "spooky and uncanny quality" of stop-motion animation, suggesting that "animated objects . . . [embody] a repetition, a recurrence, an uncanny replay of repressed activity; [they convey] life where we expect stillness, and stillness where we expect liveliness" (177). Similarly, Catherine Lester argues that animation is akin to resurrection, since it gives "the illusion of movement and 'life' to figurines and objects that would otherwise be still and 'lifeless'" ("Children's Horror" 35).[9] This seems truer of stop-motion than the 2D animation technique that *Big Mouth* employs; stop-motion's potentially uncanny effects, too, would risk undoing the incongruity so fundamental to *Big Mouth*'s operation. Nonetheless, animation as form permits *Big Mouth*'s young protagonists to remain in a state of perpetual puberty. Unlike "real" child actors, cartoon kids do not necessarily grow up. This is a quality that *Big Mouth*'s cartoon heroes share with horror cinema's revolting child. Scahill explains: "The horror of the revolting child is that [they] are locked in a liminal stasis predicated on contradiction," he writes, arguing that they are "already-arrived, both-at-once, growing—but not growing up—in a land of never-never. . . . Revolting children," he concludes, "are in a state of permanent impermanence" (5). What could be more horrific, *Big Mouth* indirectly asks, than having to perpetually endure the flux of pubescence? Think Sisyphus, but teenaged and eternally, agonizingly horny, forever betrayed by his rapidly changing body and tormented by hormones. Yet as Kristeva indicates, there is much pleasure to be found in the rediscovery and vicarious reliving of adolescence's "incompleteness," the opportunity to dwell in a queer space that may never culminate in sexually stable adulthood. We might also recall the temporality of anxiety as outlined in this book's introduction, which sees stasis and forward motion in perpetual tension with one another. This rhythm is embodied by *Big Mouth*'s animated pubescent protagonists, who are, in Scahill's words, forever "growing—but not growing up." As animated creations, they are technically static images, providing only the illusion of motion when they are sequenced and played at a rate of twenty-four frames per second. *Big Mouth*'s form, then, underscores the tension between stasis and motion also present in its adolescent themes and characters, while allowing audiences to encounter these themes and characters with horror, anxiety, and delight.

For younger viewers, however, *Big Mouth*'s effects are less likely to be rooted in retrospection, and more in line with how children's horror typically operates. As McCort explains, "The fantasy of horror offers young readers and viewers a dreamscape that parallels their reality, sometimes making it easier to cope with the monsters they must face in the real world" (22). *Big Mouth*'s younger fans (those who are skilled enough to bypass Netflix's parental controls, that is) might find relief from those anxieties attached to pubescent experience. The camping of horror, I suggest, is what provides such relief.[10] Julie Cross argues that "Many texts aimed at older junior readers (around ten years of age and above), most part of a series or which have sequels, now incorporate the mix of 'horror,' 'humour,' and the Gothic," and *Big Mouth* is arguably adjacent to this trend (57). The Gothic, too, has much in common with camp: as Jackson et al. explain, the Gothic's appeal "has something to do with unrestraint, transgression, and the overturning of normalcy"; moreover, the comic Gothic "achieves its humour through excess; it presents a vision ridiculous in its extremes" (11). Animation, too, nicely serves this "dethroning" function of camp humor in the context of horror. Lester, for example, reminds us that animation "marks an aesthetic distance from reality," and thus "can help to signal films . . . with potentially frightening imagery as not real, and therefore of no danger to child viewers" ("Subversive Horror"). Insofar as *Big Mouth* is interested in horrifying its audiences, it is equally if not more invested in helping viewers manage its horrors.

Thus, to offset the show's more terrifically anxious moments, *Big Mouth* gives us camp: the singing tampon in "Everybody Bleeds"; the ghostly cabaret number of "Am I Gay?"; and the mutant dildos and surreal *Apocalypse Now* satire of "The PornScape." As a genre that "examines our fear of desire," the Gothic—and its interest in those horrors that emerge from our selves—are well-suited to *Big Mouth*'s exploration of puberty and the losses of bodily control brought about by surging hormones (Jackson et al. 14). Yet because the show is so campy, it ultimately undoes these fears. The comic Gothic, Cross explains, relies on "the incongruous—fear-inspiring characters and terrible situations which may cause reader anxiety, but which are often also seen to be humorous and comically incongruous" (65). Here, again, we are reminded that incongruity is also central to camp and the basic premise of *Big Mouth*. "What Is It about Boobs?" in particular, takes body horror (Missy's anxiety about the size of her breasts, manifested by her evil double) and deploys the musical to neutralize any dread. This episode's song-and-dance number references camp musical classics like MGM's *Gold Diggers of 1933*, which feature large female ensembles in glamorous attire performing elaborate routines. "The abundant scale of the numbers is an abundance of piles of women," writes Richard Dyer about *Gold Diggers*, in which women are literally costumed as currency; "the sensuous materialism is the texture of femaleness" (28). In lieu of a number that offers only what Dyer would call a "subservient" female ensemble offered up for male consumption, however, we get "I Love My Body," an anthem to body positivity performed by Connie and a sizable chorus of physically diverse naked women at a Korean Spa, which causes Missy's evil doppelgänger to dissolve, shrieking, into a hot tub like Oz's Wicked Witch. This moment offers multiple levels of incongruity: spa clients spontaneously burst into song; the show deploys a genre that has often relied on women as aesthetic accessories to make a subversive point about female empowerment; a monster leads a musical number to conquer another monster, all of which culminates in a reference to that quintessential camp text, *The Wizard of Oz*. With assistance from the musical, campy humor ultimately defeats anxiety and horror.

Where the Wanton Things Are: Puberty's Monsters

Big Mouth's monsters, too, inspire more chuckles than screams. They are aesthetic cousins with monsters seen elsewhere in children's animation, which presents animators with the "challenge of creating [characters] that [are] clearly monstrous, yet not terrifying or discomforting" (Kunze 157). Maurice and Connie, the show's two primary Hormone Monsters, are never truly scary or threatening. They are furry, like stuffed toys; their large, wide eyes and maws are more frisky and friendly than frightening; their horns are rendered in the same subdued earth tones as their fluffy bodies. Maurice's name recalls, as Patterson points out, the beastly but ultimately amiable "wild things" of Maurice Sendak's classic children's picture book. Maurice is drawn, in Kroll's words, as "a collection of penises" (quoted in Blake): his nose is a dangling, bulbous protuberance; a single horn emerges, erect, from the center of his heart-shaped head. Mulaney describes Maurice as having a "party body." "Imagine if [Rolling Stones member] Ron Wood took his shirt off," he explains, "You'd see that" (quoted in Blake). Connie is sheer diva excess, her voice alternating swiftly between seductive, Eartha Kitt purrs and hormone-fueled squawks. The hilarious vocal performance of Maya Rudolph, known for her time on *Saturday Night Live*, only compounds Connie's campiness. Critics frequently highlight, for example, the preposterous way Connie coos the words "bubble bath" (google it—there's essentially an online fandom dedicated to Rudolph's utterance of this one phrase).

The show's other, more minor Hormone Monsters are equally comic and absurd. Rick, inept Coach Steve (and later temporarily Nick)'s Hormone Monster, is decrepit and sexually clueless; Tyler—a Hormone Monster-in-training—is naive and easily manipulated by the Shame Wizard; Gavin, who makes a brief appearance in the season two finale, is a hypermasculine caricature, somewhere between camp figures Sylvester Stallone and Gaston from *Beauty and the Beast*.[11] The most compelling feature of *Big Mouth*'s monsters is that they simultaneously perform a highly traditional horror function yet, through their unrelenting campiness, undercut this same function. In other words, *Big Mouth*'s monsters (and here I exclude the Shame Wizard, whom I will turn to later) both embody and deflate anxieties surrounding young people and (queer) sexuality. Ultimately, *Big Mouth* makes the horrors and anxieties surrounding adolescent sexuality seem silly—or, at the very least, far less serious than culture-at-large makes them out to be, and it does so by aligning the treatment of its monsters with the conventions of children's animation.

There is a large body of writing on the monster's role in horror films and in culture more broadly. Most critics agree that the monster typically functions as an avatar of abjection, an index of some kind of cultural or unconscious anxiety.[12] In *Totem and Taboo*, Freud notes that "spirits and demons . . . are only projections of man's own emotional impulses. He turns his emotional cathexes into persons, he peoples the world with them and meets his internal mental processes again outside himself" (107). McCort observes that "our cultures' monsters tend to represent our obsessions and anxieties, even in what seem to be the most innocuous of texts" (10). In "Monster Culture (Seven Theses)," Jeffrey Jerome Cohen elaborates:

> The monster is born . . . as an embodiment of a certain cultural moment—of a time, a feeling, and a place. The monster's body quite literally incorporates fear, desire, anxiety, and fantasy (ataractic or incendiary), giving them life and an uncanny independence. The monstrous body is pure culture. A construct and a projection, the monster exists only to be read: the monstrum is etymologically "that which reveals," "that which warns," a glyph that seeks a hierophant. (4)

Queer sexuality has long been figured as a fearful and desirous monster in horror film. As Peter C. Kunze notes, "Horror is largely a conservative genre in its aim to remove the threat of a marginalized outsider and restore the status quo" (149), yet the genre simultaneously "present[s] the sexually Other as fascinating and thrilling," a "nightmarish—if titillating—alternative[] to mundane reality" (Benshoff and Griffin, *Queer Images* 76–77). Benshoff's 1997 study, *Monsters in the Closet: Homosexuality in the Horror Film,* clarifies the parallels between representations of monsters and queers from classical Hollywood horror films through postmodernism. When "homosexuals" appear in popular culture, he notes, "like vampires . . . they are often filtered through the iconography of the horror film: ominous sound cues, shocked reaction shots, or even thunder and lightning" (1). As discussed above, these are the precise techniques that *Big Mouth* deploys in its second episode to introduce Connie the Hormone Monstress. In *Queer Horror*, Darren Elliott-Smith argues that "the horror film's representation of the 'Other' has long been understood to be a symbolic representation of social ills, anxieties and unease. Non-normative sexuality (bisexuality and homosexuality) is often chief among these concerns" (1), and Cohen similarly indicates that "'Deviant' sexual identity is . . . susceptible to monsterization" (9). *Big Mouth*'s Hormone Monsters are undoubtedly part of this tradition. They can be interpreted in dialogue with broader social anxieties about unruly adolescents and polymorphously perverse children; the Gothic's interest in the fear of the self, where the monster as Other is a projection of one's own latent desires; as well as the child's sexual desires and anxieties that may emerge and/or be heightened with the onset of puberty.

Drawing on Robin Wood's "Introduction to the American Horror Film," Elliott-Smith indicates that "sexuality in children" as "non-procreative desire" regularly emerges symptomatically in horror through "monstrous metaphor" (10). It follows, then, that young people themselves—sources of such tremendous social and cultural anxiety—are often monsterized in forms not limited to the revolting child. Clare Bradford points out that, in their liminality, "the changing bodies and developing subjectivities of young people constitute an almost-monstrous lability" (125). Since they are "Pathologized as deviant, ascribed with endless maladies that capitalize on societal anxieties and intolerances, and diagnosed as irrational, dependent, and non-conforming," writes Elaine J. O'Quinn, "young adults are viewed as dangerous and unpredictable aberrations" (50). Insofar as adults might project their own anxieties about adolescence into monstrous vessels, Michelle J. Smith and Kristine Moruzi propose that young people might see something of themselves in the monster: "Young adult readers, poised between childhood and adulthood," they write, "have proven especially receptive to the Gothic's themes of liminality, monstrosity, transgression, romance, and sexuality" (6).

Big Mouth's monsters, then, are conventional according to two generic traditions, but unconventional and even radical, I might suggest, in the way that one conventional deployment of the monster undercuts the other. To be more specific, on the one hand, *Big Mouth*'s monsters are avatars of unhinged, poly-morphous, queer childhood sexuality, representations that have an established history in horror film. On the other hand, the monsters are not excised from *Big Mouth*'s narrative as they might otherwise be in standard horror. Instead, *Big Mouth* is about the ongoing, symbiotic relationship between child and monster, where both monster and child are continually figured as perverse and deviant. The children and their monsters are perverts, yes, but hey, the show tells us, so is everyone—so these monsters will be sticking around.

Big Mouth's Hormone Monsters are avatars of what Stockton calls "the child queered by Freud," "a sexual child with aggressive wishes" (*Queer Child* 27), that is, Freud's polymorphously perverse child from his essay "Infantile Sexuality," the child who evinces an irreducibly infinite number of sexual processes and erotic attachments. This child "looks remarkably, threateningly precocious," Stockton writes, in its "wanting the mother to have its child . . . wanting to have its father's baby . . . wanting to kill its rival lover" (*Queer Child* 27). Of course, *Big Mouth*'s kids, horny though they are, do not actually want these particular things. And yet, their sexual urges are often so intense, and their Hormone Monsters so crude, that the show plays with the possibility that their perversions may extend to Freudian extremes. In the episode "My Furry Valentine," Connie is assigned to Nick as his new Hormone Monster. This latest stage of puberty sees his nipples swelling and becoming intensely sensitive, which causes him to lash out and blame Connie. He doesn't want a female Hormone Monster, he insists. Enraged, Connie taunts Nick and his overly affectionate parents: "Why don't you go and have a sexy-ass Valentime's [sic] Day with your momma and your daddy in a fuckin' three-way," she shouts. "I don't wanna fuck my mom!" Nick protests. "You wanna fuck your mom!" Connie insists. "And then, you wanna give your daddy a BJ!"

Later, per their annual tradition, Nick's parents take him out for Valentine's Day dinner, where they present him with a basketball-shaped locket containing photos of their faces. Nick is horrified and humiliated. "I'm not gonna have sex with her and kill you and stab my eyes out!" he shouts at his father. "Nicky," comes the calm reply, "while we are thrilled that you're reading the Greek clas-sics—it's wonderful!—your tone is unacceptable." Soon thereafter, the Ghost of Duke Ellington introduces the episode's final scenes with a Freudian pun: "And now for the third act, sponsored by Oedipal Arrangements! Your mother wants to sleep with you, so give her some fruit!"

Here, the monster is explicitly associated with one of its traditional horror functions: to embody "those sexual practices that must not be committed, or that may be committed only through the body of the monster" (Cohen 14). Connie, that is, deploys an incest fantasy—the greatest sexual taboo—to torment Nick, who then grows ever-anxious that he may, in fact, be caught in an Oedipal tangle with his parents. *Big Mouth*, however, does not proceed down the usual path of horror, wherein "the monster and all that it embodies must be exiled or destroyed" because "the monster is transgressive, too sexual, perversely erotic, a lawbreaker" (Cohen 16). In traditional horror films, Elliott-Smith explains, "the thrill is rendered safe via the narrative trajectory, . . . which demands the ejection and destruction of the monster and a realignment of identification with non-monstrous subjects" (15). In such cases, he continues, queer spectators "are eventually encouraged to 'suffer with' the monster in its destruction or have to realign themselves with a heteronormative object" (15). Instead, *Big Mouth* sabotages this trajectory by adopting the conventions of children's animated horror.

In his study of monstrosity in children's animated films (including, for example, *Monsters Inc.* and *Shrek*), Kunze indicates that there is something insubordinate in how these films treat their monsters. "Rather than the monstrous being that which must be vanquished," he writes, "the monster in these contemporary children's films must be understood, empathized with, and respected. Acceptance of the monster into and peaceful cohabitation with society are the objective" (157). "My Furry Valentine" parodies romantic comedies (*When Harry Met Sally*, in particular—including the infamous "I'll have what she's having" scene, restaged in the school cafeteria) to tell a story about how Boy Gets Monstress, Boy Loses Monstress, and then Boy Gets Monstress Back. Instead of expelling the perverse child and/or its monstrous avatars, the narrative not only permits them to stay but centers Nick and Connie's "romance," positioning their reunion as the ultimate happy ending. After Connie and Nick's falling out, Nick realizes that he cares for and needs Connie. He approaches her at Lola's Valentine's Day Party and says:

> I've been thinking a lot about you and me, and I'm just not gonna fight it anymore. I don't know why I pushed you away, I guess . . . I guess I was just scared. But Connie, I love how you take care of me and my tender nipples. I love how you inspire me to jack off! . . . I love everything about you! Because, Connie, you are the one for me. You're my Hormone Monstress. That is, of course, if you'll have me.

With a nod to *Jerry Maguire*, Connie replies, "Shut up. Shut the fuck up. 'Cause you had me at tender nipples." The episode then concludes with a *When Harry Met Sally*–style, fourth-wall-breaking interview in which Nick and Connie recounting their romance and describe their mutual affection for one another.

In his analysis of *Monsters Inc.*, Kunze argues that the film "proposes a better world for monsters and children alike founded on a symbiotic relationship, while suggesting . . . the benefits of confronting the Other, not to destroy it, but to appreciate it and work toward mutual understanding" (161). This outcome, he continues, "effectively challenges the conventions of horror" in how it settles on a "peaceful compromise" instead of "the violent annihilation of any threat" (161). *Big Mouth* differs, however, in that its monsters remain figures that awaken the show's protagonists "to the pleasures of the body" (Cohen 17). These are polymorphously perverse monsters, and equally perverse children, much unlike the animated protagonists of the films that Kunze explores. In their endurance in and centrality to *Big Mouth*'s narrative, and in the way this narrative is often focused on the "symbiotic relationship" between queer child and monster, as opposed to the marginalization and destruction of queerness through the monster's body, *Big Mouth*'s Hormone Monsters defy typical horror convention.

"I'm a Creep! I'm a Pervert!": Dark Camp, the Shame Wizard, and the Ghost of Duke Ellington

Big Mouth does, however, offer us the Shame Wizard: a creature who, through his eventual banishment from the central narrative, fulfills the monster's more traditional role. Introduced in the third episode of the show's second season, and voiced by British character actor and *Harry Potter* alum David Thewlis, the Shame Wizard appears on the scene—Dementor-like, in a cloud of smoke—to (as his name suggests) shame *Big Mouth*'s young protagonists for their desires and behavior. Although the show never loses its comedic edge, the Shame Wizard provides some of *Big Mouth*'s darker moments, as he antagonizes the show's young characters with a cruelty never demonstrated by the Hormone Monsters: "There is no doubt about it. You are irredeemable!" the Shame Wizard tells Andrew during the aforementioned trial scene ("The Shame Wizard"). The latter is resigned: "I'm a creep! I'm a pervert! And maybe at the end of the day, I'm just a bad person" (see figure 5.4). The Shame Wizard's intended effect echoes how Eve Kosofsky Sedgwick famously theorizes shame via Silvan Tomkins in "Queer Performativity: Henry James's *The Art of the Novel*": "Shame, as opposed to guilt, is a bad feeling that does not attach to what one does, but to what one is" (12). The Shame Wizard, in other words, aspires to convince *Big Mouth*'s young people that they are, at their core, shameful creatures, that their very identities are constituted by selves deserving of shame.

The Shame Wizard is so cruel, and he has such painful effects on his targets, that he may initially seem to undo the show's overall campiness. He is also drawn to appear more menacing than the Hormone Monsters: he floats, legless

Figure 5.4. In *Big Mouth* episode 2.3, "The Shame Wizard," the Shame Wizard puts Andrew on trial for perversity. Copyright Netflix Inc., 2017. Retrieved from Netflix.com.

and ghost-like; he has mismatched eyes, a scarred face, long fingers, horn-like ears, a sinister moustache, and a wicked toothy grin; he is shrouded in a dark, tattered cloak. Yet shame and camp have their own entwined history. Sedgwick hints that shame "may get us . . . further with the cluster of phenomena generally called 'camp'" (14), and in *Beautiful Bottom, Beautiful Shame: Where "Black" Meets "Queer,"* Stockton picks up on Sedgwick's observation to craft a theory of "dark camp," which is "at once violent, comic, lurid, and sad" (207), and sees "debasement [as] strange and strangely funny—a kind of black comedy" (11). "Black" here bears a double valence, since Stockton is also pointing us towards the racial dimensions of camp and shame; her book is focused on a cluster of texts by mostly Black authors. I will return to this important fact momentarily. First, however, I will illustrate how shame functions in *Big Mouth* to initially alienate and isolate the characters, but the show ultimately highlights the social dimensions of shame, yoking this affect to its vision of universal queerness.

The Shame Wizard's arc unfolds over the majority of *Big Mouth* season two, beginning with his appearance in episode three ("The Shame Wizard") and culminating in a two-part climax that features a sleepover in the school gym gone perversely awry (episodes eight and nine, "Dark Side of the Boob" and "Smooch or Share"). Through the season, the Shame Wizard materializes to taunt *Big Mouth*'s young protagonists when they are at their most vulnerable, reinforcing whatever shame they might be feeling. Unlike the Hormone

Monsters, who often appear to multiple characters simultaneously, the Shame Wizard only reveals himself to one protagonist at a time, thus feeding their sense of alienation and convincing them that their adolescent freakishness yields only solitude. "Yes, everybody's got their fun little secrets," the Shame Wizard cackles to himself prior to the sleepover at the school gymnasium, delighting in the havoc he is planning to wreak.

And, indeed, what havoc he wreaks. Toward the end of "Dark Side of the Boob," the Shame Wizard takes advantage of the students' proximity to one another and launches a full-on assault on each individual student. He upbraids Andrew for his horniness, blames Jessi for her parents' separation, slut-shames Gina (Gina Rodríguez), labels Missy a pervert for masturbating with her toy Glow Worm, and reduces Matthew to "a vicious little queen" who doesn't "fit in anywhere." The shame frenzy culminates, naturally, in a musical number, a parody of Ursula the Sea Witch's "Poor Unfortunate Souls" of Disney's *Little Mermaid* fame. The Shame Wizard sings: "That why I'm here to steer you right / And to shine a naked light / On all the horrid things you do / And fill you with shame, shame / Make life just a little bit lame / A healthy dose of sweet self-loathing / Shame!"

Although the Shame Wizard endeavors to isolate each character, he simultaneously and ironically unites *Big Mouth*'s protagonists through their shared shame. The "you" of his song is both singular and plural, individual and communal. The social dimension of shame in *Big Mouth* aligns itself with both Sedgwick and Stockton's theory of this affect; the latter writes that shame might be "an invaluable if also painful form of sociality, even when debasement seems lonely and interior" (*Beautiful Bottom* 26). Gradually, over the course of the episode, the sociality of shame becomes clear. *Big Mouth*'s characters eventually realize that the Shame Wizard has been tormenting them all, and their collective awareness of shame becomes a source of connection and empowerment. Humiliated at being caught masturbating with her Glow Worm, for example, Missy flees to the school washroom. "I'm a horny spaz and everyone knows it," she sobs. To comfort her, Andrew confesses that, as we witnessed in the pilot episode, he ejaculated in his pants while they were dancing. "It was so brave of you to share with me," Missy replies; "And you know what? It actually does make me feel better." "I feel better, too," Andrew says, "telling you that . . . makes me feel less alone." Moments later, gathered in the gym, the students all confess that they have been visited by the Wizard: "I thought *I* was the only one who could see him," Andrew exclaims. United in this newfound consciousness, the students banish the Shame Wizard by declaring they would be better off without him. Maurice announces, triumphantly, "Welcome to a world without shame, baby!"

With that, the school sleepover descends into depraved pandemonium. Missy's worm comes to life and the two begin humping unrepentantly. Andrew gives his fellow students a tour of the various locations where he has clandestinely masturbated. Nick, naked, rides a Segway through the gym. Someone sets the school on fire. Various students kiss and grope each other. The otherwise homophobic Jay initiates a kiss with Matthew. Seemingly untethered from shame, *Big Mouth*'s adolescents are free to indulge in their horniest fantasies. Here, *Big Mouth* offers another salacious twist on children's horror, a genre which, as McCort explains, allows young people "to experience [the] disruption of and resistance against authority and to judge the moral law to which they are held accountable" (20). This defiance of moral law entails, notably, very few displays of sexuality in the form of heterosexual coupling, despite the predominance of ostensibly heterosexual protagonists. Instead, the show focuses our attention on girl-on-worm action, exhibitionism, public masturbation, and a gay pairing. Here, we have the show's universalizing of queerness and perversity at its most clear. "Queer," as Sedgwick argues, "might usefully be thought of as referring in the first place to . . . an overlapping group of infants and children, those whose sense of identity is for some reason tuned most durably to the note of shame" (13). Indeed, shame—as central affective register of *Big Mouth*—is what has thus far unified the show's young protagonists, and what continues to unite them even as they attempt to disavow and banish the Wizard who embodies this affect. So central to every character's experience of adolescence, shame—and the queerness that Sedgwick associates with shame—is a universal experience, the universal affect from which a "sense of identity" and relationality emerges.

Sedgwick argues, however, that it is in fact impossible to fully cleave shame from the queer psyche. In response to self-help literature that aspires to "heal" shame, she writes, "There's no way that any amount of affirmative reclamation is going to succeed in detaching ['queer'] from its associations with shame and with the terrifying powerlessness of gender-dissonant or otherwise stigmatized childhood" (4). On one level, the liberation of adolescent sexuality from shame and the celebration of universal queerness appears to be *Big Mouth*'s primary pedagogical objective. On another, however, the show is unable to completely rid itself of shame, and it offers shame as integral to both relationality and sexuality. Although the Shame Wizard receives the treatment of most monsters in horror—he is banished, remarginalized—he nonetheless endures in the season's final episode, "The Department of Puberty," albeit as a lonely, sad-sack office worker. Moreover, the show also allows for the eroticization of shame—for moments of "dark camp," as Stockton might call them, which illuminate the lurid features of debasement.

In "Steve the Virgin," for example, Andrew and Lola antagonize one another in a lightly sadomasochistic back-and-forth that takes a sexual turn. Both Maurice and the Shame Wizard are on the scene as Andrew and Lola trade insults following a failed first date. The Shame Wizard eggs them both on, and Maury observes: "I think I can work with this . . . All this verbal abuse is making my nips hard." "You're just a disgusting, slimy, little worm," taunts Lola, and Andrew replies, "Come here, you big block," before the two kiss messily and Maury begins hopping around on all fours, barking like a dog. "Wait," Andrew interjects, "say something mean about how clammy my hands are!" "I'm gonna wring you out like a sponge!" Lola offers. Andrew to Lola, lustily: "You're a sociopath." They kiss passionately again, the Shame Wizard cackles, and Maury howls, wolf-like, silhouetted by a full moon. In this scene, *Big Mouth* delivers a rare moment of cooperation between Maurice and the Shame Wizard, between arousal and debasement. Shame, here, provides nearly as much erotic fodder as does shamelessness in the show's post-Wizard world, as seen in "Smooch or Share." We see another glimpse of such erotics in that episode, when the Shame Wizard places a "cone of shame" on Tyler, the Hormone-Monster-in-training, in an attempt to prevent him from gnawing at his genitals. "Ooh, you're such a good master!" Tyler coos. The Shame Wizard begins swatting Tyler with a folded newspaper, and Tyler begs for more: "What about my tushy??" "Stop enjoying this!" the Shame Wizard scolds as he spanks. "But I love it!" exclaims Tyler.

The show's representation of debasement as the site of sexual arousal for adolescents (and one adolescent Hormone Monster) is provocative. Shame and sexuality fuse, here, to fortify the show's universal queerness. In the world of *Big Mouth*, everyone is embarrassed and ashamed (recall Andrew and Nick's "everything is so embarrassing" exchange from the pilot), yet sometimes shame is also kind of sexy. Queerness is yoked to shame, just as Sedgwick suggests, yet the show's iteration of "queer" is one that extends to all characters in their polymorphously perverse glory. The show offers a social model of shame, a structure that, as Stockton writes, might help "make debasements possible, bearable, pleasurable, creative, even in their darkness" (*Beautiful Bottom* 26). The Shame Wizard's effects endure and extend, then, far beyond his banishment from the school gymnasium. The monstrous effects of shame may be temporarily cast away, along with the monster who acts as their avatar, but shame has still made its mark as *Big Mouth*'s primary social mode, an affect integral to its queerness, and even the source of some sexual pleasure.

I would be remiss if I concluded without addressing the racial dimensions of camp, particularly since race is fundamental to Stockton's work on dark camp. As Noah Fields points out, "camp theorists have consistently failed to address race." Often, such theorists—including, but not limited to Sontag—tend to whitewash camp discourse, attributing its origin to "urban gay male communities during the classical Hollywood era," as do Benshoff and Griffin in *Queer Images* (68), and/or entirely glossing over its roots in communities of color, as does Babuscio when he suggests that camp is "a means of illustrating those cultural ambiguities and contradictions that oppress us all, gay and straight, and, in particular, women" (128). In *Queer as Camp*, Kidd and I acknowledge camp's history of "white privilege and even structural racism," but we too "fail entirely to offer critique of such in Camp productions and criticism" (16). Such violent omissions were spotlighted following the 2019 Met Gala, themed "Camp: Notes on Fashion," to which actor/comedian Lena Waithe wore a jacket emblazoned with the phrase "Black Drag Queens Inventend [sic] Camp"—an outfit that spawned a range of conversations about Black culture's formative contributions to camp. Sequoia Barnes, for example, writes that "camp is inherent in black style. We have a cultural symbiosis with the highly stylized. There is a . . . seemingly innate emphasis on the adorned body to exercise one's blackness" (685). A *Teen Vogue* piece by Scarlett Newman explains that

> camp as an aesthetic that relates to blackness spans many disciplines, from Vaudeville and minstrelsy performances and the golden age of Hollywood cinema to black beauty traditions like the Bronner Brothers International Beauty Show and the Detroit Hair Wars to the gay ball cultures of the 1980s and the exaggerated, gaudy fashion ideals that came out of hip-hop.

These critics, among others, remind us that academic writing tends to place Sontag and White gay men at the origins of camp, erasing and further marginalizing the way racialized communities have so profoundly shaped the contours of camp aesthetics and practices.

Notably, *Big Mouth* features a Black character who unites many of the themes discussed in this chapter, including the Gothic, sexual anxiety, and "dark camp": the ghost of famous jazz musician Duke Ellington, who dwells in Nick's attic and is approached by Andrew and Nick whenever they require advice about one of their many horrific adolescent experiences (see figure 5.5).[13] At first glance, Duke risks replicating several racist tropes that pervade popular media. Duke might recall the "magical negro," which "situates blacks as mascots, inspirations, and/or surrogates for the celebration or affirmation of white humanity" (Ikard 10). This character exists "almost exclusively to usher whites through emotional, social, or economic crises" (Ikard 10), and often draws on "mystical powers" in service of this function (Benshoff and Griffin, *America on Film*). In his role as mentor to Andrew and Nick, Duke might also remind us of "the familiar story . . . of a black man who is sexually savvy and

Figure 5.5. In *Big Mouth* episode 1.2, "Everybody Bleeds," the Ghost of Duke Ellington gives Nick some characteristically bad advice. Copyright Netflix Inc., 2017. Retrieved from Netflix.com.

slick teaching a white man how to get a girl," as seen in films like *Hitch* and *The 40-Year-Old Virgin* (Childs 112).

Insofar as Duke references these tropes, however, he largely upends them. It is noteworthy that Duke is voiced by Jordan Peele, the actor/director known for his remarkable achievements at the intersections of horror and comedy, including the groundbreaking, Oscar-winning horror film *Get Out* (2017), a terrifying (yet often funny) allegory of White supremacy and anti-Black racism. *Big Mouth*'s Duke is an absurd, excessive character, undoubtedly one of the show's campiest creations. Duke typically gives terrible advice, and he is mostly interested in sharing tales of pansexual debauchery from his lifetime. He often catalyzes the show's musical numbers, many of which feature the ghosts of other dead celebrities (Freddie Mercury and Whitney Houston, for example, also voiced by Peele and Rudolph). Duke is central to how *Big Mouth* deploys the kind of "dark camp" theorized by Stockton, wherein "a social embrace of debasement" is central to its operation (*Beautiful Bottom* 26). Duke is an eager vessel for the boys' most humiliating experiences. He embraces or reinforces the shame the boys feel, often replying with a ridiculous and debased story of his own. On rare occasions when he offers anything approximating sincere advice, he immediately undermines it with something outrageous. Take, for example, "What Is It about Boobs?" which sees Nick seeking counsel from Duke about his crush on classmate Gina. Duke opens with some sensible words: "Let me tell you a little Duke-y secret when it comes to the ladies. . . . Listen. When they speak, listen to the words they say. And for extra credit, retain the details, and drop them in at a later date to prove you were listening! It's shockingly effective! It took me a lifetime to realize that women—get this—just want to be treated like human beings." Then, he continues, singing this time: "Oh, listen to the ladies and you'll be rolling around in a big field of titties, but don't trust the titties, the nipples are tiny cameras!" The absurdity of his song might not entirely undo the wiser advice, but it certainly puts into question Duke's effectiveness as a mentor to *Big Mouth*'s impressionable protagonists.

Mostly, however, Duke's advice is terrible or just ludicrous, and it rarely (if ever) yields positive results for his mentees. In the show's pilot, for example, Nick approaches Duke for help managing his insecurity about penis size ("Ejaculation"). Duke replies by sharing a story about "the Cotton Club, 1938," when "I saw Charlie Parker's penis in a bathroom, and, good lord, I felt inferior." His reaction: "I went out and made sweet love to Eva Gabor. That's right, I balled a white woman back when it really meant something!" Nick interprets Duke's advice: "So I should find the prettiest girl in school and ask her out?" Replies Duke: "Bingo-bango, furry triangle! If you know what I'm saying." This, of course, does not end well for Nick: he is abandoned by his date Olivia and, humiliated, reduced to tears. There are many such instances of Duke's failed mentorship. In "Pillow Talk," Duke accompanies Nick and Andrew to New York City, ostensibly as a chaperone, but he winds up on a depraved bender. In "The Head Push," Nick—confronted with the (deluded) possibility that he might receive a blowjob from Tallulah, his current crush—seeks advice for his penile insecurity from an array of celebrity ghosts, all of whom encourage Nick to drop his drawers and show them what he's working with. "Do you think it's too small for Tallulah Levine?" asks Nick. Duke replies, "Does she have a gap between her two front teeth? Because then it might work out fine!" Nick, exasperated, replies, "Okay, haha, well you're all dead." Duke, again: "And you've got a little dick!" Overall, Duke refuses the traditionally affirming function of the magical negro, and his advice to the show's White protagonists culminates not in sexual success but rather in failure and further humiliation. Duke takes Andrew and Nick's debasement and mirrors it, reflecting it back at them by recounting his own debased experiences (e.g. the Cotton Club anecdote) or refusing to allay their anxiety (e.g. ridiculing Nick's penis). Ultimately, Duke's dark camp aligns itself with the show's overall approach to shame. By highlighting and heightening shame, Duke invites us to laugh at it—this, paradoxically, has the potential effect on audiences of defusing those feelings of debasement that he reinforces in Nick and Andrew. When we laugh at Duke's mocking of Nick's shame, in other words, we are invited to laugh at similar anxieties we might have about our own bodies. Shame, here, remains a highly social affect, inviting the show's characters and its audience into relation with one another.

In response to the whitewashing of camp, Fields proposes a theory of "black queer camp," which "represents an insurrection against not just homophobic discourses but also anti-black racist discourses. Simultaneously," he continues, "it is involved in a project of racial and sexual uplift by recentering and rendering visible the bodies and narratives of marginalized black queer subjects." I am not certain that this is, exactly, what *Big Mouth* accomplishes. Duke does, however, represent an impertinent rejoinder to racist figures like the magical negro in his insistent refusal to fulfill this trope's conventional functions. Instead of buttressing the show's White protagonists, Duke prompts them to fail; in lieu of sage counsel he offers dark camp and its embrace of debasement. Significant, too, is how *Big Mouth* places a Black character at the intersection that is so fundamental to the show: camp, horror, sexuality, and the sociality of shame. *Big Mouth*'s project is indeed one of "sexual uplift," and the series accomplishes this in large part through the rendering visible (if ghostly) a Black character who is as polymorphously perverse as every other character on the show. Duke's dark camp is certainly comic and lurid, as per Stockton's criteria (*Beautiful Bottom* 207), and it is often a bit sad, too. Between comic anecdotes, Duke will often evince a melancholy befitting a specter who is trapped between two worlds. "Jazz is like life," he tells Andrew in the episode "Pillow Talk." "It goes on for longer than you think, and then as soon as you're like, 'I get it,' it ends." Although *Big Mouth*'s protagonists endure in a state of perpetual flux, Duke reminds audiences that the delights and horrors of incompleteness are, ultimately, fleeting—and perhaps time should be spent lingering in the pleasures and sociality of shame instead of losing ourselves to anxiety.

On the one hand, *Big Mouth*'s sexual politics may appear banal. Like Stockton's argument in *The Queer Child*, the show risks flattening queerness by universalizing it. If every child is queer, then is "queer" left with any kind of political or critical clout? If a sense of queerness is established through a shared shame that affects all adolescents, then who or what is *not* queer, if anything or anyone? On the other hand, however, something feels radical about a show that embraces the polymorphous perversity of twelve- and thirteen-year-old children and uses camp to critique the anxieties that swarm so feverishly around the sexuality of young people. Like *Grasshopper Jungle*, *Big Mouth* both amplifies and undermines Hall's concept of *Sturm und Drang* through satire. Instead of pushing queerness to its margins, however, *Big Mouth* allows queerness to proliferate, spreading itself over every character. Far from being unbearable, queerness in *Big Mouth* is visibly at the very core of relationality. The series makes a clear connection between queerness, shame, and the universality of childhood perversity, and then sends up those negative affects—shame, anxiety, horror—that so often attach themselves to adolescence. Through camp, *Big Mouth* exposes *Sturm und Drang* to be itself a kind of naïve camp. "In naïve, or pure, Camp," Sontag writes, "the essential element is seriousness, a seriousness that fails" (59). *Big Mouth* assembles those elements of adolescence that are so often taken seriously and causes them to fail repeatedly, quite effectively "dethroning" them.

Ultimately, *Big Mouth* is an invitation to dwell in the pleasures of adolescent polymorphous perversity and the perpetual pubescent incompleteness of the revolting child, while—like many of the queer YA protagonists we've seen thus far—resisting linear growth and development. As seen elsewhere, too, stasis and growth are in constant tension with one another; the temporality of anxiety persists. Like John Donovan and Isabelle Holland's novels, as explored in this book's first two chapters, *Big Mouth* functions in part to convincingly defy some queer YA critics' desire for coherent queer visibility and sexual teleology. Although the show provides an openly gay character and others who seem heterosexually inclined, most of *Big Mouth*'s erotic attachments are decidedly queer and definitively nonreproductive: masturbation, primarily, to and with a variety of nonhuman objects (pillows, Glow Worms, a tomato, a bathing suit, etc.), while shame itself becomes a source of erotic pleasure. Through its deployment of children's horror conventions, the show also offers us another queer twist on the feral tale, which would have a child protagonist abandon their association with "nature" in favor of growth into civilized, heterosexual adulthood. Just as Donovan's Davy refuses to readily relinquish his attachment to his queer childhood companions (Fred the dachshund and the stuffed coyote), *Big Mouth*'s animated revolting children learn to work with (or, in Nick's case, "romance") their feral companions instead of abandoning them and the queerness they represent. The show and its characters linger in depravity and debasement, asking us as audience members to do the same. And here, I would agree with Maurice: there's "something beautiful" about that—something perversely, horrifically beautiful.

CHAPTER 6

Getting Better: Children's Literature Theory and the *It Gets Better* Project[1]

In response to the devastating rash of reported queer youth suicides in the fall of 2010, writer Dan Savage and his partner Terry Miller founded the *It Gets Better* project, a website inviting adults to submit videos that offer messages of hope and encouragement to youth who may be struggling with their sexualities in difficult environments.[2] Fueled by contributions from public figures like Barack Obama and a host of celebrities including Ellen DeGeneres, *It Gets Better* has garnered widespread attention and received over sixty thousand user-created video submissions that have been viewed more than fifty million times. The *It Gets Better* book, edited by Savage and Miller, was released in March 2011 and appeared on the *New York Times* bestseller list within weeks, and in the same year the project launched a Global Affiliate Network that "now represents nearly 20 countries around the world" and has received over 625,000 pledges of support ("About Our Global Movement"). Additionally, an *It Gets Better* documentary special profiling several queer teens was broadcast on MTV and Logo in February 2012. The project's website, radically revamped in 2017 (with the support of Google), now boasts of major partnerships with corporations as varied as Adobe, Converse, Doritos, NBC/Universal, and Uber, and curates a variety of multimedia content in addition to *It Gets Better* videos. Visitors to the site can learn how to incorporate queer content into public screenings and educational workshops ("Engaging Your Community"), contemplate "10 Ways to Boost Someone Else's PRIDE This Season," or discover how "It Gets Better w/ American Eagle Outfitters!"

As *It Get Better*'s popularity initially surged, however, critiques of the project quickly surfaced.[3] Tavia Nyong'o notes that *It Gets Better* primarily hails an upwardly mobile class of White gay youth while excluding those for whom adulthood does not necessarily bring a reprieve from forms of anti-queer violence—particularly, Nyong'o writes, "gender nonconforming and/or trans" people. Sponsored by the Gay-Straight Alliance of San Francisco, the *Make It Better* project took aim at the passivity implicit in *It Gets Better*—the idea that simply enduring adolescence will result in improved social conditions—by offering practical tools for taking action against homophobia in schools and communities and on a national level.[4] In a *Guardian* article, Jasbir Puar expresses concern with the narrowing of queerness's significance for both adults and youth: she argues that *It Gets Better* showcases a narrow class of successful adults and reinforces the idea that queer youth are inevitably prone to suicide and bullying. For Puar, many adult *It Gets Better* contributors are invested in versions of the family that stray little—if at all—from the heteronormative, and in narratives of upward mobility that "[echo] the now discredited 'pull yourself up from the bootstraps' immigrant motto" ("In the Wake"). She concludes that *It Gets Better* "might turn out to mean, you get more normal" ("In the Wake"). And in a frank Facebook post, queer activist Charlotte Cooper challenges the idea that queer youth require adult stories to survive, writing, "I wish there was some kind of an *It Gets Better* campaign in which fucked up queer teenagers give reassurance and advice to windy and pompous bourgie grown-up homos."

There is a provocative tension between *It Gets Better*'s stated purpose and the way it seems to circulate. On one hand, *It Gets Better* claims to be about queer youth: the project directly addresses itself to this audience and the ostensible crisis in which it finds itself.[5] As Savage notes in his introduction to the *It Gets Better* book, "the point of the project is to give despairing LGBT kids *hope*. The point is to let them know that things *do* get better, using the examples of our own lives" (6). On the other hand, taking into account the ever-growing array of responses to and critiques of *It Gets Better*, the project appears to be more about adult anxieties surrounding how queer youth should be addressed than about queer youth themselves. As it circulates through a variety of media, *It Gets Better* accumulates mostly adult-authored personal stories that echo the project's primary, teleological narrative of development and resilience, and an expansive body of mostly adult-authored critical interventions that interrogate the pedagogical value and appropriateness of the message that "it gets better" while gesturing, more broadly, to the project's political failings. In other words, *It Gets Better* does not circulate according to the ways that it imagines its audience.

My focus here is this tension between *It Gets Better*'s purported objective of providing youth with hope and its circulation as a venue for adults to rehearse their anxieties about the relationship between adulthood, visible queerness, and queer youth. *It Gets Better* addresses youth, but its narrative is not solely aimed at or even about youth: the stories also serve their own authors by affirming a stable adult-identified subject position in opposition to a narrative of tumultuous queer adolescence, while repeatedly asserting an ostensibly "correct" didactic approach to queer youth. Jen Gilbert also explores this disjunct between *It Gets Better*'s stated mission and its pedagogical function in "Histories of Misery: *It Gets Better* and the Promise of Pedagogy," which convincingly illustrates that queer adults require the project's narrative structure and "the figure of . . . the pathological gay youth" in order to provide themselves with a "sense of having a history, rather than an affliction" (60). Insofar as the project's "you" conjures a troubled queer youth audience, Gilbert explains, "the 'you' also reaches back: the other 'you' to whom these narratives are addressed is the 'you' that is me, albeit in another, earlier age" (55). This might bring to mind the queer double-take I discuss elsewhere in this book: *It Gets Better*'s adult, anxious about their own subjectivity and the future of queerness (as embodied by the figure of queer youth in crisis), turns back to self-narrate in an attempt to fix the present. Gilbert offers the optimistic conclusion that this shared history of suffering, transmitted through the web, might in fact enable us to imagine "new modes of relationality" between generations of queers (60).

While *It Gets Better* borrows conventions from a variety of genres—essay, confession, autobiography, and, as Gilbert points out, the orphan tale or "foundling text" (48)—in my view, the adult/youth relationship it evinces suggests above all else children's literature.[6] This is perhaps most evident in how Puar, Nyong'o, Cooper, and other critics of the project unknowingly critique *It Gets Better* using an approach associated with the study of children's literature: as Karín Lesnik-Oberstein writes, children's literature scholarship is often overly invested in improving existing strategies for finding the ideal book for the child reader (4). Although *It Gets Better*'s critics are not necessarily in pursuit of "the right book" for queer youth, they are most definitely concerned with illustrating how and why *It Gets Better* includes, for a variety of political and pedagogical reasons, the wrong set of stories to be circulating among its imagined audience. Indeed, it seems, the project functions as an assemblage of narratives that might serve the investments and attachments of its adult participants and its adult critics more than its young queer audience.

In *The Case of Peter Pan, or the Impossibility of Children's Fiction* (1984), Jacqueline Rose asserts that children's fiction "rests on the idea that there is a child who is simply there to be addressed and that speaking to it might be simple" (1). This genre, she continues, "sets up a world in which the adult comes first (author, maker, giver) and the child comes after (reader, product, receiver), but where neither of them enter the space in between" (1–2). As a result, Rose claims, children's literature is impossible: not because it cannot be written, but because it rests on "the impossible relation between adult and child" (1). In other words, the child of children's literature is always a product of adult fantasies about what childhood is or should be; there is no real child to whom children's literature is addressed (Rose 10). While acknowledging the tragic fact that real queer youth are taking their own lives as a result of hostile and oppressive social conditions, I want to put Savage and Miller's project into conversation with Rose to consider the (im)possibility of *It Gets Better*. The project addresses itself to troubled queer youth, but, as I will illustrate, it is ultimately more about the anxious relation between adult-identified storyteller and imagined audience than anything else. Yet *It Gets Better*'s circulation suggests that Rose's "middle space" between adult and child is not as untouched as she claims. The project is founded on an impossible adult/youth relationship, yes, but this impossibility—and the exclusions produced through the limited way that *It Gets Better* imagines its audience—is what drives *It Gets Better*'s widespread circulation across media and the large body of critique it has generated from a variety of sources. In other words, *It Gets Better* both supports and complicates Rose's argument about impossibility. The project is structured around fantasies about a particular young queer audience, and critics meditate anxiously about whether or not *It Gets Better*'s pedagogical approach is the correct one given this same audience, but these responses and critiques produce a discursive space that interrogates the adult/youth relation on which the project rests. While we could say that *It Gets Better* enters Rose's untouched middle space, drawing again on Kathryn Bond Stockton's *The Queer Child* enables us to acquire a different metaphor that conceptualizes the project's circulation and its effects with greater nuance while enriching our critical approaches to children's literature: the notion of "growing sideways" (11).

Queer theorists including Stockton have leveled critique at sites that, like *It Gets Better*, privilege futurity as a normative temporal orientation. Puar reads *It Gets Better* through Lauren Berlant's concept of slow death, a "concomitant yet different temporality of relating to living and dying" ("The Cost").[7] As discussed in chapter four, Lee Edelman's *No Future* attacks the ideology of "reproductive futurism" that functions as the "organizing principle of communal relations" (2), and Jack Halberstam's *In a Queer Time and Place* positions the AIDS crisis and youth subcultures as disruptive forces in heteronormative and capitalist ideologies of reproduction and longevity. Recall that in *The Queer Child*, Stockton argues that we require a new spatial metaphor for growth since our language of child and adolescent development is impoverished. To account for how queer or "proto-gay" children grow and delay growth in ways that exceed what she calls "the vertical, forward-motion metaphor of growing up," Stockton introduces the metaphor of "growing sideways," which "suggests that the width of a person's experience or ideas, their motives or their motions, may pertain at any age, bringing 'adults' and 'children' into lateral contact of surprising sorts" (11). Using sideways growth as a heuristic for conceptualizing *It Gets Better*'s accumulation of critiques and responses helps us imagine how the project draws youth and adults into the kind of proximity Stockton describes.

Rose maintains that children's literature "is clearly about [the impossible relation between adult and child], but it has the remarkable characteristic of being about something which it hardly ever talks of" (1); what Stockton provides, in the context of *It Gets Better*, is a method for thinking about how the sideways growth of a text—or even an entire genre—creates space that *does* address and critique this relation in meaningful and productive ways. Examining *It Gets Better*'s sideways growth allows us to conceive of the project's circulatory accumulations as part of the project itself. As Stockton brings adults and children into contact, so too am I putting the project's "inside" and "outside" into conversation, interrogating not only the stories published directly within *It Gets Better* but also how (if at all) the project circulates amongst and is responded to by audiences of all ages. In other words, this is not a linear mode of analysis that traces the development of *It Gets Better*'s adaptation from website to book to documentary and focuses only on the project's adult-authored and youth-aimed stories. Instead, I offer a method for textual analysis that considers nonlinear circulations and accumulations—including affective structures—that may occur and accrue outside of how a text seems to imagine its own circulation.

In what follows, I will illustrate the following claims about *It Gets Better*: (1) as a work of children's literature, *It Gets Better* rests on an impossible adult/youth relation in that it anxiously invents the youth it seeks to address (there is no "real" youth behind the idea of *It Gets Better*); (2) this impossibility is responsible for the project's political failure since the youth *It Gets Better* imagines is limited and exclusionary, or to paraphrase Rose, the project believes that there is a queer youth who is simply there and easily spoken to; (3) precisely because of its impossibility and political failure, the project succeeds as productive cultural discourse in its generation of countless responses and critiques; and (4) the circulation of *It Gets Better* troubles Rose's argument about the middle space between child and adults, since the project demonstrates a sideways growth that brings adults and youth into contact with one another. Thinking *It Gets Better* as children's literature permits a critique of the project that points to its (im)possibilities, failures, and successes, and it also has the potential to reshape our approaches to children's literature more broadly.

Political Failure and the Impossibility of *It Gets Better*

Before addressing *It Gets Better*'s political failures, which spring from the limited version of queer youth the project imagines, I want to acknowledge some of the project's strengths, many of which are shared with queer YA. Without a doubt, the wide reach and popularity of the *It Gets Better* campaign contributes to increased awareness about homophobia, bullying, and queer youth suicide, social issues that persist in spite of the ostensible progress in the realm of liberal gay rights in our North American context. We can safely speculate that many queer youth who regularly confront homophobia or feel isolated due to an uneasy fit with normative expectations surrounding gender and sexuality have been touched by an *It Gets Better* video, just as they may have been affected by a YA novel with visible queer content. As Savage writes in the introduction to the *It Gets Better* book, "thousands of LGBT adults who thought they were going to contribute a video found themselves talking with LGBT youth, offering them not just hope but advice, insight, and something too many LGBT youth lack: the ear of a supportive adult who understands what they're going through" (6). Since, as Savage notes, many *It Gets Better* videos are created by openly queer adults, we can also credit the project for heightening the visibility of nonheterosexual identities, which might in turn provide young people with a broader sense of sexual possibility. For youth who grow up in areas where queerness seems invisible, *It Gets Better* may provide them with a sense that a nonheterosexual existence is, in fact, possible. As Gilbert explains, "For the LGBTQ youth who suffer from a lack of narrative possibilities as well as from physical harassment, the compromised promise of *It Gets Better* is that shared histories of misery might be the tendon of intergenerational conversation" (59). Moreover, given that the project "helps queer adults turn their experience of being miserable into history," the project may prove therapeutic and self-affirming for those who create videos (Gilbert 57). We might be reminded, here, of Kristeva's argument that writing enables authors to experience adolescent incompleteness while simultaneously, momentarily cohering an anxious self. In the Kristevan sense, the *It Gets Better* project is an adolescent novel as much as it is children's literature.

Critics concerned with the political failure of *It Gets Better*, on the other hand, primarily emphasize two points. First, as Puar puts it, the project has undeniable "affective attachments to neoliberalism" ("The Cost"): investments in the growth, development, and productivity of the individual as opposed to a broader interest in forging social collectivity and creative modes of relationality. *It Gets Better* largely suggests that the ideal telos of an individual's development is a monogamous relationship, stable career, and family—all of which constitute a heteronormative model of existence according to queer theorists, and when replicated by people in queer communities, is frequently dubbed "homonormative" and understood to have close ties with neoliberalism.[8] The queer critique of neoliberalism and hetero/homonormativity is lucidly articulated by Michael Warner: "Like most stigmatized groups," he asserts, "gays and lesbians were always tempted to believe that the way to overcome stigma was to win acceptance by the dominant culture, rather than to change the self-understanding of that culture" (50). Critics of *It Gets Better* take issue with the project's emphasis on acceptance and conformity, and its overall disavowal of queerness's potential to create and reshape nonnormative social worlds. Next, and most important to this chapter, these critics gesture to a longstanding critique of how queer youth identity gets narrated and interpreted, as discussed in chapter two of this book: adults often understand queer youth as Eric Rofes's "Martyr-Target-Victims"—the voiceless, passive, suicide-prone victims of inevitable anti-queer violence and bullying (41). As Susan Talburt argues, this trope not only limits the complexity of the discourse surrounding queer youth, but it also "[constitutes] a production of subject positions in which adults administer a group with problems and needs—and participate in inventing those whom we would help" (18). Indeed, *It Gets* Better's coherence around a very specific idea of queer youth structures the project's impossibility and causes its political failure. *It Gets Better*, that is, imagines a limited and exclusionary version of queer youth that is ultimately more about shoring up its adult authors. Inspired by Rose, "instead of asking what children want, or need, from literature," I ask "what it is that adults, through literature, want or demand of the child" (137)? More specifically, I want to explore what adults ask of queer youth through *It Gets Better*. What investments, in other words, do adults have in the pedagogical approach to and representation of certain narratives of queer youth, and what are the anxieties—as manifested in *It Gets Better* narratives—that these investments make apparent?

It Gets Better presumes a queer youth audience with specific kinds of mobility.[9] According to the project, to survive the transition into adulthood queer youth must be (1) physically and geographically mobile, moving from small towns to big cities that are ostensibly more accepting of nonheterosexuals; (2) upwardly mobile in terms of class and career; and (3) able to move through a now-familiar linear and teleological narrative, one that sees queer youth grow from troubled martyr-target-victims into successful adults who openly embrace an essential and stable sexual identity. While Savage notes the centrality and importance of hope to *It Gets Better*, the project's version of hope has particular content that can be accessed only by making particular movements through time and space that are available only to particular individuals. *It Gets*

Better fails politically in part because of these exclusionary spatial and temporal assumptions: spatial in that the project suggests that queer youth must physically relocate in order to survive, and temporal in the project's insistence on futurity and rehearsal of a simplistic, linear narrative of progression from tumultuous adolescence into stable adulthood.

The narrative framework of the vast majority of *It Gets Better* stories can be described as follows: I was raised in a conservative small town and/or in a conservative family and/or as part of a conservative religious community. I was bullied violently at school, felt isolated as a result, and contemplated suicide. I endured high school and moved to a big city and/or attended a college with a diverse campus. I found a community of like-minded queers, accepted my true self, and came out. Love, a successful career, and a family followed. Many queers have lived and/or are living lives that echo this narrative, and I do not intend to diminish the real experiences of *It Get Better*'s storytellers. However, with a few small exceptions, reading the *It Gets Better* book cover to cover is like reading and rereading this story over and over again. Under the guise of telling one hundred and five stories, the *It Gets Better* book essentially tells only one, and its characters are almost always the same: adult-identified authors who have made the transition from troubled adolescence into the safety and sexual stability of adulthood, a place from which they can look back, directly address their audience of martyr-target-victims, and didactically advise them to follow a specific narrative.

A key plot point in almost every chapter is the narrator's relocation from a small town to a city or college. Brinae Lois Gaudet explains that "the cool thing about high school . . . is it doesn't last forever. . . . Once you get out of high school you are free. . . . You can go see the world. You can do things; you can get an education; you can make something of your life" (28). Joseph Odysseus Mastro counsels queer youth to move as soon as possible: "If you're in high school and you're gay, bisexual, or transgender, and you're being tormented, find some way to get through school and then get to San Francisco, get to the Bay Area, get to Miami or Chicago or New York City" (209). And A. Y. Daring stresses the critical importance of this type of mobility: "I can attest to the fact that I honestly, legitimately, literally do not know of a single queer adult who graduated from high school and went on to bigger cities and bigger schools and didn't eventually find a place where they belong" (65). In Daring's story and many others, nonmobile queer youth, youth unable to readily relocate, youth who simply choose to stay put, and their opportunities for finding acceptance and community are left excluded and unimagined.

Of the hundred and five stories in the *It Gets Better* book, there are only two that deviate from the standard "move, or else" story. Stephen D. Lorimor is the lone contributor who claims that "college was worse" (238). In her playful story entitled "Rockin' the Flannel Shirt," Krissy Mahan extols the virtues of being a rural-dwelling queer. "As a person who lives in the country and doesn't have a lot of money, I can tell you that not all gay people are urban or rich," she writes; "I've been really happy being a big rural dyke. So, if you want to live in the country, or just can't move away, you'll be fine" (71). Mahan's narrative is also noteworthy for the way it encourages movement away from community and into relative isolation: "One of the nice things about being in the country is you don't have to deal with people all the time. There's land out there, and you can just get away. Go build yourself a little fort in the woods. . . . You'll be a butch dyke and you'll be hot. Everyone will love it. It will be good" (71). It is striking that stories like Mahan's are so rare in *It Gets Better*; her account is lost in a mass of pro-urban narratives that demand particular types of physical and geographic movements from queer youth.

In the standard *It Gets Better* story, moving to an urban center enables upward-mobility, career growth, and the accumulation of physical, emotional, and financial assets. "Do what you love to do," writes Dave Holmes, "and I guarantee you there is a place in this world where someone will pay you to do it. So find it" (191). While it is undeniably important for young queers to recognize that they too can obtain employment, the problem as Puar illustrates it lies in the simplistic way that successful queer adulthood is equated with a successful career and particular forms of neoliberal relationality ("In the Wake"). "I am a gay man who loves his life," proclaims Darren Hayes, former member of pop duo Savage Garden; "I have a career that I love. I've got a partner that I adore beyond all comprehension. And I am surrounded by friends and family and a community who accept me and support me for who I am" (151). Jenn and Erika Wagner-Martin advise readers that "we're not so different from those kids from high school who used to harass us and pick on us for being different. . . . I have my family. I have my life. I get up and go to work every morning" (97). And Jessica Leshnoff claims that she and her partner are "ridiculously normal. As in: We fall asleep on the couch together and watch movies and go grocery shopping and do laundry and go to Starbucks and make meat loaf. . . . And you'll have that one day, too. You really will. I promise" (252). In his introduction, Savage remarks: "without gay role models to mentor and support them, without the examples our lives represent, [youth] couldn't see how they might get from bullied gay teenager to safe and happy gay adult" (3). Indeed, *It Gets Better* imagines that queer youth must make the exact transition from precarious adolescence to the sanctuary of adulthood that Savage describes. Conversely, however, I ask of Savage's dialectic: can "happy gay adults" imagine themselves as such without enacting a retrospective turn towards the image of the "bullied gay teenager"? Is it the troubled gay teen who requires the image of the happy gay adult to survive, or vice-versa?

The more *It Gets Better*'s grand narrative is staged, the more the adult-identified speaker's fragile subject position and, concurrently, the project's impossibility become clear. Through its direct address to an imagined audience of young martyr-target-victims, *It Gets Better* functions primarily as a medium for the anxious rehearsal of fixed and resolved adult identities that exist by virtue of their self-opposition to this audience. As Kenneth B. Kidd explains, "the young adult embodies and perhaps even restores to the old adult a weird sort of innocence, representing both past and future stability of the self" ("A Case History" 167). The project's retrospective narratives of movement through space, class, and time, told with the distinct pedagogical force of a second person address, evince contributors who imagine themselves as having navigated the martyr-target-victim/out-and-proud narrative and achieved an ending that enables them to become *It Gets Better* storytellers. Adulthood is a vantage point from which they look knowingly back on youth as a period of flux and turmoil that ultimately produces a complete adult self.

In this way, the turning-back of adult-identified *It Gets Better* contributors mirrors the turning-back of queer YA critics, as previously discussed in this book. As Gilbert explains, "the insistence that 'you' will get better or stronger becomes less a prediction or promise than a historical reconstruction of experience" (55). Just as YA critics (like Hartinger, Cart and Jenkins, and others, as discussed in my introduction and first chapter) reflect on the "adolescence" of queer YA—i.e. the problem novel—with the intent of asserting the superior state of contemporary queer YA, so do *It Gets Better* contributors turn back to their own adolescences—most of which read like problem novel excerpts—in order to assert and buttress a similar narrative of progression and improvement. Moreover, similar to critics like Hartinger who describe the ideal queer YA character as sexually resolved, *It Gets Better* is rife with the language of essentialism, as though sexuality concretizes once uncovered and is never again subject to change. "Finding my true sexuality has changed my life and I wouldn't change anything that I went through for the world," writes Hunter Brady, for example; "I have found who I really am and I am happy now. And that is all that matters" (144). Brady is a 16-year-old, not an adult in the traditional sense, and yet she qualifies as an *It Gets Better* storyteller because she has successfully progressed from martyr-target-victim to stable, confident bisexual. The "I" in *It Gets Better* is adult-identified, if not conventionally so: a subject position that has earned the pedagogical capacity to imagine and address an audience of queer youth, an audience that serves to shore up the speakers themselves.

The speaker's adult-identified position, however, is ultimately always a precarious one; the repetitive rehearsal of the *It Gets Better* backwards turn serves as an attempt to mask this underlying anxiety. Again, similar to critics who are concerned about the potential effects of queer YA on its readers, the anxiety of *It Gets Better* storytellers stems in part from a desire for the project to remedy the ongoing crisis of queer youth suicide and repair the future of queerness that this crisis represents. Queer YA critics want to fashion the genre into something hopeful that represents a particular version of a queer future; *It Gets Better* contributors want the project to function in a similar manner. For this objective to be accomplished, however, stories must be made to fit the provided mold: queer YA stories must contain visibly queer and sexually resolved characters; *It Gets Better* stories must be recounted from a sexually resolved adult-identified position that can turn back and narrate an overcoming of the martyr-target-victimhood and *Sturm und Drang* of adolescence. Anxieties are most palpable—in criticism of *It Gets Better* and the stories themselves—when these stories are seen to not fit or are interpreted as pedagogical misfires.

The anxious cracks in the rickety foundation of the *It Gets Better* storyteller's position slip to the surface in Lynn Breedlove's story. He writes, "When I heard about this project, I thought, 'I never got bullied so I have nothing to offer,' but then I remembered they always called me 'weird' in grammar school, and I didn't have many pals" (228). *It Gets Better* requires a martyr-target-victim narrative in order to assume the position of the pedagogical "I." This is what enables Barack Obama—who was president when homophobia remained institutionalized on numerous levels—to tell an *It Gets Better* story, in which he claims that "I don't know what it's like to be picked on for being gay. But I do know what it's like to grow up feeling that sometimes you don't belong" (9). All individual differences may apply, so long as they narrate hardship, culminate in resilience and success, and participate in the address to *It Gets Better*'s imagined audience. Gilbert claims that the "emptiness" of the project's title, "its capacity to mean almost anything and to be said by almost anyone in any situation," is what permits "conservative politicians, queer icons, 'ordinary LGBTQ adults,' and members of queer youth groups to promise, in all earnestness, 'It Gets Better'" (52). Breedlove, however, goes on to deviate slightly and tell one of the few stories in the *It Gets Better* volume that celebrates queer creativity and its potential for imagining nonheteronormative social forms: "If I had had a family who said they would love me only if I pretended to be someone I wasn't, things might have turned out differently," he writes; "but if you have that kind of family, you can make your own family who will love you unconditionally. That's why queers call each other Family. We create one that will love us for who we are. We have drag moms and dads, dyke uncles, and matriarchal mamas"

(230). Breedlove's version of the family differs dramatically from the others in the collection in its view of social and sexual relations as fluid and malleable: queers can remain relationally creative instead of accepting *It Gets Better*'s telos and insisting on the sedimentation of their sexual selves.

It Gets Better's repetitiveness recalls Judith Butler's "Imitation and Gender Insubordination," in which she describes heterosexuality as "an incessant and *panicked* imitation of its own naturalized idealization" (314). Butler continues:

> That heterosexuality is always in the act of elaborating itself is evidence that it is perpetually at risk, that is, that it "knows" its own possibility of becoming undone: hence, its compulsion to repeat which is at once a foreclosure of that which threatens its coherence. That it can never eradicate that risk attests to its profound dependency upon the homosexuality that it seeks fully to eradicate and never can or that it seeks to make second, but which is always already there as a prior possibility. (314)

In this case, *It Gets Better*'s repetition functions to sell the project's grand narrative, disavow its exclusions, reinforce its imagined audience, and sustain the fantasies of stable sexual identity expounded by the project's adult storytellers. In terms of the impossible relationship between adult and youth the project evinces, minor narrative variations like Mahan and Breedlove's stories are relatively insignificant. All *It Gets Better* stories are about how adults (or adult-identified youth) imagine pedagogical and temporal relationships to the youth on the other end of *It Gets Better*. The project's dominant repetition of this primary narrative produces the exclusions and adult/youth relationship that are responsible for *It Gets Better*'s impossibility and political failure.

A tragic example of this failure involves Jamey Rodemeyer, who committed suicide weeks after having uploaded an *It Gets Better* video.[10] Rodemeyer's death is a brutal illustration of Puar's point (and the message inherent to the *Make It Better* project) that *It Gets Better*'s focus on futurity "lets the politics of the now off the hook" ("The Cost"). According to Puar, *It Gets Better* disregards "what suicide might actually be, which is an inability to reconcile the current moment with some projection of the future itself. It's an impassive temporality" ("The Cost"). The consequence, according to Robert Lipscomb, is that "the queer teen is relegated to a virtual, temporal realm—as a being/identity/life that might be accepted/seen as normal *in the future*" (356). In other words, *It Gets Better* attempts to force a temporal identification between adult and youth where one may be impossible. As I have illustrated, *It Gets Better* rehearses a linear, largely adult-authored, future-oriented narrative of growth and development in service of an imagined audience of young queers who have access to the forms of mobility that survival ostensibly requires. What Rodemeyer's case demonstrates is that it is possible to participate in the repetition of this narrative—to speak from the position of the adult-identified pedagogical "I"—without being able to live it. Rodemeyer, it would seem, could believe in the possibility of getting better but could not reconcile this subject position with the daily torment and bullying he was experiencing; the future-oriented mobility and stability the project demands might have been incompatible with how Rodemeyer was experiencing the present. Tragically, Rodemeyer's story illuminates the impossible relationship that structures *It Gets Better*. *It Gets Better*'s youth is children's literature's child, "the [child] which the category itself sets in place," in Rose's words, "the one which it needs to believe is there for its own purposes" (10). The project's imagined youth audience failed to properly bolster Rodemeyer's adult-identified "I," the subject position that, according to *It Gets Better*, is supposed to be secure and hopeful.

Returning to my earlier point, although Mahan and Breedlove's stories mark moments of dissonance in *It Get Better*'s dominant narrative that are nonetheless part of the impossible relationship that structures the project, these stories also have a different simultaneous effect. They cause *It Gets Better* to grow sideways, producing critique, indicating the project's overall exclusions, and enabling the project to circulate in ways that contribute to its success as productive cultural discourse. As I have argued, the critical attention *It Gets Better* receives has as much to do with the project's status as a cultural phenomenon as it does with the concerns of children's literature and YA criticism: that it is teaching (or attempting to teach) young people the "wrong thing." Precisely because *It Gets Better* is founded on an impossible relation and fails politically on a number of levels, the project circulates in a way that makes something possible. This possibility is the work of critical cultural discourse, accomplished by Breedlove and Mahan's stories—which provide us with narratives about creative social relations that challenge hegemonic notions of age, family, community, and sociality—and political critiques from the likes of Nyong'o and Puar. This commentary takes place both inside and outside *It Gets Better*, in a space that is best understood as *It Gets Better*'s sideways growth, which I explore in the following section. These moments are noteworthy interruptions of the forward-oriented progression of *It Gets Better*'s narrative. We return, again, to the anxious rhythm of the queer double-take explored throughout this book. These are moments of delay that see the future as queer question mark instead of a zone of stability, and they challenge and disrupt the project's teleological conceptions of growth and growing.

Children's Literature, Sideways Growth,
and the Possibility of *It Gets Better*

It Gets Better is striking in its ready and frequent adaptation and mutation into a variety of forms—from web-based project into book into documentary film into "Global Movement"—and from these core *It Gets Better* texts spring countless responses, ranging in tone from critical to satirical to celebratory, which themselves take multiple shapes. *It Gets Better* circulates feverishly though and across media and technology so that the project grows sideways, bringing adults and youth into a kind of "lateral contact" that Rose suggests is impossible in children's literature, and generating something of an odd temporal space. Through the project, Gilbert explains, "adults recount histories of suffering and redemption, rhetorically place themselves in a didactic relation to youth, and—in that rhetorical move—pasts, presents, and futures are collapsed" (54). Mapping *It Gets Better*'s sideways growth not only sheds new critical light on the project itself, but also provides us with a useful methodology for children's literature that approaches the ostensibly untouched middle space between child and adult.

Several children's literature scholars have taken issue with this "space in between" aspect of Rose's argument. Karen Sánchez-Eppler and Robin Bernstein assert that the child at the other end of children's literature is engaged in critical, material reading practices that transcend Rose's "reader, product, receiver" version of the child (Rose 2). Sánchez-Eppler argues that tracking how children destroy, scribble in, and cut up books provides new insight into the literary history of childhood (151). She claims that child readers repurpose and resignify texts through material destruction while remaining deeply entrenched in broader cultural narratives. Taking a similar tack, Bernstein draws on Frances Eliza Hodgson's recollection of how she used dolls to reimagine and stage moments from *Uncle Tom's Cabin*. Bernstein posits a triangulation of play, literature, and material culture as an entry point into Rose's middle space between the empowered adult author and the passive child reader: "it is precisely these connections that deliver children's literature beyond the paradigm of 'impossibility,'" she writes (167). "*Pace* Rose," Bernstein continues, "children not only receive literature, they receive the co-scripts of narratives and material culture and then collectively forge a third prompt: play itself" (167).

In addition to material evidence of children's interaction and play with texts, the sideways growth of a text or a genre includes what Peter Hunt calls "the peritext—that is, the written (and graphic) material that 'surrounds' the story" as well as "the relationship of the meaning made to things 'outside' the text:

the ideological implications of the children's book—indeed, the implications of reading at all" (4). Along these lines, Marah Gubar uses children's theater as an example of how material outside of a dramatic text itself (i.e. playbills and children's documented responses to productions) and a consideration of the actual theatergoing practices of children are integral to determining whether or not analysis of a text under the children's literature aegis will be productive. "Cutting children out of the loop closes down inquiry," she writes, "whereas acknowledging that their reading, viewing, and playing practices can function as one of the fibers that help determine whether a text counts as children's literature opens it up" (215). As described in chapter one, Nat Hurley also explores the possibility of a "murky middle" space between adults and the child of children's literature. In an essay that describes the potential productivity of ambiguity, impossibility, and readerly play, Hurley writes:

> One of the aspects of children's literature that I have always found fascinating is its insubordinations: its sites of dissident or non-conforming children, its failures, its surprising circulations, its appropriations—even its misuses—and especially, to invoke Jacqueline Rose, its impossibilities. The stretch for impossibility makes for some of the best and unruly works of children's literature. ("Perversions" 119)

These circulations, appropriations, and misuses, along with the narrative destruction, reconfiguration, and play examined in Sánchez-Eppler, Bernstein, and Gubar's essays, are aptly described as the sideways growth of particular texts and—in the case of children's literature—an entire genre.[11] These approaches to children's literature speak to sideways growth without naming it as such, given how they track the nonlinear circulation and productivity of texts, the material contact between text and child, and analyze the significance of this contact.

It Gets Better's sideways growth includes not only its official adaptations (website into book into documentary), but also how the project is reshaped and reimagined across media by people in addition to Savage, Miller, and other authors of *It Gets Better* stories, all the while accumulating and producing anxiety through its circulation. In a way, *It Gets Better*'s sideways growth is the most interesting, productive, and successful thing about it. Gabrielle Rivera's story, for example, not only brings the ostensible inside and outside of the project into lateral contact, but also critiques the adult/youth relationship at the core of *It Gets Better*. Rivera's clip first made the rounds on social media when it was posted to a blog under the title "It Doesn't Get Better. You Get Stronger" (Cage). Rivera's story drew attention because her message seemed to fly in the face of *It Gets Better* while challenging the project on its scant treatment of race and class issues. "As a gay woman of color," Rivera begins,

I just want to let the youth know that it kind of doesn't get better. All these straight, rich celebrities: they can tell you that it gets better because they've got money and people don't care what they do.... But I'm gonna be real, because I live this life and I'm not rich and I'm brown and I probably look like most of you. (45)

Although it directly challenges the project on the levels of authorship and ideology, Rivera's story still echoes the narrative of many of the other *It Gets Better* passages: "I'm a normal person that lives her life as a gay individual, has a relationship, and just tries to make it in the world," she maintains (45). The edited text of this video was subsequently published in Savage and Miller's book under the title "Getting Stronger and Staying Alive"—an attempt, it seems, on behalf of Savage and Miller to contain one of *It Gets Better*'s rogue circulations, to demonstrate that even critiques of the project drive it forward. In spite of this text's normative elements, it remains an uneasy fit with the rest of *It Gets Better*: Rivera declares that it does not get better in a book entitled *It Gets Better*, and her video continues to live online outside of the project under its original title, which points more directly to *It Gets Better*'s exclusions and failures. The inclusion of this text in Savage and Miller's book, while reinforcing some aspects of *It Gets Better*'s narrative of mobility, gestures to the incompatibility of *It Gets Better*'s adult-identified storytellers with its imagined audience while simultaneously demonstrating that the project's political failures fuel critical discourse.

There are many other (and significantly more perverse) critiques and parodies of *It Gets Better* circulating on the internet: the "It Gets Bigger" parody, the "It Gets Worse" project (Moylan), and the *It Gets Betterish* web comedy series all poke fun at Savage and Miller's campaign, while the website *Splitsider* offers a list of the "best" *It Gets Better* parodies (Hoban). Created mostly by adults, these parodies reinforce how *It Gets Better*'s actual circulation contradicts its own self-understanding: these are adult-identified subjects, not youth, who are largely responding and writing back to the project. What the sideways growth of *It Gets Better* exhibits, in fact, is an overall absence of youth-identified voices. Adult-identified subject positions dominate the project itself and the body of response, critique, and parody that *It Gets Better* accumulates. So while sideways growth as a spatial and temporal metaphor for examining a text and/or genre has the potential to bring adults and children into contact (and does, in essays from Sánchez-Eppler, Bernstein, and Gubar), in *It Gets Better*'s case, it is a challenge to find traces of youth-identified readers responding and writing back directly to *It Gets Better*. In this sense, again, the project provides an apt illustration of Rose's argument about why children's literature is impossible: it fails to circulate according to its own expectations, demonstrating instead the messy ways in which adult authorship, fantasies, desires, and anxieties are inextricably enmeshed with how children's literature produces meaning. Yet the stories that fail to conform to its grand narrative and the critiques that point to the project's political failures are the most productive parts of *It Gets Better*: those moments that indicate discord or slippage in *It Gets Better*'s otherwise feverish repetition of near-identical stories. This is where *It Gets Better* becomes possible. It fails politically but succeeds as cultural discourse, growing sideways into a body of work that addresses the adult/youth relationship represented in the project's stories.

Although there is little evidence of young people directly critiquing *It Gets Better* in widely circulated forums, the project has demonstrated traction in one particular space popular with youth: online fanfiction communities. In the chapter that follows, I consider how fanfic mash-ups of *It Gets Better* and *Glee* further demonstrate the sideways growth of the project, the "lateral contact" between *It Gets Better* and a community generally associated with young people, and material evidence of the tangibility of Rose's "middle space."

CHAPTER 7

Not Getting Better: Sex and Self-Harm in *It Gets Better* / *Glee* Fanfiction

The *It Gets Better* project makes a cameo appearance in a season five episode of *Glee* entitled "The End of Twerk." Rachel (Lea Michele) and Kurt (Chris Colfer)—both high school glee club graduates living in New York—decide to get tattoos as a means of celebrating life following the death of Finn (Cory Monteith, whose real-life death prompted the sudden plot twist), who was Rachel's ex-boyfriend and Kurt's step-brother. Kurt, whose arc over the show's six seasons hinges primarily on his sexuality—coming out as gay to friends and his initially anxious father; contending with homophobic bullying at the hands of closeted jock Dave Karosfky (Max Adler); experiencing his first relationship—decides to tattoo "It Gets Better" on his back as a tribute to the project. Buzzed on the limonata he downs to provide liquid courage, Kurt misspells the phrase for the artist and winds up with "It's Get Better" permanently inked on his back. In a panic, Kurt returns to the tattoo parlor the next morning and laments his failed attempt at rebellion: "My path has been different and exciting considering my background," he explains, "but considering who I think I am and how I see myself, it's like I've taken the streetcar named predictability." The tattooist replies, "Why don't you give me another shot at it? I'm starting to get a sense of who you are." The result: Kurt's tattoo is transformed to read "It's Got Bette Midler."

Glee's tongue-in-cheek shout out to *It Gets Better* feels appropriate for several reasons. For one, *Glee* reached peak popularity in 2010–2011,[1] the moment I flag in my introduction as crucial to the development of contemporary queer YA and its commentary. During this time, the *It Gets Better* campaign was launched, news and concerns about queer youth suicide and bullying were being widely disseminated, and queer YA began undergoing a publishing boom. Additionally, the show's *It Gets Better* reference speaks to the many synergies between the two texts. *Glee* contains a number of plot lines that read like *It Gets Better* narratives—especially Kurt's, whose arc involves coming out, overcoming bullying, finding love, moving from small-town Lima, Ohio to big-city Manhattan, being accepted to the performing arts college of his dreams, and eventually marrying his high school boyfriend (Blaine, played by Darren Criss) and having a child thanks to Rachel's surrogacy. Both *Glee* and *It Gets Better* have become landmark contemporary queer-themed popular culture texts, and in a sense, they enabled each other's circulation. *Glee*'s characters can be read vis-à-vis *It Gets Better* narratives, and several *Glee* cast members—including Jane Lynch and Chris Colfer, both openly gay, and Max Adler, who plays Karofsky, the closeted bully—have contributed videos to the project. It is unsurprising that *Glee* and *It Gets Better* have accumulated so many traces of one another.

On another level, Kurt's botched tattoo is a comical illustration of what I argued in my previous chapter: *It Gets Better* rarely circulates as it intends. Kurt's initial attempt at reiterating the project's message results in a version skewed—slightly, but skewed nonetheless—from Savage and Miller's original, and his effort to restore the message produces a phrase completely removed from the project, queer only through the semiotic chain that links Bette Midler to gay culture. In short, whatever efforts *It Gets Better* makes to signify as such, the project's sideways growth always produces an excess of meaning through stories and interpretations that lie outside the scope of the project's stated objectives. Within this sideways growth, however, lie compelling examples of how this excess of meaning is taken up and reworked by readers, including those young audiences whose desires, in Jacqueline Rose's view, are legible only as the products of adult fantasies and anxieties. The resonances between *Glee* and *It Gets Better* also enable the perverse "rogue circulations" (Hurley) and reappropriations of *It Gets Better* that take place in fanfiction, which provide an example of youth writing back to the project in forms not limited to outright criticism or videos narrated from the perspective of an adult-identified "I." While we could read *It Gets Better/Glee* mashup fanfiction as part of the project's success as cultural discourse, *It Gets Better* is here further repurposed so that it opens a space that both deviates from and exists concurrently with the project's grand narrative of progression. And, crucially, slash authors bring critical elements to *It Gets Better* that are missing from its official stories: sexual pleasure, and the possibility that it doesn't always get better.

This is not to say that the activities described in *It Gets Better*—going to Starbucks with one's partner, adopting children together—do not provide forms of pleasure. But these are relatively palatable pleasures compared to what Edelman describes as those "sterile, narcissistic enjoyments understood as . . . responsible for the undoing of social organization, collective reality, and, inevitably, life itself"—those forms of queer sexuality that dwell in the negative and eschew hetero/homonormative models for relationality and reproductivity (*No Future* 13). Here, we might be reminded of my discussion in chapter four of Andrew Smith's *Grasshopper Jungle* and its representation of the apocalyptic effects of queer sex, or the polymorphous perversity of *Big Mouth*'s child protagonists, as discussed in chapter five. Similarly, Stockton coins "'sideways growth' to refer to something . . . that locates energy, pleasure, vitality, and (e)motion in the back-and-forth connections and extensions that are not reproductive" (*Queer Child* 13). Sex is crucial to thinking about queerness: "nonstandard sex," as Warner writes in *The Trouble with Normal*, "has none of this normative richness, this built-in sense of connection to the meaningful life, the community of the human, the future of the world," and as a result "it brings queers together" (47). "How ironic," Warner continues, "that so often the first act of gay political groups is to repudiate sex" (48). Part of my intention in this chapter is to bring sex back into the conversation, since it has indeed been largely ignored by *It Gets Better*.

Fanfiction is loosely defined as "fiction that utilizes preexisting characters and settings from a literary or media text," and is most widely read and disseminated on the Internet through forums like fanfiction.net and archiveofourown.org. It is this "unofficial" method of circulation, in fact, that distinguishes fanfiction from what Catherine Tosenberger calls "other forms of 'recursive' fiction" (329). Although fanfiction is not written and consumed solely by young people and fan culture (or "fandom") is not their exclusive domain, "fandom as a space of engagement" is widely recognized to be "especially valuable for young fans," and its distribution online grants "younger writers access to a wider audience than ever before" (Tosenberger 329–330). Likewise, Karen Hellekson and Kristina Busse note that the "demographics" of fan culture "have shifted: ever-younger fans who previously would not have had access to the fannish culture except through their parents can now enter the fan space effortlessly," since computer and Internet access are the only tools required (versus the financial resources required to print and distribute fan zines prior to the emergence of the web) (13). This is a significant change from Henry Jenkins's early writings on fan culture; in his introduction to *Textual Poachers* (1992, reissued in 2013), Jenkins observes that fan culture's primary demographic "is largely female, largely white, largely middle class" (1). Although Jenkins concedes that fandom "welcomes into its ranks many who would not fit this description," the average "fan" he imagines is also implicitly adult, and *Textual Poachers* does not address young people's participation in fandom (1).

In "Homosexuality at the Online Hogwarts: Harry Potter Slash Fanfiction," Tosenberger provides insight into the increasing participation of young people in a particular genre of fanfiction: slash, which "generally functions in fandom as the binary opposite of 'het' (heterosexual) fic, which features romantic and sexual relationships between characters of different genders" (331). The term "slash," Tosenberger points out, "arose in *Star Trek* fandom in the 1970s, referring to the punctuation mark separating the characters' names (Kirk/Spock)"; although heterosexual fanfiction pairings use identical punctuation, "slash . . . retain[s] its original meaning of homoerotic romance" (330–331).[2] For Tosenberger, who resists attempts by fans and academics to narrow its definition, slash can consist of "canonical" relationships—those that exist in the original text (i.e. *Glee*'s Kurt/Blaine, or "Klaine")—and the noncanonical, those "slash stories and pairings [that] build upon a reading of subtext that fans claim is present in the canon" (331). In *Glee*'s case, popular noncanonical pairings include Kurt with various straight-identified characters: classmates Finn and Puck, and his teacher Will, for example. Tosenberger insists that we require further analyses of how slash provides "adolescent fans [with] the potential to encounter and experiment with alternative modes of sexual discourse, particularly queer discourse" (330).[3] "Fandom," she argues, "offers young people the opportunity not simply to passively absorb queer-positive (and adult-approved) messages, but to actively engage with a supportive artistic community as readers, writers, and critics" (334). In other words, fanfiction provides illuminating examples of lateral contact between adult authors and young audiences.

To lay the foundation for her analysis of Harry Potter fandom, Tosenberger conceives of "slash as a space," which she argues is "the most useful way of understanding it; what slash writers have done is to carve out a space for themselves where they are free to tell the narratives they wish, linked only by the common thread of queerness" (334–335). She cites at length a fan's theory of slash as space, which warrants repeating here:

> Slash is not so much queer in the act as it is queer in the space. . . . Slash is a sandbox where women come to be strange and unusual, or to do strange and unusual things, or to play with strange and unusual sand. The women may be queer or not, strange or not, unusual or not. The many different acts and behaviors of slash may be queer or not, strange or not, unusual or not. The queerness may be sexualized or it may not, and what is sexual for one woman may not be for another. The space is simply that: a space, where women can be strange and unusual and/or do strange and unusual things (Julad, quoted in Tosenberger 334).[4]

Tosenberger's conception of slash as a space for the practice of queerness is reiterated throughout her essay. She writes, for example, that "Potter slash readers and writers have access to a space where queer sexuality, whether teen or adult, can be depicted in its full, messy, exuberant glory, and the emphasis is on jouissance" (346), while maintaining that this messy space is nonetheless "a safe space for [young people] not only to improve their writing skills, but also to explore discourses of sexuality, especially queerness, outside of the various culturally official stances marketed to them, and with the support of a community of like-minded readers and writers" (347). Tosenberger's article advanced academic discourse on the queer work of slash and young fan communities, but her conception of slash as "space"—as well as the temporal implications of this argument—remain unexplored. How, for example, can we conceive of the space of slash as relative to the space of the original narrative? Moreover, what temporal relation does slash bear to the canon?

Building on claims I have made throughout this book, I want to posit a theory of slash as a space of delay and, counter (or perhaps parallel) to Tosenberger's assertion of slash as a safe space, I understand it as a risky one—where readers risk encounters with queerness that may, in fact, become avenues to new desires and relations. Recall Deborah Britzman's theory of "risking the self," as discussed in chapter two of this book: at stake in this risk is the foundation upon which our sense of self rests, and the narratives we use to interpret ourselves and our relations to others ("Queer Pedagogy" 94). In this sense, slash is also potentially a pedagogical space, where critical strategies for reading and writing are taught, learned, and rehearsed through narratives that are, in many cases, created by young people.[5] Further, I propose sideways growth as the most apt spatial/temporal trope for thinking through slash. As it circulates within queer YA's affective economy of anxiety, the space of slash, I suggest, functions to both delay a narrative and cause it to grow sideways.[6] Slash is the equivalent of hitting "pause" during a story, cutting away, and filling in the narrative blanks; of creating stories that exist parallel to the original; of causing the canon to grow sideways by imagining supplemental queer narratives and rendering them material.[7] Moreover, slash is a space where young people can enact, in addition to their sideways desires, forms of delay. Tosenberger suggests that "online fannish discourse affords fans a certain measure of concealment, which proves especially valuable for young fans who fear the consequences of expressing nonheteronormative desires" (334). In this sense, in addition to using slash to express queer desire, young people might use slash to delay real-life queer sexual activity or the pursuit thereof, as a space of exploration prior to—or in-between—the material renderings of queer desires. The temporality of slash may be thought in conversation with the queer double-take as seen, for example, in *I'll Get There. It Better Be Worth the Trip* (see chapter one). Just as Davy turns sideways to Fred and forward to the uncertain queer question mark of his relationship with Altschuler—moving, delaying, resisting movement, stalling and starting—slash might manifest itself as a sideways relation with an equally anxious relation to time and space. Slash pauses one narrative while simultaneously unfolding another in tandem. It might delay certain desires or actions on behalf of readers/writers while pushing them forward towards others, and it invites readers to risk encounters with forms of queerness that are often only latent in the texts from which they emerge.

In what follows, I track *Glee/It Gets Better* fanfiction as one of the YouTube project's many circulatory accumulations and think about how *Glee* and *It Gets Better* interact and cause each other's sideways growth. Specifically, I explore how *Glee* both buttresses *It Gets Better*'s success as cultural discourse while simultaneously enabling its perversion—a motion made manifest in Kurt's tattoo. I locate *It Gets Better/Glee* fanfic as a space that sees the project and its ostensible audience making lateral contact outside of the adult anxieties that gesture to *It Gets Better*'s many political failures. I hope as well to continue demonstrating the haziness of those anxious borders between genre, the usefulness of the critical tools of children's literature for approaching a variety of texts, and the potency of sideways growth as a trope for conceptualizing textual circulation.

Once More, with *Glee*!

Glee was once the most popular television show on fanfiction.net. In March 2014, when it was still on the air, it boasted over 103,000 stories; the next most popular series, *Supernatural*, had slightly under 93,000 (*Supernatural* has since overtaken *Glee*: in early 2020, the former had 126,000 stories versus *Glee*'s 108,000). Most fanfic that combines *Glee* and *It Gets Better* was written around 2011 when the YouTube project's circulation and *Glee*'s popularity were at their peak. The fanfic itself can be classified into a few broad and overlapping categories. First, there are stories that most directly mimic *It Gets Better*'s themes and ideas. These stories involve characters from *Glee*—including pairings both canonical and noncanonical—making an *It Gets Better* video or somehow interacting with the project. These stories tend to replicate the *It Gets Better* metanarrative, describing a transition from troubled adolescence to successful and stable adulthood. The "It Gets Better" story by author "for always forever," for example, contains two chapters, each of which describes a different *Glee* couple making a video. The first chapter features Blaine and Kurt; the former has become a successful recording artist, the latter a "rising Broadway star and also the owner of his very own fashion line" (for always forever). The story begins with the couple bickering flirtatiously about how to operate the camera before Kurt begins narrating: "Okay, so, long story short? Life sucked. I was living in a small town in *Ohio* of all places. . . . I was tormented every day. Dumpster tosses, slushy facials; you name it and it probably happened to me. I joined my high school glee club and things got better" (for always forever, chapter 1). Blaine takes a turn to describe his rise to fame, then the brief story concludes: "Blaine beams and leans in to kiss [Kurt]. When they pull back, Kurt takes Blaine's hand and then flashes his engagement ring to the camera. 'It gets better,' he says quietly" (for always forever, chapter 1). In the second chapter, canonically queer *Glee* couple Santana and Brittany make a video that ends in a similar fashion: "'It gets better,' Brittany says to the camera, and she smiles widely, 'Maybe you'll meet your own Santana and you'll be happy forever, like me. I really hope you do" (for always forever). Despite the fact that *Glee* has a massive femslash contingent, female pairings like Brittany/Santana in *Glee*/*It Gets Better* slash are rare; most stories I encountered pair Kurt with another male character.[8] Kurt's predominance is likely due to the resonances between his character arc and the shape of the *It Gets Better* metanarrative.

Author Gemmi999's story describes Finn's discovery of the *It Gets Better* project and his desire to share it with Kurt's father Burt, knowing that Kurt is having trouble with bullying at school: "Burt can make sure Kurt sees it and doesn't try to hurt himself because Finn's wanted a brother his entire life and he doesn't want to get one just to lose him again." The story concludes with Finn showing the site to Kurt, and Kurt inviting his step-brother to watch some videos with him. "[Kurt] isn't alone anymore, Finn's his brother and that means Finn's going to be there for him," Gemmi999 writes. In "It Gets Better: Jock, Glee Dork, Closet Bisexual," Anime Girl23 also describes a video made by *Glee* characters, but this author noncanonically pairs Kurt with Noah "Puck" Puckerman (Mark Salling), a football player who bullies Kurt for much of *Glee*'s first season. Moreover, the video is narrated from Puck's perspective as the coming-out story of a self-described "closet bisexual": "Things were hard and I ended up in juvie my junior year. I was struggling with not having my daughter or my best friend and I was struggling with feelings I didn't want. I was the ladies' man. I wasn't supposed to be having feelings for guys too, but I was" (Anime Girl23). The narrative then follows the pattern of most "real" *It Gets Better* stories: Puck moves from small-town Ohio to big-city New York, reconnects with Kurt, and the pair falls in love. In a passage that could be ripped from the *It Gets Better* book, Puck narrates:

> No matter what your sexuality or your situation is, know that it gets better. If you're already out or if you're in the closet like I was, know that it gets better. You'll get out of high school and you'll find your place. You'll fall in love and you'll find people that don't care about your orientation. They'll love you for you.

If you give up now, you'll never get to reach that point and that person you'll fall in love with one day won't ever get to meet you. So hold on, because there's so much more out there than high school and family drama. There's a community of people out here that understand and we love you. It gets better. (Anime Girl23)

In a final gesture to the ideal *It Gets Better* telos, the story concludes as follows: "The screen went black and a replay button popped up as Kurt wiped a tear from his eye and hugged Noah's arm. Noah ducked his head, eyes focused on the sleeping infant in his arms as his husband kissed his cheek" (Anime Girl23).

Even if the message of Anime Girl23's story is ultimately conservative in its reiteration of *It Gets Better*'s homonormative models of relationality and family, it is worthwhile noting how the project is taken up and redeployed as a narrative frame for the subversion of canonical *Glee* relationships. Here, *It Gets Better* in part enables Anime Girl23's slash reimagination of Puck as a closeted bisexual who later marries "the one out kid at school" he used to bully. *It Gets Better*'s narrative, in other words, is exported as a means of reading and rewriting Puck's character; Anime Girl23 reinterprets his bullying as an act of internalized homophobia that culminates in the outward manifestation of same-sex desire. *It Gets Better* functions not entirely as an address to an imagined audience of young queer martyr-target-victims, but instead as a means of enabling the sideways growth of *Glee*'s characters and narrative arc. The same could be said about those stories that do not necessarily subvert *Glee*'s canon, those that imagine the future of pairings like Kurt/Blaine and Santana/Brittany. Such fanfiction may be as conservative as *It Gets Better* itself in its representation of relationships, but these stories nonetheless take up the project as a tool for critical reading. In particular, they demonstrate the malleability of narrative and the refusal to accept canon as truth, and to once again channel Britzman, they deploy *It Gets Better* as a means of multiplying possibilities for identification across genre and text. *Glee/It Gets Better* slash is a moment of lateral contact between the adult-driven project and the youth-populated online spaces of fanfiction, but this contact sees the project repurposed and recirculated as a narrative frame for the subversion and sideways growth of *Glee* canon.

Another type of *Glee/It Gets Better* story does not necessarily reference the project—other than in title—but dwells instead in the martyr-target-victim period of adolescence before concluding with a hopeful turn. Most of these stories could be (and are, via fanfiction database labels and tags) classified as "hurt/comfort," a subgenre of slash stories that "open with the injury or near-death experience of one of the partners (or the death of another significant character); such moments of 'hurt-comfort' force a recognition of the fragility of their relationships, what would be lost should their friend be killed" (Jenkins

209). This particular subgenre supports Jenkins's claim that "the eroticism of slash is an erotics of emotional release and mutual acceptance; an acceptance of self, an acceptance of one's partner" (215). Writerbitch92's "It Gets Better" story, for example, describes a violent gay bashing of Kurt in his high school's washroom. He is ultimately rescued by Blaine: "Gently, Blaine placed his arms around his boyfriend, making sure not to squeeze too tight to hurt him, and placed a kiss just behind his ear, promising, 'It will get better'" (Writerbitch92). KlaineForeverLover07's story sees Kurt supporting Marley through her struggle with an eating disorder and bullying at the hands of cheerleader Kitty. "It Gets Better" by There_Was_A_Kat revisits the Kurt/Puck pairing, focusing on friendship in lieu of romance. In this story, Puck finds Kurt sitting alone in the rain in the football field bleachers, depressed due to the bullying he's enduring at school. Like the authors discussed above, There_Was_A_Kat repurposes *It Gets Better* to narrate an intimate friendship between Kurt and Puck that goes much deeper than in canon:

> Kurt's eyes were bloodshot, red lines tracing intricate designs, making his irises stand out in a brilliant contrasting green. But still, they found Puck's own multi-toned brown eyes, the two boys linking in a common bond. "I promise you, Kurt Hummel, I swear on my life. It *does* get better." Barely more than a whisper, but firm enough to hear the sincerity behind the words, Kurt finally believed.

Notably, many stories push the martyr-target-victim trope even further and tell noncanonical stories about Kurt attempting suicide. These stories all end hopefully and usually entail Kurt being "rescued" by another character, typically Blaine or Puck, who arrive on the scene just in time to summon an ambulance and/or convince Kurt that he should choose to live because it gets better. "It Gets Better" by Kyra5972, for example, sees Puck fulfilling a community service sentence by volunteering at the Trevor Project, a youth suicide prevention organization. Kurt phones in for support after overdosing on sleeping pills, and Puck dispatches an ambulance in time to save Kurt's life. The story concludes with Puck visiting Kurt in the hospital, and suggests a growing intimacy between the pair: "Puck knew that, yeah, it *does* get better. And he was going to make sure it got better for Kurt" (Kyra5972). Charlieanne's multi-chapter "It Gets Better" is a longer story that sees a very troubled Kurt attempt suicide on several occasions, even after his first attempt is foiled by Blaine. Kurt is subsequently admitted to a crisis center where Blaine confesses his love for Kurt and the bullied teen begins his recovery. The story concludes with a brief glimpse of their *It Gets Better*-esque future: "Kurt and Blaine were studying the decorating to their new house. It was two years since the night they both admitted they were both in love with each other, and they were finally going to college. It had been a hard time, but Kurt was finally better. Just after Kurt finished school, Blaine had proposed" (charlieanne, chapter 1). "It Gets Better" by AWritersLife is another multi-chapter story, where each individual chapter is written from Kurt and Blaine's alternating perspectives. Kurt's death is again prevented by Blaine, who subsequently encourages his fellow glee club members to make an *It Gets Better* video to support Kurt:

> I . . . I don't know how many of you have heard of the Trevor Project, but they have something called the 'It Gets Better' program. Part of it is that celebrities— actors, singers, athletes—they make these videos reaching out to LGBT youth, telling them that no matter how bad it seems, no matter how bad they get bullied, it will get better. I think . . . that we should put together a compilation of all of us sending our own little messages to Kurt. (AWritersLife, chapter 5)

After Kurt views the video and is comforted by Blaine ("I love you, Kurt. I love you and I'll do anything for you. It will get better, Kurt"), the story ends on an optimistic note: "Kurt nodded, feeling for the first time since he'd first started thinking about suicide, things were finally getting better" (AWritersLife, chapter 6). Interestingly, AWritersLife mistakenly attributes *It Gets Better* to the Trevor Project, evidence perhaps of how the project has become so widespread in cultural discourse that its actual origin is unclear and/or irrelevant. In other words, it is possible to know about *It Gets Better* without knowing where exactly it came from.

It is productive to think through these hurt/comfort stories in light of Peter M. Coviello's "The Pistol in the Suitcase: Motive, Temporality, Queer Youth Suicide," itself a response to *It Gets Better* and the various critiques the project has spawned (many of which—Puar and Nyong'o's, for example—I take up in my previous chapter). Coviello's eloquent and incisive essay asks us to make a radical shift and think about teen suicide not as "a culmination of motive, the action in which the slow and accretive gathering of impulsive sensations finds at last its most wholly decisive expression" but instead as "a search for motive, of an effort to concretize impulses that otherwise remain obdurately illegible and incoherent to the self in which they unfold" (67). Central to Coviello's argument is the multiply self-named adolescent Frankie/F. Jasmine/Frances of Carson McCullers's 1946 novella *The Member of the Wedding*, who, as Coviello writes, "cannot find *a* self in which to feel at home, a self she imagines she could inhabit without loss or distorting into the expanses of the future" (72). For Coviello, Frankie embodies an adolescence that entails "cyclonic self-shedding, undertaken in anxious proximity to imagined futures that seem to promise only an immobilizing identity—call it 'adulthood'—where there once had been the scary but enabling dislocations of motion" (74).

Here, Coviello reinforces two ideas that I have raised throughout this book. First, despite the emphasis placed by queer YA critics and *It Gets Better* on queer visibility and the importance of hopeful narratives of progression that culminate in stable adulthood, there remain nonetheless many fictions for and about young people that display attachments to delay and strong resistances to the telos of adulthood. Next, Coviello demonstrates that Frankie's "scary but enabling" moments of "cyclonic self-shedding" occur in "*anxious*" relation to the queer question mark of adulthood: these moments follow, in my words, the anxious stop-and-start rhythm of the queer double-take that I describe in my introduction, and they recall my engagement in chapter two with Adam Phillips's story of the swimming boy. Coviello argues that Frankie's sense of temporality is one unique to adolescence, taking Puar and Berlant to task for reading teen suicide vis-à-vis an adult temporality that disregards "the specifically temporal idiosyncrasies of childhood and adolescence," which may involve "delicacies of growth and delay, self-accretion and self-dispersal" (67). In Coviello's words, "to associate queer youth suicide too seamlessly with the wearing out of slow death . . . may be to transpose into adolescence the temporalities of an adult depletion, in a way that misplaces something of the specificity of adolescent dialectics of self-possession and self-dispersal" (74). He continues, extending this version of adolescent temporality to his reframing of teen suicide:

> Suicide, in this paradoxical framing, is an act of self-annihilation not easily dis-entangled from something like self-proliferation. Where the dispersal of ways of being in the world across a lateral array of possible selves works (as we can see it work for Frankie) as a strategy of self-protection or self-care—something like Stockton's sideways growth—suicide will, I think, come weighted with just this double valence: as the termination not just of a self but of all possible selves, yes, but also a thing undertaken in relation to the trying-out of provisional selves that so marks the temporal space of adolescence.[9] (75)

Following Coviello's nuanced approach to teen suicide and adolescent temporality, then, I conceive of *Glee/It Gets Better* slash as a space of delay and sideways growth for an anxious trying-out of suicidal impulses that *It Gets Better* aims to palliate, an experimentation with "provisional selves" via *Glee's* characters. I want to be cautious, here: I am not claiming that writing slash is a remedy to adolescent suicide, nor do I want to romanticize the effects of representing suicide.[10] Instead, I want to consider how slash marks a space for what Coviello outlines: the proliferation and trying-on of selves through narrative. As Kristeva indicates, writing allows adolescents "to reconstruct their psychic space" while also "shelter[ing] them from reality" (137). In this sense, slash is a space of risky reading that enables the proliferation of identificatory possibilities, to once again channel Britzman. Crucially, this space is not an adult-authored narrative, web project, or body of criticism. Slash is a space often created and populated by young people. In Rose's terms, it is a "middle space," but one that sees lateral contact between adult-authored narrative and young audiences. In this context, *It Gets Better* again fails to circulate as it imagines itself. The project, as I demonstrate in the previous chapter, fails politically in its anxious repetition of the same story. Instead, it provides a narrative structure for the proliferation of stories about suicide—and selves who desire self-destruction—through fanfiction and characters from *Glee*. Moreover, the slash stories about suicide do not follow *It Gets Better* in the project's positioning of happy, hopeful adulthood as the ultimate telos of adolescence. Instead, these stories choose to dwell in troubled adolescence, in bullying, suicide notes, and depression, which are emphasized over the brief, albeit consistently hopeful, endings. Often, they are stories about not getting better.

I want to offer an in-depth look at one final story that brings together many of the points I raise in this chapter: Susala's "It Gets Better." At forty-three thousand words—fifteen chapters—Susala's story is one of the longest works of *Glee/It Gets Better* slash and also one of the most popular and well-reviewed: as of May 2020, it boasts 107 reviews and 116 "favorites" from fanfiction.net community members. Susala's fanfic is set in the summertime, between seasons of *Glee*. While remaining true to canon it nonetheless grows the series sideways, imagining what some of the characters would have been up to behind the scenes. On one level, this is self-loathing, closeted bully Dave Karofsky's *It Gets Better* story as well as a post-bullying *It Gets Better* tale for Kurt and Blaine. All of the project's standard narrative elements are in place: Kurt has come out and is in a happy relationship with Blaine; together, they attend their first Pride and are surprised by the rest of the New Directions glee club cheering them on and singing Lady Gaga's "Born This Way" as the couple marches in the parade; Kurt takes the first steps towards organizing a PFLAG group for his school; Kurt and his father Burt strengthen their father-son relationship as Kurt shows signs of falling deeply in love with Blaine; Dave, on the other hand, struggles with his feelings for and attraction to Kurt, and finally concedes that he must come out to his father. He does so, and is supported by Kurt and Burt: "I know things are hard for you right now, Dave. You are kind of depressed," Kurt tells him; "Take it from me, Dave, I know what that is like. But try to hang in there. . . . It gets better, Dave" (Susala, chapter 6). Not only is this a reiteration of *It Get Better*'s grand narrative on a number of levels, but this fanfic also reproduces a number of coming-out story conventions. It features visibly gay characters comfortable with their sexuality while also attending to the "realistic" elements of Dave's internal struggles, which are resolved in a hopeful manner by story's end as Kurt and Dave's father meet and agree to work towards combatting homophobia in their community. "This is a small town, Paul," Burt tells Dave's father; "If we stick together maybe we can make it a better place for our kids. Maybe the kinds of things Dave and Kurt are going through won't have to continue. We can hope" (Susala, chapter 15).

What distinguishes Susala's "It Gets Better" from both Savage and Miller's project and conventional queer YA more generally, however, is precisely what slash enables: the inclusion of a number of graphic sex scenes between Kurt and Blaine. In tandem with a primary narrative arc that describes Kurt and Blaine's first pride, Dave's coming-out, and Kurt's quest to start a PFLAG group at McKinley High, Susala offers a second narrative describing Kurt and Blaine's summertime sexual play and experimentation. The story's sex scenes are moments of pleasurable delay—for characters and readers alike—in the forward movement of the overall narrative. And like Isabelle Holland's Chuck and McLeod (as discussed in chapter two), Kurt and Blaine find a great deal of sexual pleasure in delay itself. In the latter case, however, this is a pleasure that emerges from the delay of certain kinds of sexual activity until future chapters and, ultimately, beyond the scope of the story itself (which, of course, is also a strategy for tantalizing the reader). Kurt and Blaine's pleasurable, sexual delays bookend the story. In the first chapter, oral sex is deferred:

> "Kurt, honey, I want you in my mouth. I want to *taste* you." [Blaine] squeezed Kurt's thighs for emphasis. This was pretty close to begging.
>
> *Oh, well, since you're already down there . . . No,* wait.
>
> "Oh my god, Blaine!" Kurt Hummel finally engaged his brain and found his tongue. "Blaine, no. NO. . . . Of course I want you to. I just can't in the shower . . . not the first time anyway" (Susala, chapter 1).

By chapter thirteen, however, Kurt and Blaine are well beyond the point of deferring such activity, so they turn instead to the erotics of delaying penetrative sex:

> "Blaine, I want you to be honest with me." Kurt rolled his hips [while straddling Blaine].
>
> "What—?"
>
> "Do you ever fantasize about us having sex?" Kurt's body was still; he was waiting for the answer.
>
> "*What*? Of course."

"I mean *real* sex, Blaine." And Kurt rolled his hips.

"GOD, Kurt! Yes!"

Kurt slightly moved off of Blaine and put his hand on Blaine's erection. "In your mind, how does it work?" Kurt could feel the heat coming through Blaine's cotton shorts.

"Tell me one of your fantasies, Blaine."

. . . "This is torture." Blaine sounded almost pissed.

Kurt leaned over Blaine and whispered, "I could make you come while you are telling me about it. Come on, honey. You know you want to talk about it before we do it. You are the *talker*." Then Kurt unbuttoned and unzipped Blaine's fly. (Susala, chapter 13)

Afterwards, Kurt and Blaine further discuss the sexual activity that will be ultimately deferred to a point outside the scope of Susala's story:

"Blaine? Do you think a lot about having sex? I mean proper sex—intercourse."

"Sure. I'm curious. But I don't think I'm ready right now. I don't think *we* are ready."

Kurt nodded and smiled. He put his arm through Blaine's and leaned his head on Blaine's suntanned shoulder. "It's not like we've run out of other things to do." (Susala, chapter 13)

Like the protagonists of Henry James's *The Pupil* according to Stockton's analysis, Kurt and Blaine find pleasure in delay: specifically, the pleasures associated with talking in lieu of action. For Kurt and Blaine, this involves talking about future action as a companion to present action. Similarly, the raunchier chapters of Susala's story constitute moments of delay that interrupt the forward progression of the narrative.[11] The story's chapters are structured so that sex scenes regularly delay the overarching narrative: chapters one, five, eight, and thirteen all consist, in part or in whole, of lengthy descriptions of Kurt and Blaine's sexual romps. Susala's narrative, in other words, stalls and starts. It drives forward Kurt, Blaine, and Dave's stories, pausing for sex while talking about and imagining future sex, progressing the narrative, delaying it, rinsing (literally), and repeating. This anxious rhythm, by this point in the book, is a familiar one.

If we put Susala's "It Gets Better" into conversation with Savage and Miller's *It Gets Better*—and, certainly, the story's title and content invite us to do so—then we can read Susala's story as enacting a critique of the project on several levels, contributing to *It Gets Better*'s sideways growth and highlighting its dissonances and resonances. First, the story serves as an ironic reminder to widely syndicated sex columnist Savage that the pleasures of queerness are not limited to those associated with marriage, family, and the accumulation of material assets. These pleasures also include sex, which remains palpably absent from *It Gets Better*. Next, while the project positions adulthood as an ultimate source of stability and an escape from the pain of adolescence, Susala inserts delay and its erotics into the forward progression of the *It Gets Better* narrative structure she takes up and partially imitates. Susala's story, in other words, dwells in the sexual pleasures and discoveries of adolescence instead of emphasizing, like *It Gets Better*, the telos of growing up into adulthood. Susala, that is, demonstrates the thrills that come from lingering in adolescent sexuality (and in reading, writing, and rewriting it) and its forms of delay. This, as I have discussed, is reflected in the form of Susala's slash, which asks its readers to delay pleasure if they want to follow the narrative in a linear manner, while pleasure-seekers are, of course, free to skim through and skip chapters in search of sex. Helpfully, Susala's chapters include "an unrepentant SMUT ALERT" whenever appropriate (ch. 13).

Alongside the other stories discussed in this section, Susala's "It Gets Better" points to the pleasures of slash more broadly: those associated with dwelling in the interval of a canonical narrative; "pausing" a story to linger in its murky middle while growing it sideways; and the anxious, risky experimentation with and multiplication of temporary selves. This returns us to what I earlier suggested is the most productive effect of *It Gets Better*: its sideways growth, the way it does not inherently move queer youth forward through a narrative of progression as it intends to, but instead lingers—stuck, somewhat—in a space of critique, political failure, and the anxious rehearsal of its own singular story. *It Gets Better* and its sideways growth through *Glee* thus invite us to further reconsider some broader assumptions about children's literature and YA.

Getting Better at Doing Children's Literature?

Philip Nel and Lissa Paul point out that children's literature is one of the few genres named after its imagined audience, the child it attempts to shape based on the desires and anxieties of its adult authors (1). As I have illustrated, the impossibility of this adult-child relationship produces starkly different effects and responses than those ostensibly intended. Tison Pugh makes a similar point, arguing that children's literature attempts to teach children about normative sexuality while simultaneously keeping them innocent of sexuality: "A recalcitrant ideological conflict . . . emerges within the genre," he writes, "in which innocence and heterosexuality clash and conjointly subvert its foundations"

(*Innocence* 1). For Savage and Miller, *It Gets Better* necessitates repetition and reiteration to disguise its impossibility and failure. For critics—like Gabby Rivera, for example—*It Gets Better*'s failure invites intervention that results in the project's sideways growth and success as cultural discourse. For slash writers, *It Gets Better* and *Glee* intersect to provide a narrative frame for risky reading and writing, the subversion of canonical stories, and experimentation with sexuality and relationality. Texts like *It Gets Better* that attempt to secure a stable adult-identified subject position by iterating normative forms of childhood often, by virtue of the impossibility of their project, have the most potential for sideways growth. It is precisely through the project's repeated attempts to normalize a specific adult/youth relationship and its failure to do so that *It Gets Better* invites response and critique.[12]

It Gets Better speaks to an ongoing investment in the perceived power of storytelling, especially as it relates to the growth and development of children and adolescents. There are always stories that remain untold, however, stories that in this case could set up much more radically creative ways of being in the world that don't privilege individual movements through a specific, linear, forward-oriented narrative. As Hurley points out, however, "the productive failures of normalization" generate creative new approaches to children's literature, allowing us to think "more about the narratives of sociability and the acts of world-making at play in texts for young people" ("Perversions" 128). *It Gets Better*'s failures are what render it a productive site for thinking about and critiquing the relationship between its adult-identified authors, imagined young audience, and sideways growth. As contemporary critics of children's literature illustrate—and as *It Gets Better* itself demonstrates—children's literature is much more than printed words on a page. It also includes the material reading practices of its audience, spontaneous play, the physical destruction of books, the creative resignification of a text at the hands of its readers, and its own compelling impossibilities and failures. Ernest L. Bond and Nancy L. Michelson aptly describe how fanfiction is reshaping the contours of children's literature: "The abundance of child-authored literature on the World Wide Web takes the concept of expanded literacies a step farther than the environments of most literary theorists," they explain, since prior to the emergence of the web "it could be argued that there was no real 'children's literature'—published narratives written by young people for young people. However, Internet browsing and publishing software have made this genre a reality" (316). Through its failures and attendant anxieties, *It Gets Better* invites us to take new approaches to children's literature that call for different conceptions of temporality, circulation, and the relationship between author, text, and audience.

Briefly, I want to return to Lesnik-Oberstein's claim that "children's literature criticism as it stands, and as it defines itself, cannot succeed in achieving its own aim: finding the good book for the child, through knowing the child and the book" (19), a methodology that Hunt dubs "childist criticism" (191). When it comes to *It Gets Better* and critics of queer YA, this goal of finding the "good book"—or the right story—for the young (queer) person clearly persists. Instead of childist criticism, Lesnik-Oberstein proposes "writing and thinking about children's literature that does not rest on—or re-introduce at some point, overtly or indirectly—the real child, and a wider real of which it is a part" (19). Yet reading *It Gets Better* as children's literature reminds us that there *is* a real child—and real queer youth—out there, and some are taking their own lives, which is a very real issue that demands some kind of response. The urgency of this situation contributes to the anxious discourse that circulates so feverishly around *It Gets Better*. Coviello reflects on the problems and dilemmas that attend what he calls "the confusion of tongues between the potentially non-invidious generosities of adult care and the scenes of queer adolescent turmoil on which they might appear" (66):

> How do we begin to address ourselves to queer youth, whose futures we might want there to be room for, without defaulting to the cheap promises of bourgeois ascendancy or, for that matter, to the presumption that we know what ails these kids, after all, better than they do, or could? How do we sustain an exchange with queer kids whose refusal of our terms however bright with care—in fact, whose outpacing distance from those terms—may feel to them most like freedom, like authentic possibility, like breathable air? (79–80)

To add to Coviello's questions, can we think about children's literature, queer YA, the anxieties and impossibilities of genre, *and* consider the real child/young person on the other end of the text? Can we imagine queer YA as part of an address to queer youth without consistently privileging visibility and stable, resolved sexuality? Can we further our investigation of those middle spaces of lateral contact between adult and youth? As Coviello insists, "There may finally be no way of banishing entirely these urgencies and insistences from the scene of the encounter between the older and the younger. But we might try at least to reorganize and redeploy them, in ways that are, perhaps, generative" (79). In terms of queer YA, this entails a richer sense of those terms and ideas that often accumulate at the site of the encounter Coviello describes. What does it mean to read anxiously and read for anxiety, to risk the self, to approach growing up with ambivalence, to desire stasis and delay over forward motion?

These are the questions I have been posing throughout this book and, I argue, questions we should continue posing to the discipline of children's literature.

As a means of conclusion, I want to reassert my belief in the critical importance of children's literature and culture, and reiterate why I think the study of children's literature is so crucial to thinking broadly about cultural manifestations of the anxieties surrounding the relation between adults and young people. First, as I have demonstrated throughout this book, children's literature criticism operates as an index of adult anxieties about childhood and a site for the dissemination and circulation of these anxieties. Children's literature itself is also indexical in this sense, as Rose intimates, but the queernesses, queer readings, and "rogue circulations" of children's literature—the genre's sideways growth—will always be in excess of the adult desires and anxieties that children's literature might seem to express. As Hurley argues, these are among the most fascinating, provocative, and productive aspects of the genre ("Perversions"). What children's literature and its criticism succeeds in doing is providing us with the tools for thinking through these anxieties and, as Coviello illustrates, the stakes of the moment of address between adults and young people—a moment at the very center of *It Gets Better*. Children's literature and its methodologies cannot—and should not—be ignored in the broader study of culture because, as Edelman demonstrates in *No Future*, the figure of the child is at the very heart of politics. Children's literature invites us to consider how we attempt to address that child through literature and criticism, and how our modes of addressing that child are related to our own desires, anxieties, and relations. In an era when real queer youth continue to take their own lives, these questions continue to be of undeniable importance.

Immaturity: Reflections on the "Great (Queer) YA Debate"

"I didn't much mind [J. K.] Rowling when she was Pottering about. I've never read a word (or seen a minute) so I can't comment on whether the books were good, bad or indifferent. I did think it a shame that adults were reading them (rather than just reading them to their children, which is another thing altogether), mainly because there's [sic] so many other books out there that are surely more stimulating for grown-up minds."
—LYNN SHEPHERD, "If JK Rowling Cares About Writing, She Should Stop Doing It." *Huffington Post Culture*, 21 February 2014.

"Although my book is intended mainly for the entertainment of boys and girls, I hope it will not be shunned by men and women on that account, for part of my plan has been to try to pleasantly remind adults of what they once were themselves, and of how they felt and thought and talked, and what queer enterprises they sometimes engaged in."
—MARK TWAIN (from the preface to *The Adventures of Tom Sawyer* (1876), quoted in Clark 80).

In her February 21, 2014 post on the *Huffington Post UK* Culture Blog, Lynn Shepherd advises *Harry Potter* author J. K. Rowling to put away the pen and paper and clear some shelf space for other aspiring authors. Purportedly speaking on behalf of all struggling writers, Shepherd pleads, "We can't wave a wand and turn our books into overnight bestsellers merely by saying the magic word. By all means keep writing for kids, or for your personal pleasure—I would never deny anyone that—but when it comes to the adult market you've had your turn." A poorly argued and carelessly written rant infused with palpable bitterness, Shepherd's piece is transparent clickbait, ready fodder for impassioned bloggers and the vitriol innate to online comment threads. Nonetheless, perhaps because Shepherd brazenly attacked one of the world's most beloved and bestselling contemporary children's authors, the essay went viral, drawing responses from *Interview with the Vampire* author Anne Rice (who calls it a "vicious, cynical, resentful, and thoroughly ugly article"), many literary blogs, and BBC News (see Rice and Zurcher).

My interest in Shepherd stems not from her assault on Rowling, but rather the attitude towards children's literature she evinces and the widespread attention she received. Shepherd, who openly admits to never having read the *Harry Potter* series, nonetheless relegates the books to a realm of fiction reserved for the immature (i.e. children), even insisting that it's a "shame" for adults to waste time with these books instead of consuming other, more "stimulating" titles. J. K. Rowling is free to "keep writing for kids" in Shepherd's view, presumably because children are not the target audience for "stimulating" books, and more obviously because children's literature doesn't fill the shelf space that Shepherd, herself an author of genre fiction, so desperately pursues. Unsurprisingly, Shepherd's piece was eviscerated by critics for these claims. Writer Steven Salvatore Shaw, for example, points out how "it's obvious that Shepherd hasn't bothered to understand the genre that she's trying—and failing miserably—to critique" (quoted in Zurcher). Indeed, Shepherd seems to oppose, blindly and wholeheartedly, the sentiment behind Mark Twain's comments in his preface to *Tom Sawyer*: that adults, in spite of their ostensibly mature and sophisticated tastes in stimulating literature, can be challenged and provoked by the queernesses of children's literature.

Regardless of Shepherd's folly, the article's publication and the widespread attention it received are symptomatic of persistent cultural anxieties surrounding genre, some of which take the shape of elitism and condescension directed towards children's literature.[1] These anxieties and elisions, as Beverly Lyon Clark points out in *Kiddie Lit* (2004), are a relatively recent phenomenon: "nineteenth-century observers did not make the sharp differentiations between literature for children and literature for adults that we do now," she explains; "Writing for an audience of boys and girls—or, better yet, writing for boys of all ages—did not necessarily diminish a writer's stature. And the audience for all fiction was still conceived of as encompassing both young and old" (81). The twentieth and twenty-first centuries, however, have seen a repudiation of the nineteenth-century belief that "children's reading should overlap with adults' reading" (Clark 57), and the condescending dismissal of children's literature within academic circles (Clark 50).[2] This desire to keep children's literature fenced off, Clark maintains, is partially the product of what she calls a "cultural anxiety of immaturity" that disavows those provocative childhood queernesses that Twain places at the heart of *Tom Sawyer*'s broad appeal (49). My goal in these final pages is to return to my argument from the introduction, wherein I position queer YA as an anxious genre that perpetually rehearses a nervous uncertainty about its own constitution. Here, I take a step back to consider queer YA's relation to children's literature more broadly, entering the discussion via another node in queer YA's affective economy: its "anxiety of immaturity."

In June 2014, I had the pleasure of presenting some of my research to a friendly and receptive audience at the Children Literature Association's annual conference in Columbia, South Carolina. After outlining what I understand to be contemporary critics' anxiety about visibility in queer YA, I presented portions of my first chapter—in particular, my reading of Donovan's *I'll Get There. It Better Be Worth the Trip*—to sketch my concept of an affective economy of anxiety and gesture to those temporalities, ambiguities, and ambivalences that, throughout this book, I argue present an alternative method for conceiving of queer YA. During the discussion period, I fielded a thought-provoking question from a colleague, Gwen Athene Tarbox, who questioned whether or not contemporary queer YA critics—and the genre itself—were indeed as invested in visibility as I seemed to suggest.[3] Did I find any evidence, Gwen wondered, that more recent queer YA is returning to an iteration of the ambiguity and/ or wholesale rejection of identity seen in *I'll Get There*? Moreover, are critics embracing these thematic changes instead of continuing to push for characters who, to once again borrow from Brent Hartinger, just "happen to be gay"? In a follow-up conversation over email, Gwen cited two acclaimed novels featuring characters with particularly fluid and ambiguous relationships to gender and sexuality—David Levithan's *Every Day* (2012) and Bill Konigsberg's *Openly Straight* (2013)—to suggest

> a growing sense of confidence among YA authors that it's okay to present gender and sexuality in fluid terms. Even 10 years ago, the idea of presenting queer characters was perceived as . . . putting enough pressure on publishers—but obviously, the idea of a queer YA novel is now solidified enough that authors are moving beyond the traditional coming out narrative . . . or even Levithan's traditional LGBT romances [e.g. *Boy Meets Boy*] in order to ask other sorts of questions (Tarbox, "Re: LGBT Visibility").

Indeed, as Gwen's comments indicate, queer YA and its criticism have shifted significantly since I first began imagining this project as my doctoral dissertation in 2009. It has been an immense challenge to remain astride the explosion of queer YA titles while keeping a steady finger on the pulse of YA criticism both inside and outside of academia. In this brief conclusion, I hope to use Gwen's remarks as a springboard to address some developments in queer YA and YA criticism more broadly, putting them into dialogue with the arguments I have made throughout this book.

It strikes me that Kenneth B. Kidd's 2011 claim—made as queer YA discourse was beginning its rapid spread—that "queer theorists don't seem to know much about children's literature" is becoming less accurate as children's literature and queer theory grow increasingly conversant with one another ("Queer Theory's Child" 184). As I was in various stages of writing this book, Kidd's own co-edited 2011 collection *Over the Rainbow: Queer Children's and Young Adult Literature* appeared in addition to a number of other volumes that probe the intersections between queer theory and children's literature. To name just a few, in winter 2012, Lance Weldy and Thomas Crisp edited an issue of *Children's Literature Association Quarterly* that "address[es] contemporary issues related to sexuality and sexual identity in children's and young adult literature" ("From Alice to Alana" 372); Nat Hurley's special issue of *English Studies in Canada*, "Childhood and Its Discontents," contains essays that consider queerness and sexuality in relation to childhood and works of children's literature, including *Peter Pan* and Orson Scott Card's *Ender's Game*; in January 2014, Laura Robinson edited an issue of *Bookbird* that "explore[s] the queerness in texts intended for children and youth very specifically" ("Queerness and Children's Literature"); 2016 saw the publication of a collection of essays, edited by Darla Linville and David Lee Carlson, entitled *Beyond Borders: Queer Eros and Ethos (Ethics) in LGBTQ Young Adult Literature*.[4] Most recently, in 2019, Angel Daniel Matos and Jon Michael Wargo edited a special issue of *Research on Diversity in Youth Literature* entitled "Queer Futurities in Youth Literature, Media, and Culture," in which they raise questions similar to those posed in this book. Matos and Wargo trouble YA critics' attachment to positive affect and ask, in their introduction to the issue, "By abandoning the equation between queerness, violence, and negative affect, are we not doing a disservice or injustice to people, readers, and communities who cannot escape the negative and harmful experiences commonly tethered to queer life and representation?" (9). My brief, inadequate overview of such scholarship says nothing of the many other publications at the intersections of queer theory and children's literature. Clearly, these are hot topics that promise to inspire exciting and groundbreaking work over the years to come. I hope that this book, which speaks to some broad questions about genre while (re)considering individual works of queer YA across media, helps to advance these conversations.

Outside of academic circles, interest in children's literature—and, specifically, YA—has also been intensifying over the past decade. With the global success of multiple YA franchises and their highly lucrative film adaptations, YA is under a particularly bright spotlight as readers of all ages flock to purchase these titles. A 2012 Bowker Market Research study, cited by *Publishers Weekly*, found that "55% of buyers of works that publishers designate for kids aged 12 to 17—known as YA books—are 18 or older, with the largest segment aged 30 to 44," and "78% of the time they are purchasing books for their own reading" ("New Study"). Yet despite—or precisely because of—the fact that YA has been booming, discourse that evinces our "cultural anxiety of immaturity" seems to be surfacing with growing intensity (Clark 49). Even publishers themselves seem anxious about the effectiveness of the "YA" label as a strategy for marketing books to adults. In late 2009, St. Martin's Press announced a pitch contest to launch the category "new adult fiction," which describes "great, new, cutting edge fiction with protagonists who are slightly older than YA and can appeal to an adult audience" (Jae-Jones). Yet, the publisher concedes, the actual differences between YA and New Adult Fiction are few: "Since twenty-somethings are devouring YA," the contest page explains, "St. Martin's Press is seeking fiction similar to YA that can be published and marketed as adult—a sort of an 'older YA' or 'new adult'" (Jae-Jones).[5] Literary critics, too, are demonstrating those age-old anxieties that have been tenaciously haunting children's literature: who should and shouldn't be reading children's literature and/or YA? What are the pedagogical stakes of these books, if any?

In September 2014, as I was completing a draft of my dissertation, the massive success of John Green's *The Fault in Our Stars*—a YA novel published in 2012 and adapted into a film in 2014—generated a heated debate that received coverage in the *New York Times Magazine*, the *New Yorker*, and just about every corner of the blogosphere. If, as Gwen suggested to me, audiences, authors, and publishers are becoming increasingly comfortable with a broad array of themes being represented in YA, it appears that the widespread appeal and success of YA remains a source of discomfort and anxiety for many critics regardless of what these books might contain. This anxious dialogue sprung from an article written by Ruth Graham that appeared in the *Slate Book Review*, entitled "Against YA: Yes, Adults Should Be Embarrassed to Read Young Adult Books." Like Shepherd's essay, Graham's polemic relies on a series of generalizations. Graham writes, for example, that "YA books present the teenage perspective in a fundamentally uncritical way" and "these books consistently indulge in the kind of endings . . . which adult readers ought to reject as far too simple. YA endings are uniformly *satisfying*, whether that satisfaction comes through weeping or cheering." Clearly, Graham hasn't read any early queer YA titles, which contemporary critics critique on the basis of their unsatisfying endings, as I demonstrate in the first two chapters of this book. Graham concludes that there's a special reward in that feeling of stretching yourself beyond the YA mark, akin to the excitement of graduating out of the kiddie pool and the rest of the padded trappings of childhood: It's the thrill of growing up. But the YA and "new adult" boom may mean fewer teens aspire to grown-up reading, because the grown-ups they know are reading their books.

The anxiety of immaturity is everywhere in Graham's piece, demonstrating the persistence and potency of the affective economy within which YA and its criticism continues to circulate.

Certainly, it is easy enough to critique Graham's piece, and many columnists and bloggers took it upon themselves to do so.[6] Laura Miller's *Salon* piece, for example, calls Graham out for flattening an entire genre's potential and for her reductive reading of Green's novel. "It's perplexing," Miller writes, "to read a complaint about the lack of literary sophistication in Young Adult fiction from a critic who seems insensible to how literary effects are achieved." However, I am less interested in critiquing Graham than I am in considering the impressive traction her piece received, the conversation it generated, the anxieties about YA this conversation evinces, and how this all relates to those aspects of queer YA I have been exploring throughout this book.

The countless blog posts and articles spawned in the wake of Graham's essay include two longer essays in the *New York Times Magazine* and the *New Yorker*. In the former, published in September 2014, A. O. Scott contemplates "The Death of Adulthood in American Culture" with deep ambivalence, arguing that "in doing away with patriarchal authority, we have also, perhaps unwittingly, killed off all the grown-ups." Scott confesses to "feeling a twinge of disapproval" when he spots "peers clutching a volume of 'Harry Potter' or 'The Hunger Games,'" but also states that he's "not necessarily proud of this reaction." He claims that many YA novels "advance an essentially juvenile vision of the world" and that "adulthood as we have known it has become conceptually untenable," but concedes that adulthood "may never really have existed in the first place." Scott draws on Leslie A. Fiedler's *Love and Death in the American Novel* (1960) to consider the contemporary "antics of . . . comic man-boys" and "the bro comedy" vis-à-vis the "apparently sexless but intensely homoerotic connections" between characters who "managed to escape both from the institutions of patriarchy and from the intimate authority of women" in the likes of *Huckleberry Finn* and *Moby-Dick* (here, too, we hear echoes of the feral tale). As Fiedler suggests, "the great works of American fiction are notoriously at home in the children's section of the library" (quoted in Scott); or as Scott summarizes, "All American fiction is young-adult fiction." He concludes with consistent ambivalence by extending this desire for delay at the core of American fiction/YA to American culture as a whole, arguing that

Y.A. fiction is the least of it. It is now possible to conceive of adulthood as the state of being forever young. Childhood, once a condition of limited autonomy and deferred pleasure ("wait until you're older"), is now a zone of perpetual freedom and delight. . . . The world is our playground, without a dad or a mom in sight. I'm all for it. Now get off my lawn.

Scott's article flagged for me the centrality of sideways growth, delay, and anxious temporality to a body of texts that extend well beyond queer YA. His closest theoretical bedfellow in this moment, surprisingly, is Julia Kristeva—recall her insistence that all novels are adolescent novels. Both Scott and Kristeva point us to an archive that, alongside those texts I've explored throughout these pages, invites us to question how and where young protagonists function as figures of reproductive futurism, as Edelman contends, and/or as symbols of incompleteness and anxious resistance to a futurity that finds its telos in the kind of "adulthood" that Scott declares dead—if, that is, it ever really lived it all. Truthfully, this realization made *me* anxious. If *all* American fiction is indeed YA and all novels adolescent novels, and an ambivalence and/or anxiety about conventional notions of "growing up" is a constitutive feature of this literature, then am I doing anything at all interesting or original by pointing to queer YA's affective structures, temporal subversions, and sideways attachments? Am I simply engaged in my own anxious rehearsal of generic conventions that could be attributed, as Scott and Kristeva point out, to any number of texts contained under the massively broad umbrellas of "all American fiction" or, even worse, "all novels"?

This may in fact be a valid critique of this project. But what I find so interesting is that, despite the tenacity of characters who long for delay and resist "growing up" as visibly LGBT in YA, these themes and the YA genre continue to generate ample anxious critical discourse. I hope to have demonstrated, throughout this book, how sexuality inflects upon and shapes those desires and anxieties surrounding delay and alternative temporalities of growth, and how, when sexuality enters the picture, so does a whole new series of anxieties. Critics remain consistently anxious about the status of "growing up," who's doing it, who's doing it *properly*, and who seems to be failing—perhaps because they're consuming the wrong media. Sexuality plays an integral role in "growing up," since so much discourse on child development imagines (hetero/homo)sexual adulthood as its endpoint. Anxieties persist about what this developmental narrative should look like, how it should be represented, and the pedagogical consequences of representing various permutations of this story in texts that imagine for themselves a young audience.

Scott confesses, "I do feel the loss of something here," when it comes to his proclaimed "death of adulthood," yet he also maintains that "the best and most authentic cultural products of our time . . . imagine a world where no one is in charge and no one necessarily knows what's going on, where identities are in perpetual flux." To return to Gwen's comment, perhaps ambiguity can't be "back" because it never really went anywhere. As I illustrated throughout these pages, queer YA has long been attached to various forms of ambiguity and identities in "perpetual flux" even though various critics have maintained that visibility and coherence are integral to the genre's pedagogical potential. Just as Scott heralds the "Death of Adulthood" while simultaneously suggesting that adulthood never really existed, Brent Hartinger's declaration "We Got There"—as discussed in chapter one—assumes the demise of a particular narrative of sexuality that never quite vanished the way he imagines.

In his *New Yorker* piece entitled "Henry James and the Great Y.A. Debate," published a week after Scott's essay, Christopher Beha addresses Scott's ambivalence and initially appears to make a case for YA as a genre that addresses with nuance these blurry boundaries between child- and adulthood. "There is a difference between art that merely enacts a culture's refusal to grow up," Beha writes, "and art that thoughtfully engages with that refusal." He cites James's distinction in "The Art of Fiction" between "the artist's subject matter and his treatment of that matter" to support his claim that "if we assume that subject matter is what defines a book as 'young adult,' it doesn't make much sense to discourage adults from reading a book with that label. It is as much as saying that certain types of human experience are beneath serious adult attention, which I don't think is true." Moreover, Beha acknowledges that the YA "label" is often "simply a marketing tool, which isn't something that a critic ought to be paying attention to."

Yet by the end of his essay, Beha's anxiety of immaturity takes hold of his heretofore carefully reasoned arguments. He argues that oftentimes "giv[ing] a subject a treatment that is more appropriate for a young audience . . . involves simplifying things—first the diction and syntax, but finally the whole picture of life." Although it is not "shameful for adults to spend a lot of time reading these simplified treatments," Beha claims, "it does strike me as strange." He concludes with a paean to the work of Henry James, Beha's avatar of all supposedly mature and sophisticated works of literary fiction:

> Much is taken from us as we pass out of childhood, but other human beings who have suffered these losses have created great works of art, works that can only be truly appreciated by those who have suffered the same losses in turn. These works are among the great recompenses that experience offers us. Putting down *Harry Potter* for Henry James is not one of adulthood's obligations, like flossing and mortgage payments; it's one of its rewards, like autonomy and sex. It seems to me

not embarrassing or shameful but just self-defeating and a little sad to forego such pleasures in favor of reading a book that might just as easily be enjoyed by a child.

Here, Beha makes a series of reductive assumptions about the complexities of YA and how adults and children read. Not only does he imply that YA authors cannot create "great works of art" that deal with loss and that children cannot or do not experience loss, but he also assumes that adults and children will experience the same (fundamentally immature) "pleasures" of reading YA. Lost is any sense of nuance when it comes to genre and the myriad reading strategies people of all ages use when engaging with texts. As I have illustrated throughout, (queer) YA tackles with tremendous thoughtfulness the risks, rewards, pleasures, and subversive possibilities involved in reading texts and the world around us. As they navigate sexuality and sexual (anti-)identifications in myriad forms, the protagonists I examine call attention to reading as a strategy for multiplying identificatory opportunities or refusing identity altogether, cultivating alternative temporalities and relations, and critiquing those tropes of genre, growth, and development that obstinately govern children's literature discourse.

When we put Beha into conversation with Maria Tatar's "No More Adventures in Wonderland"—the *New York Times* essay discussed in this book's introduction—the affective economy of anxiety within which YA circulates becomes all the more tangible. Beha's use of *Harry Potter* as James's immature counterpoint is ironic given that the loss of Harry's parents is foundational to Rowling's entire series; in Tatar's delineation of today's dark and "not-so-childish . . . children's stories," she writes that the *Harry Potter* books "offer expansive meditations on mortality." YA writers like Rowling, Collins, and Philip Pullman "have successfully produced new literary contact zones for adults and children," Tatar claims, "with monumental narratives about loss, suffering and redemption." Whereas Beha might find these themes appealing, they lead Tatar to "mourn the decline of the literary tradition invented by Carroll and Barrie," who "more fully entered the imaginative worlds of children—where danger is balanced by enchantment."

The debate continues and the anxiety persists with a rhythm as repetitive as Davy's dream about the beach, as seen in *I'll Get There. It Better Be Worth the Trip.* Critics remain determined to pin down the pedagogical function of children's and YA literature, a rehearsal that points to the shaky foundation of the genre itself. This anxiety, as I have argued, presents not only a point of entry into this critical conversation, but also the tools for fashioning an alternative method for approaching and engaging with a range of cultural artifacts—including, but not limited to, the unceasingly anxious genre of queer YA.

Notes

Introduction. Notes on an Anxious Genre:
Queer Young Adult Literature and Culture

1. I follow Lydia Kokkola's assertion that "most critics do not distinguish between the use of YA, teenage, adolescent, and juvenile literature," so in this book I use "YA" as shorthand for everything that might fall under this category (11). As I will illustrate, generic and formal slipperiness is important to my project. For thoughtful analyses of the differences between "adolescent literature," "literature of adolescence," and "young adult literature," see Trites's *Disturbing the Universe* and Kidd's "A Case Study of Us All."

2. In Lo's words, "Mainstream publishers include the Big 5 (Hachette, HarperCollins, Macmillan, Penguin Random House, and Simon and Schuster); major publishers Disney Book Group, Houghton Mifflin Harcourt, and Scholastic; and general interest publishers that do not focus on LGBT books," whereas "major publishers include: Disney Book Group, Hachette, HarperCollins, Houghton Mifflin Harcourt, Macmillan, Penguin Random House, Scholastic, Simon and Schuster" ("LGBTQ YA" and "A Decade of LGBTQ YA").

3. Queer YA is booming alongside YA more generally. In the 2016 edition of *Young Adult Literature*, Cart indicates that in the late 1980s and early 1990s, 250–500 books would constitute a "good" year in YA publishing; in 2016, there were close to 7,000 (109–110). Citing a 2014 *Time* report, Cart points out that sales of books for young readers rose 22.4 percent while adult title sales decreased by 3.3 percent in that year (109). Furthermore, a 2014 *Publishers Weekly* study revealed that YA's imagined audience does not necessarily reflect its actual readership: readers eighteen years and older were responsible for 79 percent of YA purchases from December 2012 through November 2013 (Cart 146). It seems fitting, then, that the top six novels on the list of bestselling titles from January through June of 2014 were YA books (Cart 146–47).

4. See Baxter, Deloria's *Playing Indian* (1998), and Kidd's *Making American Boys* (2005) for histories of how Indigenous practices and culture were (and continue to be) appropriated and crudely adapted as means of disciplining the "savage" child and adolescent into ostensibly well-behaved and productive adults.

5. For a thorough account of the emergence of YA and "the young adult" alongside psychological and psychoanalytic discourse, see Kidd's chapter "'A Case History of Us All': The Adolescent Novel Before and After Salinger" from his *Freud in Oz: At the Intersections of Psychoanalysis and Children's Literature* (2011).

6. I would also point to Kristeva's argument that sexual identity becomes a theme central to the (adolescent) novel in the eighteenth century. "If we peruse the novels of this era," she writes, "we see that the eighteenth century explicitly formulates the notion of sexual difference as an unresolved, if not impenetrable, concept" (144). Kristeva's version of the "queer" adolescent novel, then, would align itself with those queer theorists and YA protagonists who resist sexual stability instead of those queer YA commentators who prefer coming out narratives that result in protagonists with concretized sexual selves (in other words, the *It Gets Better* narrative, which I discuss more thoroughly in chapters six and seven).

7. Freud discusses anxiety in *The Interpretation of Dreams* (1900) and *Three Essays on the Theory of Sexuality* (1905), in which he characterizes anxiety as the affective effect of various forms of repression. Freud later complicates this claim in *Inhibitions, Symptoms and Anxiety* (1926), arguing instead that repression can be the cause and/or the result of anxiety. Like anxiety, repression suggests a delayed or halted temporality—the *OED* lists among its definitions, "To prevent (a thing or occas. a person) from natural development, growth, or manifestation; to curb, inhibit, hold back" ("Repression").

8. Lacan writes: "*Impedicare* means *to be ensnared* and it's an extremely precious notion all the same. Indeed, it implies the relationship between one dimension and something that comes to interfere with it and which, in what interests us, impedes not the function, a term of reference, not movement, which is rendered difficult, but truly and verily the subject. Here then is what brings us closer to what we're searching for, namely, what happens in what goes by the name of anxiety" (10).

9. Stockton's theories rely on "philosopher Jacques Derrida's notion of delay as the inescapable effect of our reading along a chain of words . . . where meaning is delayed, deferred, exactly because we read in sequence, go forward in a sentence, not yet knowing what words are ahead of us, while we must take the words we have passed *with* us as we go, making meaning wide and hung in suspense" (*Queer Child* 4). Stockton is interested in "not just words" but also "metaphors, which a child may use as a way to grow itself, in hiding, in delay" (*Queer Child* 4).

10. Affect, according to Patricia Ticineto Clough, "refers generally to bodily capacities to affect and be affected or the augmentation or diminution of a body's capacity to act, to engage, and to connect" (2). Many affect theorists distinguish between "affect," "emotion," and "feeling"; since I draw primarily on Ahmed's theory of affective economies to consider the circulation of anxiety, "affect" is the term I will generally prefer, although I recognize that anxiety could be theorized as an emotion and/or feeling. Like Ahmed, I am more interested in asking "what do emotions [or affects] do?" than "what are emotions [or affects]?" (*Cultural Politics* 4). For more on affect theory, see *The Affect Theory Reader*, eds. Gregg and Selgworth (Duke University Press, 2010).

11. Thomas Crisp's "The Trouble With *Rainbow Boys*" is a good example of this: Crisp himself flags the popularity and widespread circulation of Alex Sanchez's *Rainbow Boys* trilogy as the primary source of his anxiety about how Sanchez represents gay teen archetypes. In other words, the anxiety is not inherent to the text itself or in Crisp as he reads the text, but is rather "produced," in Ahmed's words, "as an effect of [the text's] circulation" in tandem with Crisp's particular reading, both of which contribute to the accrual of anxious signifiers (45).

12. See Alexander Doty's "My Beautiful Wickedness: *The Wizard of Oz as Lesbian Fantasy*" and Tison Pugh's "There Lived in the Land of Oz Two Queerly Made Men" for deeper examinations of queer reading and the queerness of *Oz*.

13. We might also consider how Fredric Jameson defines genres as "social contracts between a writer and a specific public, whose function is to specify the proper use of a particular cultural artifact" (106). Queer YA commentary becomes anxious if the public feels that writers are not obeying the genre's supposed "social contract," i.e. the notion that YA does not contain enough queer visibility, or the "wrong kinds" of visibility, that is, too much "realism" in the form of homophobia and stereotype.

14. In the 1990s, queer theory distinguished itself from gay and lesbian studies, its academic predecessor, through an interrogation of identity, an embrace of sexual shame as the ground for collectivity, and a recuperation of not only the gay and lesbian voices absented from the canon, but also modes of relationality—public sex, cruising, kinks and fetishes, activism in the face of HIV/AIDS—that have been demeaned and labeled perverse. In *Queer Theory: An Introduction*, Annamarie Jagose offers an appropriately loose definition of the term: "Queer," Jagose writes, "describes those gestures or analytical models which dramatise incoherencies in the allegedly stable relations between chromosomal sex, gender and sexual desire," relations that claim heterosexuality as the normative model for sexual being (and are often described as "heteronormativity") (3). Jagose's definition draws on Eve Kosofky Sedgwick's frequently cited description of queer: "The open mesh of possibilities, gaps, overlaps, dissonances and resonances, lapses and excesses of meaning where the constituent elements of anyone's gender, of anyone's sexuality aren't made (or *can't* be made) to signify monolithically" (*Tendencies* 8). As Lee Edelman writes in *No Future*, "Queerness can never define an identity; it can only ever disturb one" (17).

15. Aside from a few texts, the relationship between anxiety and literary criticism remains under-theorized. In addition to John Michael's *Anxious Intellects* (2000), see Scott S. Derrick's *Monumental Anxieties* (1997), a study of gender and homoeroticism in nineteenth-century American literature; Jennifer Schacker's "Unruly Tales: Ideology, Anxiety, and the Regulation of Genre" (2007), which explores mid-Victorian criticism of folk and fairy tales; *My Mother's Voice: Children, Literature, and the Holocaust* (2001), in which Adrienne Kertzer concludes that YA illustrates anxiety surrounding "the possibility of learning about the past through the act of reading" (340); and Beverly Lyon Clark's *Kiddie Lit* (2003), which flags a "cultural anxiety of immaturity" as the impetus for adult disavowal of children's literature's complexity (49). I consider Clark's analysis more thoroughly in my conclusion, in the context of recent debates about adults who read YA.

16. Love focuses on authors Walter Pater, Willa Cather, Radclyffe Hall, and Sylvia Townsend Warner.

17. See Angus Gordon's "Turning Back: Adolescence, Narrative, and Queer Theory" and Claire Gross's "What Makes a Good YA Coming Out Novel?" for examples of articles that position retrospection and "the eventual realization of homosexual identity" (Gordon 1) as two fundamental "coming out" narrative conventions.

18. See Huyck and Dahlen (2019) for infographics illustrating this racial disparity in children's publishing, and diversebooks.org for more on *We Need Diverse Books*. In this book, following ideas articulated by Ann Thúy Nguyên and Maya Pendleton, I capitalize "Black" and "White" in order to emphasize "the critical importance and political permanence of these words as real, existing racial identities."

19. Defined as "a narrative form derived from mythology and folklore that dramatizes but also manages the 'wildness' of boys," the feral tale has been in circulation for centuries (Kidd, *Making* 1). In the twentieth century, Kidd explains, we see "the Western recuperation

of the feral boy as a normative subject, especially in certain genres developed for children and families" (6).

20. Like the feral tale's protagonist, queer YA characters are often liminal figures who attempt to navigate their queerness in an oppressively normal world. They are "so-called freaks," as Kidd writes, "caught between cultures or modes of life" (*Making* 191).

21. Regretfully, my book also omits discussions of characters on the asexual/aromantic spectrum, who have only recently been given meaningful treatment in YA. For more on asexuality and childhood, see Przybylo (2019).

22. Gill-Peterson made this comment following her keynote "On Wanting in the Trans Archive: A Shameful Love Story" at a University of Lethbridge symposium entitled *Queer Youth Doing Queer History* on 18 October 2019.

Chapter 1. Visibility: Growing Sideways in *I'll Get There. It Better Be Worth the Trip*

1. A previous version of this chapter appeared as Mason, Derritt, "A Phallic Dog, A Stuffed Coyote, and the Boy Who Won't Come Out: Revisiting Queer Visibility in John Donovan's *I'll Get There. It Better Be Worth the Trip." Children's Literature Association Quarterly*, vol. 41, no. 3, 2016, pp. 295–311.

2. Several critics identify Donovan's novel as the first North American young adult text to visibly represent and deal with a nonheterosexual encounter. Michael Cart and Christine Jenkins, for example, begin their survey of queer YA with Donovan's book. Kirk Fuoss describes the book as "the first problem-realism text to include a 'homosexual incident'" (162); Rumaan Alam calls it "almost certainly the first book for young adults that deals explicitly with homosexuality." As Carrie Hintz and Eric L. Tribunella point out, however, there is a long history of "same-sex loving characters" in children's fiction; they identify Edward Irenaeus Prime-Stevenson, the author of two nineteenth-century "novels for boys," as "the first known American or British author to refer to his or her own work for children as 'homosexual'" (455). For more on the prehistory of the gay and lesbian novel, see also Nat Hurley's *Circulating Queerness* (2018).

3. There are many more examples of critics discussing and debating the proper kinds of queer visibility in young adult literature, far too many to include in this chapter. Thomas Crisp's frequently cited "The Trouble with *Rainbow Boys*," a critique of Alex Sanchez's popular trilogy, is a well-known example; it prompted a response from the author himself (see Sanchez and Sipe). In this essay, Crisp positions David Levithan's *Boy Meets Boy* as an antidote to the potentially harmful, angst-ridden, stereotype- and homophobia-riddled titles; Wickens (149, 156), Tison Pugh (*Innocence* 18), and Cart and Jenkins (144–45) also contrast Levithan's novel and its unproblematically gay characters with earlier works of queer adolescent fiction. Additionally, Crisp critiques Sanchez's representation of HIV/AIDS in *Rainbow Boys*; see Robert McRuer's "Reading and Writing 'Immunity': Children and the Anti-Body" and chapter three of this book for more on HIV/AIDS in children's literature.

4. Rob Linné also critiques Donovan's ending for its ambiguity and assumes that only a single, negative reading is possible: "The sexualities of the characters remain ambiguous," he explains, "presumably just 'phases' they have struggled through, or 'choices' they reconsider by the end of the novel. . . . This trope presumably diffuses homophobic tensions in the readers by intimating that a return to 'normalcy' is always possible" (204).

5. The other three novels included in Hanckel and Cunningham's study are *The Man Without a Face* (Isabelle Holland, 1972), *Sticks and Stones* (Lynn Hall, 1972), and *Trying Hard to Hear You* (Sandra Scoppettone, 1974).

6. Joshua Whitehead (2019) has written eloquently about the colonial impulses of this moment, and how YA characters often negotiate their queerness through "green spaces" that erase Indigenous bodies and lives.

7. The erotic terms of Davy and Fred's relationship recall an interaction between John Thornton and his dog in Jack London's *The Call of the Wild* (1903), which Tribunella characterizes as "a kind of sexual encounter. The man and dog embrace roughly; there is jerking, the calling of 'ill' names, the murmuring of oaths—certainly the lewd name-calling and exclamations of rough sex" (34).

8. See the chapter "it's a dick thing" from hooks's *We Real Cool: Black Men and Masculinity* (2004), in which she traces "the history of the black male body . . . in the United States" beginning with "the imposition onto that body of white racist sexist pornographic sexual fantasies" (63). For more writing at the intersections of Blackness, masculinity, and sexuality, see Walcott; Alexander; Stockton, *Beautiful Bottom, Beautiful Shame*; and Pharr, among many others.

Chapter 2. Risk: The Queer Pedagogy of *The Man Without a Face*

1. Portions of this chapter appeared in Mason, Derritt, "Vulnerable Fictions: Queer Youth, Storytelling, and Narratives of Victimization," *Fictionalizing the World: Rethinking the Politics of Literature*, edited by Louisa Söllner and Anita Vržina, Peter Lang, 2016, pp. 19–36.

2. The site notes that "YRBS and other studies have gathered data on lesbian, gay, and bisexual youth but have not included questions about transgender and questioning/queer youth. As that changes and data becomes available, this content will be updated" ("YRBSS").

3. Rofes notes that as he was developing a course on "Gay and Lesbian Issues in Schools," he struggled to find material that took him beyond Matthew Shepard, Brandon Teena, and other queer youth who had been murdered. While his students had powerful emotional reactions to the material, in particular to discussions about Shepard's torture and murder, Rofes expresses concerns that his queer students identified closely with Shepard's martyrdom (43–44).

4. Although Britzman is perhaps the most prominent theorist to consider in depth the role of psychoanalysis—including anxiety—in education, other critics tread similar terrain, even without naming "anxiety" as such in their work. In "Queer Pedagogy: Praxis Makes Im/Perfect" (1993) for example, Mary Bryson and Suzanne de Castell describe pedagogy as always and necessarily a messy (and, one could argue, anxious) mix of success, failure, missteps, and small victories. Shoshana Felman's "Education and Crisis, or the Vicissitudes of Teaching" (1995) explores the relationship between teaching, testimonial, and crisis. Heather Sykes (2011) considers how "adult phantasies and projected anxieties" about "childhood and adolescence" play themselves out in the physical education classroom (91), and Sheila L. Cavanagh (2007) examines public anxieties surrounding teacher sex scandals, inviting us to "imagine a queer pedagogy based not on sex between teachers and students but on illicit wishes and non-normative identifications with these wishes" (27). For more, see Kumashiro's first chapter, in which he considers the anxieties he experienced when attempting to implement an anti-oppressive pedagogy in his own classroom. As Britzman asserts in "Between

Psychoanalysis and Pedagogy," "It is hardly news to observe that in the field of education words arouse anxiety. But it is news to think education through its neurotic, perverse, and psychotic symptoms" (105). The latter is the work I hope to continue in this chapter.

5. Quinlivan summarizes Britzman's primary assertion in *After-Education* as "what is educative makes us anxious," emphasizing the inextricability of anxiety from the scene of education (519).

6. Britzman's "Precocious Education" (2000) treads in comparatively positive affective territory (vs. anxiety and fear, for example), exploring the role of pleasure, desire, and love as they relate to education. She asks, "How does the experience of learning become pleasurable? How does one take joy in having ideas, in changing one's mind, in encountering the work of learning? What sorts of relation exists between learning to love and loving learning?" (44). In this essay, Britzman draws on Freud's conception of children as "little sex researchers" to associate childhood curiosity and precociousness with the desire and pleasure that surrounds learning (51).

7. Cavanagh makes a similar conscious/unconscious, articulable/displaced distinction between worry and anxiety: "A worry that is real can be dealt with and named for what it is. An unconscious anxiety . . . goes underground and resurfaces as an attachment to something seemingly more legitimate" (21–22). While there remains overlap between the two concepts, especially in terms of their shared temporality, I believe there are (hazy) lines to be drawn between the object-centered "worry" and the more generalized, perhaps directionless and/or improperly focused affect "anxiety."

8. We can further recall Lacan's assertion that anxiety "impedes . . . truly and verily the subject" (10).

9. Judith Butler famously asserts in "Imitation and Gender Insubordination" that "heterosexuality [is] an incessant and *panicked* imitation of its own naturalized ideation" (314). Given that heterosexuality, as Butler explains, "is always in the act of elaborating itself," it is simultaneously demonstrating "that it 'knows' its own possibility of becoming undone: hence, its compulsion to repeat which is a foreclosure of that which threatens its coherence" (314). In other words, heterosexuality rehearses itself in order to pin itself down, but it is this very anxious, repetitive performance that renders it unstable.

10. See, for example, the work of Paulo Freire (1998, 2004) and bell hooks's *Teaching Community: A Pedagogy of Hope* (2003)

11. For an essay that considers the queer productivity of shame in Holland's novel, see Stebbins (2014).

12. The many parallels between *The Man Without a Face* and *The Pupil* (as examined by Stockton) warrant in-depth investigation elsewhere. Among these similarities is a reversal in narrative voice and conclusion: James gives us the story from the tutor's perspective and it is the pupil who dies at the end from a "weak heart," whereas in Holland's novel, the story is narrated from the student's point of view and the tutor is the weak-hearted one.

13. As Britzman writes, queer pedagogy aims "to unsettle old centerings of the self in education: to unsettle the myth of normalcy as an originary state and to unsettle the unitary subject of pedagogy" ("Queer Pedagogy" 81). Chuck's trajectory in Holland's novel—which culminates in the very kind of "unsettling" Britzman describes—could also be read in light of Bersani's "Is the Rectum a Grave?" in which the author posits "a more radical disintegration and humiliation of the self," a "self-shattering into the sexual as a kind of non anecdotal self-debasement" as a lens for "transgressing . . . that very polarity which . . . may be the profound sense of both certain mystical experiences and of human sexuality" (217). Britzman

channels Bersani more directly in "Between Psychoanalysis and Pedagogy" when she writes that "symbolizing uncertainty involves the work of getting to know one's emotional experience from the pain and vulnerability of learning from ambiguous experience. . . . Paradoxically, getting to know one's emotional experience involves one with new ideas that may shatter what sentiments try to settle" (98). There is much to be said here, especially given that Holland's novel relies on Chuck's "pain and vulnerability of learning" from experience that is narrated as "ambiguous." A Bersani-inspired approach to Holland's novel, however, has more in common with the masochistic reading suggested by Stockton's chapter on James than what I am attempting to do through a focus on a pedagogy of anxiety. For more on Bersani and a reading of queer YA vis-à-vis queer negativity, see chapter four of this book.

14. This moment returns us to Britzman's suggestion that queer pedagogy pushes "thought . . . to think the limits of its own dominant conceptual orders," which is necessary "if new desires are to be made" ("Queer Pedagogy" 80). Here, Britzman draws on queer theory's interest in the relationship between knowledge, ignorance, and "the will not to know," or what Sedgwick calls "the relations of the closet" (*Epistemology* 3). "Silence is rendered as pointed and performative as speech, in relations around the closet," Sedgwick famously points out, "[which] highlights more broadly the fact that ignorance is as potent and as multiple a thing there as is knowledge" (*Epistemology* 4).

Chapter 3. HIV/AIDS: Playing with Failure in *Caper in the Castro* and *Two Boys Kissing*

1. Of course, since bacteria and viruses are distinct, there is no such thing as a bacterial virus. The house wine death message is the only instance in the game where the lethal substance is referred to as a "virus"—otherwise, it is called a "bacteria." The "virus" mention only further strengthens the game's resonances with HIV/AIDS.

2. For an example of the intense anxiety that emerges when young people do come into contact with HIV in popular media, see the controversy surrounding Larry Clark's 1995 film *Kids*. In a *New York Times* piece covering the film's twentieth anniversary, Ben Detrick writes, "For cultural alarmists of the 1990s Clinton era, the film 'Kids' represented a culmination of fears." Thanks to Morgan Vanek for suggesting this connection.

3. These books are J. C. Burke's *The Things We Promise* (2017), Helene Dunbar's *We Are Lost and Found* (2019), Sara Jaffe's *Dryland* (2015), Cordelia Jensen's *Skyscraping* (2015), Christopher Koehler's *Poz* (2015), Abdi Nazemian's *Like a Love Story* (2019), Jason Schmidt's memoir *A List of Things That Didn't Kill Me* (2015), and Brian Selznick's *The Marvels* (2015). Our searches yielded these titles because "HIV" or "AIDS" appear in the book summary and/or Goodreads user comments or questions about the title. It is of course possible that this cursory search missed titles that deal with HIV/AIDS but did not meet our limited criteria. See also Jenkins and Cart for a list of nonfiction titles for young people on HIV/AIDS published between 2006 and 2015 (216), and recent work by Gabriel Duckels (2020) on how the "romantic fantasy of AIDS" in queer YA "enables the expression of other nostalgic yearnings."

4. In addition to Matos, see Carlson and Linville's "The Social Importance of a Kiss," and Hutton.

5. Schulman understands "AIDS of the past" as the years between 1981 and 1996, "when there was a mass death experience of young people. Where folks my age watched in horror as our friends, their lovers, cultural heroes, influences, buddies, the people who witnessed our

lives as we witnessed theirs, as these folks sickened and died consistently for fifteen years" (45). Thanks to Vivek Shraya for bringing Schulman's outstanding book to my attention.

6. On July 10, 2019, as I was revising this chapter, a second review was added that provides a clever solution to the hyphen problem. I find myself simultaneously buoyed by the cunning of the *Castro* gaming community, and moderately dismayed that this workaround may in part dismantle my argument. Now, it seems, I feel like I'm failing at providing a sound argument about failure. Ultimately, I suppose, the new review doesn't change the fact that I failed endlessly at this game. Moreover, this tip further illuminates the necessity of "networking" oneself to solve the game, which I address later in this chapter.

7. Spoiler alert/protip: when the Club 102 bouncer asks you where the money is, he will only accept "in trunk" as a correct answer. Typing "trunk" or "in the trunk" or "car trunk" or "car" will get you killed.

8. Thanks to Angel Daniel Matos for pointing out, in his generous comments on this chapter, that this passage and Cooper's entire arc judgmentally repudiate not only digital technology, but also the kinds of (often anonymous) sexual encounters that technology facilitates. Such moralizing is in line with YA's treatment of HIV/AIDS more broadly and the genre's persistent attempts to preserve the innocence of its protagonists.

9. The objects of their critique, among others, include José Esteban Muñoz's *Cruising Utopia* and Halberstam's in *In a Queer Time and Place*.

Chapter 4. Dystopia: Queer Sex and the Unbearable in *Grasshopper Jungle*

1. Definitions of "dystopia" vary widely and range from strict to relatively open-ended. In "The Origins of Dystopia," for example, Gregory Claeys claims that "conquest by alien beings, or robots, or the final calling of time by God at Judgment Day, may portray dystopic elements. . . . But texts portraying such events are not 'dystopias' as such" (109). I take a looser approach to dystopia and am more interested in the themes and questions raised by dystopic elements in children's literature. I follow Basu et al, who suggest that "dystopian writing engages with pressing global concerns: liberty and self-determination, environmental destruction and looming catastrophe, questions of identity, and the increasingly fragile boundaries between technology and the self" (1).

2. See Hall, *Adolescence* (1904). As discussed in the introduction, Hall proposes that *Sturm und Drang* (storm and stress)—emotional turbulence, vulnerability, risk-taking tendencies, etc.—is a fundamental attribute of adolescence.

3. In August 2018, long after I had completed a draft of this chapter, the *Wall Street Journal* published another clickbait-y piece similar to the essay by Gurdon discussed here. Written by Steve Salerno, it is entitled "The Unbearable Darkness of Young Adult Literature" (but has nothing to do with Berlant and Edelman). I promise, dear reader: I thought of it first.

4. For a comprehensive investigation of this popular subgenre, see Basu et al. See also Ebony Elizabeth Thomas's *The Dark Fantastic* (2019) for an incisive look at race and the racial dimensions of "darkness" in several speculative YA texts, including *The Hunger Games*.

5. See, for example, Gayle Forman's essay and Mary Elizabeth Williams's "Has Young Adult Fiction Become Too Dark?" in *Salon* (2011).

6. For more examples of critics who embrace dark themes, see Sian Cain's "YA Books on Death: Is Young Adult Fiction Becoming Too Dark?" (2014) and Maureen Johnson's "Yes, Teen Fiction Can Be Dark—But It Shows Teenagers They Aren't Alone" (2011).

7. The hype surrounding Gurdon's essay is captured in the byline to Mary Elizabeth Williams's response: "Has young adult fiction become too dark? A scorching Wall Street Journal editorial rips apart the genre—and lights up the Internet."

8. See "The Dangers, Values of Dark Teen Lit" and Linda Holmes's essay.

9. An exception is Mary Elizabeth Williams's article, which cites a teen blogger named Emma: "Good literature rips open all the private parts of us—the parts people like [Gurdon] have deemed too dark, inappropriate, grotesque or abnormal for teens to be feeling—and then they stitch it all back together again before we even realize they're not talking about us."

10. In Berlant and Edelman's words, "Sex is exemplary in the way it powerfully produces such encounters, but such encounters exceed those experiences we recognize as sex" (viii).

11. Many critics have addressed the censoring and repression of queer desire in children's literature—this was a common theme of queer YA criticism in the 1990s and 2000s, when YA books with queer content were being published with increasing frequency. See, for example, Roberta Seelinger Trites's chapter on "Sex and Power" in *Disturbing the Universe*, in which she argues that gay YA novels "are very Foucauldian in their tendency to privilege the discourse of homosexuality over the physical sexual acts of gay men, defining homosexuality more rhetorically than physically" (103). See also Kirk Fuoss's "A Portrait of the Adolescent as a Young Gay" and the first two chapters of this book.

12. Shann's relative silence and apparent lack of agency in the epilogue is disconcerting—she is reduced to the role of (unhappy) mother, and Austin notes that she resents the time he spends with Robby ("Shann is quietly pouting; no doubt hiding inside her bedroom. She does not like it when Robby and I go out on our runs") (384). Eden, which is something of a utopia for Austin, seems be Shann's dystopia.

13. The many additional resonances between *Grasshopper Jungle*, queer sex, and HIV/AIDS are not lost on me, and would warrant more thorough examination in another place.

Chapter 5. Horror & Camp: Monsters and Wizards and Ghosts (oh my!) in *Big Mouth*

1. I am grateful to Peter C. Kunze for his generous comments on this chapter, which shaped this idea and many others throughout.

2. My discussion includes the first two seasons of *Big Mouth*, as well as the special episode "My Furry Valentine." Season three was released in October 2019, and as of November 2019, Netflix had renewed the show for an additional three seasons.

3. Kunze disagrees with me here, indicating in his comments on this chapter that *Big Mouth* is an extension of Kroll's work in *The League* and *The Kroll Show*, as well as Mulaney's stand-up, all of which targets an audience of straight, White men aged approximately 18–39 years. I would counter, however, that the show's adolescent themes and subtle didacticism, in combination with animation as a signifier of children's media, all function to obscure an obvious audience. This ambiguity is also reflected in the deep ambivalence of critics when it comes to the show's potential pedagogical value (or lack thereof) where young audiences are concerned.

4. Other theorists make similar connections between horror, musicals, and/or camp. Babuscio, for example, notes that "the musical comedy, with its high budgets and big stars, its open indulgence in sentiment, and its emphasis on atmosphere, mood, nostalgia, and the fantastic is, along with horror, a film genre that is saturated with camp" (125). Mallan and McGillis point out that "music and camp go together" as "it is in the song and dance numbers that camp is often given the spotlight" (15).

5. Certainly, *Big Mouth* is not the first to combine a child-like animation style with adult content. Several critics compare the show to Trey Parker and Matt Stone's long-running animated series *South Park* (1997–), for example. As Glen Weldon writes, "*Big Mouth* is arguably a filthier show [than *South Park*] with even cruder jokes and an obsession with sex that's more relentless. Crucially, however, it's also a much more sincere, more sweet, more intensely empathetic series that—even as it's visiting horrors and humiliations on its characters— never fails to side with them."

6. As Weldon's comments in the above note indicate, and as I will argue later in this chapter, *Big Mouth* aims in many ways to "satisfy" audiences, especially when it comes to defusing those anxieties surrounding puberty and its attendant shame. The show is not, in other words, entirely camp as "trash" à la John Waters—or, in other words, crudeness for the sake of crudeness (Cohan 8). *Big Mouth* does, however, have its moments of absurd vulgarity that are not somehow didactically recuperated. See, for example, the subplot that involves Jay impregnating his pillow ("Pillow Talk") or perhaps the show's crudest moment to-date, Maury's debasing of Garrison Keillor's decapitated head ("Requiem for a Wet Dream").

7. See also Francesca Donovan's "Netflix's Big Mouth is Redefining How We Learn About Sex" for more on conservative responses to the show.

8. Films covered in Scahill's book include *The Bad Seed* (1956), *Village of the Damned* (1960), *Rosemary's Baby* (1968), *Night of the Living Dead* (1968), *The Exorcist* (1973), *It's Alive* (1974), *The Omen* (1976), *Halloween* (1978), *Children of the Corn* (1984), *Firestarter* (1984), *The Good Son* (1993), and *Orphan* (2009). Scahill emphasizes the double valence of "revolting"—repulsive on the one hand, rebellious on the other.

9. Thanks to Pete Kunze for pointing out that this paradox—the way animation simultaneously gives life yet distances itself from "real life"—is why early scholars of animation (e.g. Walter Benjamin, Sergei Eisenstein) saw such promise in the form.

10. A Freudian reading of *Big Mouth* might suggest that the show's humor permits younger viewers to laugh, cathartically, at the visceral shame associated with puberty that they would otherwise repress (see *The Joke and Its Relation to the Unconscious*).

11. See Sean Griffin's *Tinker Belles and Evil Queens*, in which the author describes Gaston's solo number in Disney's *Beauty and the Beast* as a campy, "hysterical '*male* impersonation' number" (146).

12. See Julia Kristeva's *Powers of Horror* for more on the abject.

13. Duke, ghostly but not particularly monstrous, nonetheless resembles a Gothic villain as described by Jackson et al: he is "flamboyant and irrepressible" with a desire that "refuses to be contained" (13). We can think, too, about how Duke is not only a play on the Gothic "haunted house" trope, but also a cleverly perverse spin on the function of ghosts in children's fiction, which sometimes deploys specters as devices for exploring the anxieties and desires of young protagonists. Of course, in *Big Mouth*, these possibilities are typically absurd and debased. For more on ghosts and children's literature, see Judith Armstrong's "Ghosts as rhetorical devices in children's fiction."

Chapter 6: Getting Better: Children's Literature Theory and the *It Gets Better* Project

1. Portions of this chapter and chapter seven appear in Mason, Derritt, "On Children's Literature and the (Im)Possibility of *It Gets Better*," *ESC: English Studies in Canada* vol. 38, no. 3–4, 2012, pp. 83–104.

2. In the fall of 2010, five American gay teens took their own lives in the span of three weeks (see "Raymond Chase," McKinley, and the introduction to this book). For the project website, see itgetsbetter.org.

3. Although many of these critiques are authored by academics, most have been published in online venues that seek to mirror *It Gets Better*'s broad reach.

4. As of September 2014, the project's url (www.makeitbetterproject.org) had expired. The *Make it Better* YouTube channel, however, endures at www.youtube.com/user/MakeIt-BetterProject/ (accessed 14 June 2018).

5. *It Gets Better*, I argue, is more invested in an identity-based LGBT politic than a queer one. Nonetheless, in this chapter (as in the other chapters of this book), I use "queer" in tandem with "youth" to describe a range of nonheteronormative sexual identifications, counter-identifications, and practices that do not necessarily result in a concrete sense of sexual identity.

6. *It Gets Better*'s audience, as imagined by Savage and Miller, might be better described as "teenagers" or "youth" rather than "children" (although Savage uses the word "kids" to describe his audience in the introduction to the *It Gets Better* book), so it may be more accurate to call *It Gets Better* "young adult literature" instead of "children's literature," especially given that *It Gets Better* stories often reiterate the *Bildungsroman*'s "home-away-home" narrative pattern. For the purposes of this chapter, however, since I draw on critical tools emerging from the field of children's literature, I use this term to describe *It Gets Better* and "youth" to categorize its audience while recognizing nonetheless that the project circulates among children, teenagers/youth, and adults alike. Categorizing *It Gets Better* as children's literature, in a sense, also reinforces the anxious boundaries that divide these genres: *It Gets Better* is children's literature and queer YA and a book for adults, but its status within each genre is slippery and tenuous.

7. Puar, summarizing Berlant's argument, explains that "slow death describes populations that are marked out for wearing out." For more, see Berlant's "Slow Death (Sovereignty, Obesity, Lateral Agency)."

8. See, for example, Warner's *The Trouble with Normal* and Duggan's "The New Homonormativity."

9. For the purposes of this chapter, I have limited my analysis to the hundred and five *It Gets Better* stories contained in Savage and Miller's book. Featuring transcripts of videos curated by Savage and Miller as well as a handful of original contributions from public figures, the book also functions as an archive of core texts, those deemed by Savage and Miller as truest to the project's central narrative. In the book, there are undeniable similarities across stories that raise questions about who gets to be a representative teller of an *It Gets Better* tale and why, how contributors reimagine and renarrate their lives in relation to an imagined audience of young queer martyr-target-victims, and the significance of moments of disruption in the repetition of these stories. The *It Gets Better* book is an embodiment of the project's impossibility: it exists to reinforce and sell the project's foundational message while containing the possibilities for resistance to this message that circulate readily through other media, including the project's own YouTube site. In other words, the *It Gets Better* book seeks to widen the middle space between youth audience and adult author.

10. See Praetorius for coverage of this incident and a link to Rodemeyer's *It Gets Better* video.

11. An example of reader appropriation and "misuse" in the context of children's literature is slash fanfiction, erotic stories that feature same-sex character couplings. For more on

slash, see Catherine Tosenberger's "Homosexuality at the Online Hogwarts: Harry Potter Slash Fanfiction," and the next chapter of this book.

Chapter 7. Not Getting Better: Sex and Self-Harm in *It Gets Better* / *Glee* Fanfiction

1. *Glee*'s second season, which aired from September 21, 2010, to May 24, 2011, averaged 10.11 million viewers according to Nielsen ratings. This is compared to 9.77 million for season one (May 19, 2009–June 8, 2010) and 8.71 million for season three (September 20, 2011–May 22, 2012). See "Full Series Rankings" and Gorman for sources.

2. Many critics have written at length on fan culture, fanfiction, and slash. Along with Janice Radway, author of the groundbreaking *Reading the Romance: Women, Patriarchy, and Popular Literature* (University of North Carolina Press, 1984), Henry Jenkins is among the critics who first established fan culture as a site of academic inquiry. In *Textual Poachers*, Jenkins draws on Eve Sedgwick's theory of homosociality to suggest that "genre conventions create highly romantic representations of male-male friendship even as they seek to wall off those feelings from erotic contact between men" (xxiii). "The basic premises of 'slash' fiction," according to Jenkins, include "the movement from male homosocial desire to a direct expression of homoerotic passion, the exploration of alternatives to traditional masculinity," and "the insertion of sexuality into a larger social context" (186). Foundational critical work on fan culture that emerged alongside *Textual Poachers* includes Camille Bacon-Smith's *Enterprising Women: Television Fandom and the Creation of Popular Myth* (University of Pennsylvania Press, 1992), Lisa A. Lewis's *The Adoring Audience: Fan Culture and Popular Media* (Routledge, 1992), and Constance Penley's "Feminism, Psychoanalysis, and the Study of Popular Culture" (in *Cultural Studies*, editors. Grossberg, Nelson, and Treichler; Routledge, 1992).

3. Many slash stories contain explicit sex, and some critics have attempted to draw clear distinctions between slash and pornography. Jenkins, for example, writes, "If, as [John] Stoltenberg (1989) claims, pornography represents 'sex that has no past (the couplings are historyless), no future (the relationships are commitmentless), and virtually no present (it is physically functional but emotionally alienated)' (107), slash is centrally concerned with how sexual experience fits within the characters' pasts, presents, and futures" (190). Others, like Constance Penley, argue for a view that acknowledges and embraces the pornographic content of slash, claiming that disavowing slash's explicitness "slights [its] pornographic force" (167); see also Anne Kustritz's "Slashing the Romance Narrative" (2003). Similarly, Ika Willis's "Keeping Promises to Queer Children" (2006) argues that slash "can be experienced as *both* a hedonistic, erotic practice which could even be opposed to a thoughtful or critical relation to a text, *and* . . . a politically loaded practice of decontextualization that reorients a text in order to demonstrate that it bears the trace of a desiring structure not wholly congruent with the most . . . ideologically obedient reading" (156). For more on slash and its relationship to porn, see Catherine Driscoll's "One True Pairing: The Romance of Pornography and the Pornography of Romance" (in Hellekson and Busse, 79–96), Carola Katharina Bauer's *Naughty Girls and Gay Male Romance/Porn* (Anchor, 2012), and Paul Booth's "Slash and Porn: Media Subversion, Hyper-Articulation, and Parody" in *Continuum* 28.3 (2014).

4. Tosenberger points out that many scholars of fan culture—including Jenkins, Bacon-Smith, and Penley—"report that slash (like most fanfiction in general) is written primarily

by women. . . . The existence of slash complicated conventional notions about women's interest in erotica in general, and the types of erotic material women were supposed to be interested in (i.e., heterosexual romance novels)" (333). Slash, however, has evolved to be a much less gendered space; as Tosenberger argues, "In the Potter fandom, it is not just adult women, but young people as well who have a safe space in which to be 'strange and unusual'" (335). I would make the same claim about the spaces of *Glee* fanfiction.

5. I say "potentially" because, like Julad, I do not want to insist that slash is inherently subversive, queer, or pedagogical. Jenkins, in *Textual Poachers*, insists that "not all of slash is politically conscious; not all of slash is progressive; not all of slash is feminist; yet one cannot totally ignore the progressive potential of this exchange and the degree to which slash may be one of the few places in popular culture where questions of sexual identity can be explored outside of the polarization that increasingly surrounds this debate" (221).

6. Jenkins identifies fan culture as a site of anxiety for some critics and scholars, claiming that those "with little direct knowledge or emotional investment within the fan community have transformed fandom into a projection of their personal fears, anxieties, and fantasies about the dangers of mass culture" (6).

7. Willis notes that "it is only through [the] idea of *supplementation* . . . that fan fiction can be understood as 'filling in the gaps' in canon. For these gaps may only become visible—may only, indeed, *be* gaps—when the text is read from a position that refuses the illusion of continuity; and textual gaps are filled in according to an associative, not a deductive, logic" (158).

8. See Meyer and Wood for interviews with "emerging adults" about their relationship to *Glee*, including one with a participant who "labels the *Glee* narrative as a 'girls' show'" (443). For more on *Glee* fandom and convergence culture, see Wood and Baughman. Thanks to one of my anonymous readers for flagging the centrality of femslash to *Glee* fandom.

9. Coviello reminds his readers of an important quote from Stockton's *The Queer Child*: "Our futures grow sideways whenever they can't be envisioned as futures—due to forceful obstacles, forms of arrest, or our wish to be suspended in the amplitude of 'more,' as in our simply wanting more time, more pleasure, more leisure, more luxury, more destruction (as odd as that may sound)—just 'more'" (quoted in Coviello 76).

10. The controversial Netflix series *13 Reasons Why* (2017–2020), an adaptation of a YA novel by Jay Asher, has spawned impassioned debate about the potential effects of representing suicide in media for young people. One study links the show, which features an explicit suicide scene, to increases in teen suicide (see Niederkrotenthaler et al). In 2019, this scene was removed from the show. Debates similar to these have taken place surrounding the representation of sexual assault in fanfic. Jenkins writes, "Heated discussion surrounds works . . . which some fans charge romanticize rape and others insist allow them to work through the powerful emotions surrounding sexual violence in a less immediately threatening context" (220).

11. As the author herself writes in a footnote to chapter thirteen, "I know we have poor Dave hanging out there, but I just thought our boys needed a day for themselves."

12. Fairy tales are another example of what I am describing. We can think, for example, of queer/feminist revisionist tales seen in collections like Francesca Lia Block's *The Rose and the Beast* (2000), Emma Donoghue's *Kissing the Witch* (1997), and Angela Carter's *The Bloody Chamber and Other Stories* (2006). For more examples of such recursive fiction, what Hurley calls "writing back to children's literature" (126), see "The Perversions of Children's Literature."

Conclusion. Immaturity: Reflections on the "Great (Queer) YA Debate"

1. Thanks to Nat Hurley for indicating that Shepherd's article also bespeaks a number of anxieties surrounding the novel as commodity, the state of the publishing industry, celebrity culture, and the convergence of "high" and "low" culture.

2. Similarly, Karín Lesnik-Oberstein suggests that "the idea that it is somehow suspect to study children's literature in an academic context persists widely, both in the general media, in wider academia, and in some children's literature criticism itself" (1). Of course, the scholarly field of children's literature has grown significantly in the time since Clark and Lesnik-Oberstein's books were published, especially since queer childhood studies has become somewhat à la mode in academia. Clark herself concedes, "Now, at the turn of a new century, the positioning of children's literature seems to be entering a new phase. Thanks to literary criticism that has questioned the received canon, thanks to feminist and other criticism that has explored and celebrated the hitherto marginal, the academy may be becoming more willing to take children's literature seriously again" (76). Nonetheless, the circulation of articles like Shepherd's point to a persistent cultural uncertainty about the "seriousness" of children's literature and its relevance for adult readers, whether their interest is casual or academic.

3. I am grateful to Gwen for posing the question and for her generosity in our email conversation that followed the conference.

4. Queer theory and children's literature are also coming into contact in educational contexts. See, for example, Caitlin L. Ryan and Jill M. Hermann-Wilmarth's "Already on the Shelf: Queer Readings of Award-Winning Children's Literature" (2013), in which the authors "theorize a model of reading literature with children that helps a wide variety of children's literature texts become fruitful sites for opening up more inclusive conversations about gender and sexuality" (144). In particular, the authors look at "Sendak's (1963) *Where the Wild Things Are*, Woodson's (2001) *The Other Side*, DiCamillo's (2003) *Tale of Despereaux*, and Patterson's (1977) *Bridge to Terabithia*" (144).

5. The launch of New Adult Fiction initially earned a significant amount of media coverage, most of which is neatly curated by the "New Adult Fiction" Wikipedia page. See, for example, "'New Adult' Fiction Is Now an Official Literary Genre Because Marketers Want Us to Buy Things," published on 15 November 2012 by Katie Baker of *Jezebel*; and *Publisher Weekly*'s 14 December 2012 piece "New Adult: Needless Marketing-Speak or Valued Subgenre?" (both articles accessed 8 October 2014). Anecdotally, I first learned of this new genre when, in an Edmonton Chapters in March 2013, I stumbled upon a shelf of books with a sign that read, "New Adult Fiction: Take the emotional intensity of all your favourite teen titles, mix in the higher stakes of life as an adult, and you have what everyone is calling New Adult Fiction."

6. See, for example, Mark Medley's satirically titled *National Post* column "Ruth Graham Doesn't Go Far Enough: Adults and Kids Should Only Read Books Aimed Directly at Their Demographic" (11 June 2014); the entry "Is it OK to Read YA?" on the literary blog *The Anxiety of Authorship* (30 June 2014); Alyssa Rosenberg's "No, You Do Not Have to Be Ashamed of Reading Young Adult Fiction" in the *Washington Post* (6 June 2014); the "Should You Be Embarrassed to Read YA?" debate staged on the *Barnes & Noble Book Blog* (12 June 2014); the June 8, 2014, interview with Graham on NPR; Kat Kinsman's CNN piece "Don't Be Ashamed of Your YA Habit" (8 June 2014); and many, many others. An essay that echoes Graham's perspective—much less common than those who critique her—is John Patterson's

Guardian essay "The Maze Runner and the Blight of 'Young Adult' Movies," in which the author claims that "I was never much for what's now called young adult lit. . . . These days, young adult seems like the only genre that matters" (4 October 2014). All texts cited are available online and were last accessed on 14 July 2018.

Works Cited

"10 Ways to Boost Someone Else's PRIDE This Season." *It Gets Better Project*, 2018, itgetsbetter.org/initiatives/pride-boost-2018/. Accessed 14 June 2018.

Abate, Michelle Ann. "A Role for Children's Literature." *New York Times*, 26 December 2011, www.nytimes.com/roomfordebate/2010/12/26/the-dark-side-of-young-adult-fiction/a -role-for-childrens-literature. Accessed 18 June 2018.

Abate, Michelle Ann, and Kenneth Kidd, eds. *Over the Rainbow: Queer Children's and Young Adult Literature*. University of Michigan Press, 2011.

Abate, Michelle Ann, and Kenneth Kidd, eds. Introduction. Abate and Kidd, *Over the Rainbow*, pp. 1–11.

"About Our Global Movement." *It Gets Better Project*, 2018, itgetsbetter.org/about. Accessed 14 June 2018.

Ahmed, Sara. *The Cultural Politics of Emotion*. Routledge, 2004.

Alam, Rumaan. "Worth the Trip." *Los Angeles Review of Books*, 23 September 2014, lareviewofbooks.org/article/worth-trip/. Accessed 19 June 2018.

Alexander, Bryant Keith. *Performing Black Masculinity*. AltaMira, 2006.

Alexie, Sherman. "Why the Best Kids Books Are Written in Blood." *Wall Street Journal*, 9 June 2011, blogs.wsj.com/speakeasy/2011/06/09/why-the-best-kids-books-are-written -in-blood/. Accessed 18 June 2018.

"Am I Gay?" *Big Mouth*, season 1, episode 3. 29 September 2017. *Netflix*, www.netflix.com/ title/80117038.

Anable, Aubrey. *Playing with Feelings: Video Games and Affect*. University of Minnesota Press, 2018.

Anime Girl23. "It Gets Better: Jock, Glee Dork, Closet Bisexual." *FanFiction.net*, 15 November 2011, www.fanfiction.net/s/7553852/1/It-Gets-Better-Jock-Glee-Dork-Closet-Bisexual. Accessed 18 March 2014.

AWritersLife. "It Gets Better." *Archive of Our Own*, 5 October 2012, www.archiveofourown. org/works/529267/chapters/937740. Accessed 18 March 2014.

Babuscio, Jack. "Camp and the Gay Sensibility." *Queer Cinema: The Film Reader*, edited by Harry Benshoff and Sean Griffin. Routledge, 2004, pp. 121–136.

Baccolini, Raffaella. "'A Useful Knowledge of the Present Is Rooted in the Past': Memory and Historical Reconciliation in Ursula K. Le Guin's The Telling." *Dark Horizons: Science Fiction and the Dystopian Imagination*, edited by Raffaella Baccolini and Tom Moylan. Routledge, 2003, pp. 113–134.

Bacigalupi, Paolo. "Craving Truth-telling." *New York Times*, 17 December 2012, www.nytimes .com/roomfordebate/2010/12/26/the-dark-side-of-young-adult-fiction/craving-truth -telling. Accessed 18 June 2018.

Barnes, Sequoia. "'If You Don't Bring No Grits, Don't Come': Critiquing a Critique of Patrick Kelly, Golliwogs, and Camp as a Technique of Black Queer Expression." *Open Cultural Studies*, vol. 1, no. 1, 2017, pp. 678–689. https://doi.org/10.1515/culture-2017-0062.

Barnes, Tyrone. "Big Mouth: The Terror of Adolescence." *Geeks Under Grace*. 9 December 2017, www.geeksundergrace.com/tv/big-mouth/. Accessed 19 June 2019.

Basu, Balaka, Katherine R. Broad, and Carrie Hintz, eds. Introduction. *Contemporary Dystopian Fiction for Young Adults: Brave New Teenagers*. Routledge, 2013, pp. 1–15.

Baxter, Kent. *The Modern Age: Turn-of-the-Century American Culture and the Invention of Adolescence*. University of Alabama Press, 2008.

Bayard, Louis. "A Chorus of Ghosts Watches over David Levithan's 'Two Boys Kissing.'" *Los Angeles Times*, 20 August 2013, www.latimes.com/books/jacketcopy/la-ca-jc-david -levithan-20130901-story.html. Accessed 11 April 2019.

Beha, Christopher. "Henry James and the Great Y.A. Debate." *New Yorker*, 18 September 2014, www.newyorker.com/books/page-turner/henry-james-great-ya-debate. Accessed 18 June 2018.

Benshoff, Harry M. *Monsters in the Closet: Homosexuality and the Horror Film*. Manchester University Press, 1997.

Benshoff, Harry, and Sean Griffin, eds. *Queer Cinema: The Film Reader*. Routledge, 2004.

Benshoff, Harry M., and Sean Griffin. *America on Film: Representing Race, Class, Gender, and Sexuality at the Movies*. 2nd ed. Wiley-Blackwell, 2009. *Google Books*, books.google.ca/ books?id=8PwiBBLhwGEC. Accessed 25 July 2019.

Benshoff, Harry M., and Sean Griffin. *Queer Images: A History of Gay and Lesbian Film in America*. Rowman & Littlefield, 2006.

Berlant, Lauren, and Lee Edelman. *Sex, or the Unbearable*. Duke University Press, 2014.

Berlant, Lauren. "Slow Death (Sovereignty, Obesity, Lateral Agency)." *Critical Inquiry*, vol. 33, no. 4. University of Chicago Press, 2007, pp. 754–780.

Bernstein, Robin. "Children's Books, Dolls, and the Performance of Race; or, the Possibility of Children's Literature." *PMLA*, vol. 126, no. 1, 2011, pp. 160–169.

Bersani, Leo. "Is the Rectum a Grave?" *AIDS: Cultural Analysis, Cultural Activism*, edited by Douglas Crimp. MIT Press, 1989, pp. 197–222.

Blake, Meredith. "Netflix Animated Comedy 'Big Mouth' Provides a New Take on Adolescence." *Los Angeles Times*, 21 October 2018, www.latimes.com/entertainment/ tv/la-et-st-big-mouth-netflix-20181011-story.html. Accessed 19 June 2019.

Block, Francesca Lia. *The Rose and the Beast: Fairy Tales Retold*. HarperTeen, 2001.

Blumenreich, Megan, and Marjorie Siegel. "Innocent Victims, Fighter Cells, and White Uncles: A Discourse Analysis of Children's Books about AIDS." *Children's Literature in Education*, vol. 37, no. 1, 2006, pp. 81–110.

Bond, Ernest L., and Nancy L. Michelson. "Writing Harry's World: Children Co-authoring Hogwarts." *Critical Perspectives on Harry Potter*, 2nd ed., edited by Elizabeth E. Heilman. Routledge, 2009, pp. 309–327.

Boulton, Jim. "Hypercard." *100 Ideas that Changed the Web*. Laurence King, 2014, search. credoreference.com/content/entry/lkingideas/hypercard/0?institutionId=261. Accessed 8 April 2019.

Bradford, Clare. "Monsters: Monstrous Identities in Young Adult Romance." *(Re)Imagining the World: New Frontiers of Educational Research*, edited by Y. Wu et al. Springer-Verlag, 2013, pp. 115–125.

Brady, Hunter Adeline. "Finding Who I Am." Savage and Miller, pp. 142–144.

Breedlove, Lynn. "Haters Can't Hate Someone Who Loves Themselves, and If They Do, Who Cares." Savage and Miller, pp. 228–231.

Britzman, Deborah P. *After-Education: Anna Freud, Melanie Klein, and Psychoanalytic Histories of Learning*. SUNY Press, 2003.

Britzman, Deborah P. "Between Psychoanalysis and Pedagogy: Scenes of Rapprochement and Alienation." *Curriculum Inquiry*, vol. 43, no. 1, 2013, pp. 95–117.

Britzman, Deborah P. "Is There a Queer Pedagogy? Or, Stop Reading Straight." *Educational Theory*, vol. 45, no. 2, 1995, pp. 151–165.

Britzman, Deborah P. "Precocious Education." Talburt and Steinberg, *Thinking Queer: Sexuality, Culture, and Education*, pp. 33–59.

Britzman, Deborah P. "Queer Pedagogy and Its Strange Techniques." *Lost Subjects, Contested Objects: Toward a Psychoanalytic Inquiry of Learning*. SUNY Press, 1998, pp. 79–95.

Britzman, Deborah P. "The Very Thought." *The Very Thought of Education: Psychoanalysis and the Impossible Professions*. SUNY Press, 2009, pp. 1–26.

Brophy, Sarah. *Witnessing AIDS: Writing, Testimony, and the Work of Mourning*. University of Toronto Press, 2004.

Bruhm, Steven. "Nightmare on Sesame Street; or, The Self-Possessed Child." *Gothic Studies*, vol. 8, no. 2, 2006, pp. 98–113.

Bruhm, Steven, and Nat Hurley, eds. Introduction. *Curiouser: On the Queerness of Children*. University of Minnesota Press, 2004, pp. ix–xxxviii.

Bryson, Mary, and Suzanne de Castell. "Queer Pedagogy: Practice Makes Im/Perfect." *Canadian Journal of Education*, vol. 18, no. 3, 1993, pp. 285–305.

Butler, Judith. "Imitation and Gender Insubordination." *The Lesbian and Gay Studies Reader*, edited by Henry Abelove, Michèle Aina Barale, and David M. Halperin. Routledge, 1993, pp. 307–320.

Cage, Diana. "It Doesn't Get Better. You Get Stronger." *Velvetpark: Dyke Culture in Bloom*, Velvetpark Media, 2 October 2010, qa.velvetparkmedia.com/blogs/it-doesnt-get-better -you-get-stronger. Accessed 20 June 2012.

Cain, Sian. "YA Books on Death: Is Young Adult Fiction Becoming Too Dark?" *The Guardian*, 11 May 2014, www.theguardian.com/childrens-books-site/2014/may/11/ ya-books-on-death-is-young-adult-fiction-becoming-too-dark. Accessed 18 June 2018.

Campbell, Joseph. "'The Treatment for Stirrings': Dystopian Literature for Adolescents." *Blast, Corrupt, Dismantle, Erase: Contemporary North American Dystopian Literature*, edited by Brett Josef Grubisic, Gisèle M. Baxter, and Tara Lee. Wilfrid Laurier University Press, 2014, pp. 165–180.

Caper in the Castro. C. M. Ralph, 1989. *Internet Archive*, 20 December 2017, archive.org/ details/hypercard_caper-in-the-castro. Accessed 12 April 2019.

Carlson, David Lee, and Darla Linville. "The Social Importance of a Kiss: A Honnethian Reading of David Levithan's Young Adult Novel, *Two Boys Kissing*." *Discourse: Studies in the Cultural Politics of Education*, vol. 37, no. 6, 2016, pp. 887–901.

Cart, Michael. *Young Adult Literature: From Romance to Realism*, 3rd ed. American Library Association, 2016.

Cart, Michael, and Christine A. Jenkins. *The Heart Has Its Reasons: Young Adult Literature with Gay/Lesbian/Queer Content, 1969–2004*. Scarecrow Press, 2006.

Carter, Angela. *The Bloody Chamber and Other Stories*. Vintage, 2006.

Castiglia, Christopher, and Christopher Reed. *If Memory Serves: Gay Men, AIDS, and the Promise of the Queer Past*. University of Minnesota Press, 2011.

Cavanagh, Sheila L. *Sexing the Teacher: School Sex Scandals and Queer Pedagogies*. UBC Press, 2007.

Chaney, Jen. "*Big Mouth* Season 2 Is a Hilarious and Vital Portrait of Puberty." *Vulture*, 4 October 2018, www.vulture.com/2018/10/big-mouth-netflix-season-2-review.html. Accessed 11 June 2019.

charlieanne. "It Gets Better." *FanFiction.net*, 14 May 2011, www.fanfiction.net/s/6991905/1/. Accessed 14 July 2018.

Chevalier, Vincent, and Ian Bradley-Perrin. "Your Nostalgia Is Killing Me." *Postervirus*, 20 November 2013, postervirus.tumblr.com/post/67569099579/your-nostalgia-is-killing -me-vincent-chevalier. Accessed 22 April 2019.

Childs, Erica Chito. *Fade to Black and White: Interracial Images in Popular Culture*. Rowman & Littlefield, 2009.

Claeys, Gregory. "The Origins of Dystopia: Wells, Huxley and Orwell." *The Cambridge Companion to Utopian Literature*, edited by Gregory Claeys. Cambridge University Press, 2014, pp. 107–131.

Clark, Beverly Lyon. *Kiddie Lit: The Cultural Construction of Children's Literature in America*. Johns Hopkins University Press, 2003.

Cleto, Fabio S., ed. Introduction. *Camp: Queer Aesthetics and the Performing Subject*. University of Michigan Press, 1999, pp. 1–42.

Clough, Patricia Ticineto. Introduction. *The Affective Turn: Theorizing the Social*, edited by Patricia Ticineto Clough and Jean Halley. Duke University Press, 2007, pp. 1–33.

Cohan, Steven. *Incongruous Entertainment: Camp, Cultural Value, and the MGM Musical*. Duke University Press, 2005.

Cohen, Jeffrey Jerome. "Monster Culture (Seven Theses)." *Monster Theory: Reading Culture*, edited by Jeffrey J. Cohen, University of Minnesota Press, 1996, pp. 3–25.

Cooper, Charlotte. *Charlotte Cooper*. Facebook.com, 20 October 2010. Accessed 13 November 2010.

Cover, Rob. *Queer Youth Suicide, Culture and Identity: Unliveable Lives?* Ashgate, 2012.

Coviello, Peter M. "The Pistol in the Suitcase: Motive, Temporality, Queer Youth Suicide." *ESC: English Studies in Canada*, vol. 38, no. 3–4, 2012, pp. 63–81.

Crary, David. "Suicide Surge: Schools Confront Anti-Gay Bullying." *Life on NBCNews. com*. NBC News, 9 October 2010, www.nbcnews.com/id/39593311/ns/us_news-life/t/ suicidesurgeschools-confront-anti-gay-bullying/#.WoFcktJKiUk. Accessed 14 November 2012.

Creekmur, Corey K., and Alexander Doty, eds. Introduction. *Out in Culture: Gay, Lesbian, and Queer Essays on Popular Culture*. Duke University Press, 1995, pp. 1–11.

Crisp, Thomas. "From Romance to Magical Realism: Limits and Possibilities in Gay Adolescent Fiction." *Children's Literature in Education*, vol. 40, no. 4, 2009, pp. 333–348.

Crisp, Thomas. "The Trouble with Rainbow Boys." Abate and Kidd, *Over the Rainbow*, pp. 215–254.

Cross, Julie. "Frightening and Funny: Humour in Children's Gothic Fiction." *The Gothic in Children's Literature: Haunting the Borders*, edited by Anna Jackson, Karen Coats, and Roderick McGillis. Routledge, 2008, pp. 57–76.

"The Dangers, Values of Dark Teen Lit." NPR, 14 June 2011, www.npr. org/2011/06/14/137174977/the-dangers-values-of-dark-teen-lit. Accessed 18 June 2018.

Daring, A. Y. "This I Know for Sure." Savage and Miller, pp. 64–66.

"Dark Side of the Boob." *Big Mouth*, season 2, episode 8, 5 October 2018. www.netflix.com/title/80117038.

"The Dark Side of Young Adult Fiction." *New York Times*, 26 December 2010, www.nytimes.com/roomfordebate/2010/12/26/the-dark-side-of-young-adult-fiction. Accessed 18 June 2018.

Deloria, Philip J. *Playing Indian*. Yale University Press, 1998.

Denisoff, Dennis. *Aestheticism and Sexual Parody, 1840–1940*. Cambridge University Press, 2001.

"The Department of Puberty." *Big Mouth*, season 2, episode 10, 5 October 2018. www.netflix.com/title/80117038.

Derrick, Scott S. *Monumental Anxieties: Homoerotic Desire and Feminine Influence in 19th-Century U.S. Literature*. Rutgers University Press, 1997.

Detrick, Ben. "'Kids,' Then and Now." *New York Times*, 21 July 2015, www.nytimes.com/2015/07/23/fashion/kids-20th-anniversary-chloe-sevigny-rosario-dawson.html. Accessed 19 April 2019.

Donoghue, Emma. *Kissing the Witch: Old Tales in New Skins*. H. Hamilton, 1997.

Donovan, Francesca. "Netflix's Big Mouth Is Redefining How We Learn about Sex." *Unilad*, 8 November 2018, www.unilad.co.uk/featured/netflixs-big-mouth-redefining-sex-ed/. Accessed 10 June 2019.

Donovan, John. *I'll Get There. It Better Be Worth the Trip*. 1969. Flux, 2010.

Doty, Alexander. "My Beautiful Wickedness: The Wizard of Oz as Lesbian Fantasy." *Hop on Pop: The Politics and Pleasures of Popular Culture*, edited by Henry Jenkins, Tara McPherson, and Jane Shattuc. Duke University Press, 2002, pp. 138–157.

Duckels, Gabriel. "(Re)turning to AIDS in Queer Young Adult Fiction." *The Polyphony: Conversations Across the Medical Humanities*, 24 March 2020, thepolyphony.org/2020/03/24/returning-to-aids-in-queer-young-adult-fiction/. Accessed 15 May 2020.

Duggan, Lisa. "The New Homonormativity: The Sexual Politics of Neoliberalism." *Materializing Democracy: Toward a Revitalized Cultural Politics*, edited by Russ Castronovo and Dana D. Nelson. Duke University Press, 2002, pp. 188–194.

Dyer, Richard. *Only Entertainment*. Routledge, 2002.

Edelman, Lee. *No Future: Queer Theory and the Death Drive*. Duke University Press, 2004.

"Ejaculation." *Big Mouth*, season 1, episode 1, 29 September 2017, www.netflix.com/title/80117038.

Elliott-Smith, Darren. *Queer Horror Film and Television: Sexuality and Masculinity at the Margins*. I.B. Tauris, 2016.

"The End of Twerk." *Glee*, written by Ryan Murphy, Brad Falchuk, and Ian Brennan, directed by Wendy Stanzler. Fox Network, 14 November 2013.

"Engaging Your Community: Screenings and Book Readings." *It Gets Better Project*, 2018, itgetsbetter.org/lesson/screenings-readings/. Accessed 14 June 2018.

"Everybody Bleeds." *Big Mouth*, season 1, episode 2, 29 September 2017, www.netflix.com/title/80117038.

Felman, Shoshana. "Education and Crisis, or the Vicissitudes of Teaching." *Trauma: Explorations in Memory*, edited by Cathy Caruth. John Hopkins University Press, 1995, pp. 13–60.

Fields, Noah. "Slave Chains and Faggots and Camp . . . Oh My!" *Bluestockings Magazine*, 4 November 2015, bluestockingsmag.com/2015/11/04/slave-chains-and-faggots-and-camp-oh-my/. Accessed 13 July 2019.

for always forever. "It Gets Better." *FanFiction.net*, 12 May 2011, www.fanfiction.net/s/698 5975/1/It-Gets-Better. Accessed 18 March 2014.

Forman, Gayle. "Teens Crave Young Adult Books on Really Dark Topics (and That's OK)." *Time*, 6 February 2015, time.com/3697845/if-i-stay-gayle-forman-young-adult-i-was -here/. Accessed 18 June 2018.

Foucault, Michel. *The History of Sexuality, Volume 1: An Introduction*. 1978. Translated by Robert Hurley. Vintage Books, 1990.

Fox, Rose. "Authors Say Agents Try to 'Straighten' Gay Characters in YA." *Genreville*, 12 September 2011. www.publishersweekly.com. Accessed 14 November 2012.

Fox, Rose. "Riposte and Counter-riposte." *Genreville*, 15 September 2011, www.publishers weekly.com. Accessed 14 November 2012.

Fraustino, Lisa Rowe. "The Comfort of Darkness." *New York Times*, 21 December 2011, www.nytimes.com/roomfordebate/2010/12/26/the-dark-side-of-young-adult-fiction/ the-comfort-of-darkness. Accessed 18 June 2018.

Freire, Paulo. *Pedagogy of Indignation*. Paradigm Publishers, 2004.

Freire, Paulo. *Teachers as Cultural Workers: Letters to Those Who Dare Teach*. Westview Press, 1998.

Freud, Sigmund. *Inhibitions, Symptoms, and Anxiety*. 1926. Translated by Alix Strachey. Martino Fine Books, 2013.

Freud, Sigmund. "Infantile Sexuality." *Three Essays on the Theory of Sexuality*. 1905. Translated by James Strachey. BasicBooks, 1975.

Freud, Sigmund. *The Interpretation of Dreams*. 1900. Translated by James Strachey. BasicBooks, 2010.

Freud, Sigmund. *The Joke and Its Relation to the Unconscious*. 1905. Translated by Joyce Crick. Penguin, 2003.

Freud, Sigmund. *Totem and Taboo: Some Points of Agreement between the Mental Lives of Savages and Neurotics*. 1913. Translated by James Strachey. Routledge, 2001.

"Full Series Rankings for the 2009–2010 Broadcast Season." *Deadline Hollywood*, 27 May 2010. deadline.com/2010/05/full-series-rankings-for-the-2009–10-broadcast-season -44277/#more-44277=*. Accessed 18 June 2018.

Fuoss, Kirk. "A Portrait of the Adolescent as a Young Gay." *Queer Words, Queer Images: Communication and the Construction of Homosexuality*, edited by Ronald Jeffrey Ringer. NYU Press, 1994, pp. 159–74.

Gaudet, Brinae Lois. "You Are a Rubber Band, My Friend." Savage and Miller, *It Gets Better*, pp. 27–29.

Gemmi999. "It Gets Better." *Archive of Our Own*, 1 April 2011, www.archiveofourown.org/ works/211392. Accessed 18 March 2014.

Gilbert, Jen. "Histories of Misery: It Gets Better and the Promise of Pedagogy." *Sexuality in School: The Limits of Education*. University of Minnesota Press, 2014, pp. 45–61.

Gill-Peterson, Jules (published as Gill-Peterson, Julian). *Histories of the Transgender Child*. University of Minnesota Press, 2018.

"Girls Are Horny Too." *Big Mouth*, season 1, episode 5, 29 September 2017, www.netflix.com/ title/80117038.

Goldman, Linda. *Coming Out, Coming In: Nurturing the Well-Being and Inclusion of Gay Youth in Mainstream Society*. Routledge, 2008.

Gordon, Angus. "Turning Back: Adolescence, Narrative, and Queer Theory." *GLQ*, vol. 5, no. 1. Duke University Press, 1999, pp. 1–24.

Gorman, Bill. "2010–11 Season Broadcast Primetime Show Viewership Averages." *TV by the Numbers*, 20 June 2011, tvbythenumbers.zap2it.com/1/2010–11-season-broadcast -primetime-show-viewership-averages/94407/. Accessed 18 June 2018.

Gorman, Bill. "Complete List of 2011–12 Season TV Show Viewership." *TV by the Numbers*, 25 May 2012, tvbythenumbers.zap2it.com/1/complete-list-of-2011–12-season-tv-show -viewership-sunday-night-football-tops-followed-by-american-idol-ncis-dancing-with -the-stars/135785/. Accessed 18 June 2018.

Graham, Ruth. "Against YA: Yes, Adults Should Be Embarrassed to Read Young Adult Books." *Slate Book Review*, 5 June 2014, www.slate.com/articles/arts/books/2014/06/against_ya_ adults_should_be_embarrassed_to_read_children_s_books.html. Accessed 18 June 2018.

Griffin, Sean. *Tinker Belles and Evil Queens: The Walt Disney Company from the Inside Out.* NYU Press, 2000.

Gross, Claire. "What Makes a Good YA Coming-Out Novel?" *The Horn Book*, 26 March 2013, https://www.hbook.com/2013/03/choosing-books/what-makes-a-good-ya-coming-out -novel/. Accessed 27 January 2014.

Gross, Melissa. "What Do Young Adult Novels Say About HIV/AIDS?." *Library Quarterly: Information, Community, Policy*, vol. 68, no. 1, 1998, pp. 1–32.

Gross, Melissa, Annette Goldsmith, and Debi Carruth. "What Do Young Adult Novels Say about HIV/AIDS? A Second Look." *Library Quarterly: Information, Community, Policy*, vol. 78, no. 4, 2008, pp. 397–418.

Gross, Melissa, Debi Carruth, and Annette Y. Goldsmith. "How Can I Tell You This? The Developing Discourse on HIV/AIDS in Young Adult Novels." *New Review of Children's Literature and Librarianship*, vol. 15, pp. 67–87, 2009.

Gross, Melissa, Annette Y. Goldsmith, and Debi Carruth. *HIV/AIDS in Young Adult Novels: An Annotated Bibliography*. Scarecrow Press, 2010.

Grosz, Elizabeth. "Animal Sex: Libido as Desire and Death." *Sexy Bodies: The Strange Carnalities of Feminism*, edited by Elizabeth Grosz and Elspeth Probyn. Routledge, 1995, pp. 278–99.

Gubar, Marah. "On Not Defining Children's Literature." *PMLA*, vol. 126, no. 1, 2011, pp. 209–216.

Gurdon, Meghan Cox. "Darkness Too Visible." *Wall Street Journal*, 4 June 2011, www.wsj .com/articles/SB10001424052702303657040457637622592697038. Accessed 18 June 2018.

Gorman, Bill. "My 'Reprehensible' Take on Teen Literature; Raise Questions about Self-Mutilation and Incest as a Young-Adult Theme and All Hell Breaks Loose." *Wall Street Journal*, 28 June 2011. www.wsj.com/articles/SB100014240527023043144045764115812893119732. Accessed 5 April 2017.

Halberstam, Jack (published as Halberstam, Judith). *In a Queer Time and Place: Transgender Bodies, Subcultural Lives*. NYU Press, 2005.

Halberstam, Jack (published as Halberstam, Judith). *The Queer Art of Failure*. Duke University Press, 2011.

Halberstam, Jack. "Queer Gaming: Gaming, Hacking, and Going Turbo." *Queer Game Studies*, edited by Bonnie Ruberg and Adrienne Shaw. University of Minnesota Press, 2017, pp. 187–200.

Hall, G. Stanley. *Adolescence*. D. Appleton and Company, 1904.

Hanckel, Francis, and John Cunningham. "Can Young Gays Find Happiness in YA Books?" *Wilson Library Bulletin*, vol. 50, no. 7, 1976, pp. 528–534.

Harris, Lydia. "'Two Boys Kissing' by David Levithan." *Lambda Literary*, 8 September 2014, www.lambdaliterary.org/reviews/09/08/two-boys-kissing-by-david-levithan/. Accessed 11 April 2019.

Hartinger, Brent. "We Got There. It Was Worth the Trip." *I'll Get There. It Better Be Worth the Trip: 40th Anniversary Edition*, Flux, 2010, pp. 203–213.

Hawbaker, K. T. "'I Don't Wear Deodorant and Only Take Bubble Baths': Why 'Big Mouth' Is the Feminist Cartoon I've Been Waiting For." *Chicago Tribune*, 22 October 2018, www .chicagotribune.com/entertainment/ct-ent-big-mouth-connie-hormone-monster -feminism-1024-story.html. Accessed 10 June 2019.

Hayes, Darren. "Perfect, Just the Way You Are." Savage and Miller, *It Gets Better*, pp. 151–152.

"The Head Push." *Big Mouth*, season 1, episode 8, 29 September 2017. www.netflix.com/ title/80117038.

Healy, Mark. "Nick Kroll's (Pre)Teen Spirit." *Rolling Stone*, 21 December 2018, www.rolling stone.com/tv/tv-features/nick-kroll-big-mouth-interview-771741/. Accessed 10 June 2019.

Hellekson, Karen, and Kristina Busse, eds. Introduction. *Fan Fiction and Fan Communities in the Age of the Internet: New Essays*. McFarland & Company, 2006.

Hilton, Mary, and Maria Nikolajeva, eds. "Introduction: Time of Turmoil." *Contemporary Adolescent Literature and Culture: The Emergent Adult*. Ashgate, 2012, pp. 1–16.

Hilton, Perez. "America In CRISIS! A 3rd Teenage Boy Dies This Week! 5th Death From Suicide in Less Than Three Weeks!!!" *Perezhilton.com*, 30 September 2010, www .perezhilton.com/2010-09-30-suicide_crisis_in_america#.WoFt1NJKiUk. Accessed 14 November 2012.

Hintz, Carrie, and Eric L. Tribunella. "Genders and Sexualities." *Reading Children's Literature: A Critical Introduction (Second Edition)*, edited by Carrie Hintz and Eric L. Tribunella. Broadview Press, 2019, pp. 433–469.

Hirsch, Corinne. "Isabelle Holland: Realism and Its Evasions in *The Man Without a Face*." *Children's Literature in Education*, vol. 10, no. 1, 1979, pp. 25–34.

"HIV and Youth." *Centers for Disease Control and Prevention*, 10 April 2019, www.cdc.gov/ hiv/group/age/youth/index.html. Accessed 10 April 2019.

Hoban, Stephen. "The Better of the 'It Gets Better' Parodies." *Splitsider*, 19 November 2010, John Shankman/The Awl. Accessed 30 June 2012.

Holland, Isabelle. *The Man Without a Face*. J. B. Lippincott Company, 1972.

Holmes, Dave. "It Gets Better Because You're a Little Different." Savage and Miller, *It Gets Better*, pp. 189–191.

Holmes, Linda. "Seeing Teenagers As We Wish They Were: The Debate Over YA Fiction." NPR, 6 June 2011, www.npr.org/sections/monkeysee/2011/06/06/137005354/seeing -teenagers-as-we-wish-they-were-the-debate-over-ya-fiction. Accessed 18 June 2018.

Hong, Jun Sung, Dorothy L. Espelage, and Michael J. Kral. "Understanding Suicide among Sexual Minority Youth in America: An Ecological Systems Analysis." *Journal of Adolescence*, vol. 34, no. 5, 2011, pp. 885–894.

Hong, Jun Sung, and James Garbarino. "Risk and Protective Factors for Homophobic Bullying in Schools: An Application of the Social-Ecological Framework." *Educational Psychology Review*, vol. 24, no. 2, 2012, pp. 271–285.

hooks, bell. *Teaching Community: A Pedagogy of Hope*. Routledge, 2003.

hooks, bell. *We Real Cool: Black Men and Masculinity*. Routledge, 2004.

Horne, Jackie C. "Pulled in Opposite Directions: David Levithan's TWO BOYS KISSING." *Romance Novels for Feminists*, 10 December 2013, romancenovelsforfeminists.blogspot .com/2013/12/pulled-in-opposite-directions-david.html. Accessed 11 April. 2019.

Horning, Kathleen T. "Taking the Trip with Davy and Altschuler, and What Happened Along the Way." *I'll Get There. It Better Be Worth the Trip: 40th Anniversary Edition*. Flux, 2010, pp. 221–228.

Hunt, Peter. *Criticism, Theory, and Children's Literature*. 2nd ed. Blackwell, 1995.

Hurley, Nat. "Childhood and Its Discontents: An Introduction." *ESC: English Studies in Canada*, vol. 38, no. 3–4, 2012, pp. 1–24.

Hurley, Nat (published as Hurley, Natasha). *Circulating Queerness: Before the Gay and Lesbian Novel*. University of Minnesota Press, 2018.

Hurley, Nat. "The Perversions of Children's Literature." *Jeunesse: Young People, Texts, Cultures*, vol. 3, no. 2, 2011, pp. 118–132.

Hutton, Rebecca. "Boy Meets Music: Affective and Ideological Engagements in David Levithan's 'Boy Meets Boy,' Love Is the Higher Law,' and 'Two Boys Kissing.'" *Papers: Explorations into Children's Literature*, vol. 23, no. 2, 2015, pp. 21–37.

Huyck, David, and Sarah Park Dahlen. "Picture This: Diversity in Children's Books 2018 Infographic." *sarahpark.com blog*, 19 June 2019, readingspark.wordpress.com/2019/06/19/picture-this-diversity-in-childrens-books-2018-infographic/. Accessed 25 May 2020.

Ikard, David. *Lovable Racists, Magical Negroes, and White Messiahs*. University of Chicago Press, 2017.

"Is Young-Adult Fiction Intolerant of Gay Characters?" *Q*. CBC/Radio-Canada, Toronto, 28 September 2011.

"It Gets Better w/ American Eagle Outfitters!" *It Gets Better Project*, 2018. itgetsbetter.org/initiatives/aeo-pride/. Accessed 14 June 2018.

"It Gets Betterish Is a Webseries Well Worth Watching." *Jezebel*, 1 March 2012, jezebel.com/5889755/it-gets-betterish-is-a-webseries-well-worth-watching. Accessed 29 June 2012.

"'It Gets Bigger': Parody Of 'It Gets Better' Tells Boys That It Will Grow." *Huff Post Comedy*, 13 April 2012. www.huffingtonpost.com/2012/04/13/it-gets-bigger-parody-video_n_1423901.html. Accessed 30 June 2012.

Jackson, Anna, Karen Coats, and Roderick McGillis, eds. Introduction. *The Gothic in Children's Literature: Haunting the Borders*. Routledge, 2008, pp. 1–14.

Jae-Jones, S. "St. Martin's New Adult Contest." *Uncreated Conscience*, 9 November 2009, www.sjaejones.com. Accessed 8 October 2014.

Jagose, Annamarie. *Queer Theory: An Introduction*. NYU Press, 1996.

Jameson, Fredric. "Magical Narratives: On the Dialectical Use of Genre Criticism." *The Political Unconscious: Narrative as a Socially Symbolic Act*. Cornell University Press, 1982, pp. 103–150.

Jenkins, Christine. "Young Adult Novels with Gay/Lesbian Characters and Themes, 1969–92: A Historical Reading of Content, Gender, and Narrative Distance." Abate and Kidd, *Over the Rainbow*, pp. 147–163.

Jenkins, Christine A., and Michael Cart. *Representing the Rainbow in Young Adult Literature: LGBTQ+ Content since 1969*. Rowman & Littlefield, 2018.

Jenkins, Henry. *Textual Poachers: Television Fans and Participatory Culture*. 1992. Routledge, 2013.

Jenkins, Henry, and Suzanne Scott. "Textual Poachers, Twenty Years Later: A Conversation between Henry Jenkins and Suzanne Scott." *Textual Poachers: Television Fans and Participatory Culture*. Routledge, 2013, pp. vii–l.

Johnson, Maureen. "Yes, Teen Fiction Can Be Dark—but It Shows Teenagers They Aren't Alone." *The Guardian*, 8 June 2011, www.theguardian.com/commentisfree/2011/jun/08/teen-fiction-dark-young-adult. Accessed 18 June 2018.

Juhasz, Alexandra, and Ted Kerr. "Home Video Returns: Media Ecologies of the Past of HIV/AIDS." *Cineaste*, vol. 34, no. 3, 2014, www.cineaste.com/summer2014/home-video-returns-media-ecologies-of-the-past-of-hiv-aids. Accessed 15 April 2019.

Juul, Jesper. *The Art of Failure: An Essay on the Pain of Playing Video Games*. MIT Press, 2013.

Kertzer, Adrienne. *My Mother's Voice: Children, Literature, and the Holocaust*. Broadview Press, 2002.

Kidd, Kenneth B. "'A Case History of Us All': The Adolescent Novel Before and After Salinger." *Freud in Oz: At the Intersections of Psychoanalysis and Children's Literature*. University of Minnesota Press, 2011, pp. 139–180.

Kidd, Kenneth B. "Introduction: Lesbian/Gay Literature for Children and Young Adults." *Children's Literature Association Quarterly*, vol. 23, no. 3, 1998, pp. 114–119.

Kidd, Kenneth B. *Making American Boys: Boyology and the Feral Tale*. University of Minnesota Press, 2004.

Kidd, Kenneth B. "Queer Theory's Child and Children's Literature Studies." *PMLA*, vol. 126, no. 1, 2011, pp. 182–188.

Kidd, Kenneth B., and Derritt Mason, eds. Introduction. *Queer as Camp: Essays on Summer, Style, and Sexuality*. Fordham University Press, 2019, pp. 1–24.

KlaineForeverLover07. "It Gets Better." FanFiction.net, 26 March 2013, url no longer available. Accessed 18 March 2014.

Kokkola, Lydia. *Fictions of Adolescent Carnality: Sexy Sinners and Delinquent Deviants*. John Benjamins Publishing Company, 2013.

Kristeva, Julia. "The Adolescent Novel." *New Maladies of the Soul*, translated by Ross Mitchell Guberman. Columbia University Press, 1995, pp. 135–153.

Kristeva, Julia. *Powers of Horror: An Essay on Abjection*, translated by Leon Roudiez. Columbia University Press, 1984.

Kumashiro, Kevin. *Troubling Education: Queer Activism and Antioppressive Pedagogy*. RoutledgeFalmer, 2002.

Kunze, Peter C. "Didactic Monstrosity and Postmodern Revisionism in Contemporary Children's Films." *Reading in the Dark: Horror in Children's Literature and Culture*, edited by Jessica R. McCort. University Press of Mississippi, 2016, pp. 147–164.

Kustritz, Anne. "Slashing the Romance Narrative." *Journal of American Culture*, vol. 26, no. 3, 2003, pp. 371–384.

Kyra5972. "It Gets Better." *FanFiction.net*, 22 October 2010, www.fanfiction.net/s/6418408/1/ It-Gets-Better. Accessed 18 March 2014.

Lacan, Jacques. *Anxiety*, edited by Jacques-Alain Miller, translated by A. R. Price. Polity, 2014.

Leshnoff, Jessica. "My Own Worst Enemy." Savage and Miller, *It Gets Better*, pp. 248–253.

Lesnik-Oberstein, Karín. "Introduction. Children's Literature: New Approaches." *Children's Literature: New Approaches*, edited by Karín Lesnik-Oberstein. Palgrave MacMillan, 2004, pp. 1–20.

Lester, Catherine. "The Children's Horror Film: Characterizing an 'Impossible' Subgenre." *Velvet Light Trap*, no. 78, 2016, pp. 22–37.

Lester, Catherine. "The Subversive Horror of Fantasy and Animation." *Fantasy/Animation*, 16 July 2018, www.fantasy-animation.org/blog/2018/7/16/the-subversive-horror-of -fantasy-and-animation?rq=coraline. Accessed 25 July 2019.

Levine, Judith. *Harmful to Minors: The Perils of Protecting Children from Sex*. University of Minnesota Press, 2002.

Levithan, David. *Boy Meets Boy*. Alfred A. Knopf, 2003.

"LGBT Youth." *Centers for Disease Control and Prevention*, 21 June 2017, www.cdc.gov/lgbt health/youth.htm. Accessed 14 July 2017.

Linné, Rob. "Choosing Alternatives to the Well of Loneliness." Talburt and Steinberg, *Thinking Queer: Sexuality, Culture, and Education*, pp. 201–213.

Linville, Darla, and David Lee Carlson, eds. *Beyond Borders: Queer Eros and Ethos (Ethics) in LGBTQ Young Adult Literature*. Peter Lang, 2016.

Lipscomb, Robert. "Failure Reconnaissance: The Virtual Problem of the It Gets Better Project." *Queer Studies in Media & Popular Culture*, vol. 2, no. 3, 2017, pp. 353–364.

Lo, Malinda. "A Decade of LGBTQ YA Since Ash." *Malinda Lo*, 14 May 2019, www.malindalo.com/blog/2019/3/18/a-decade-of-lgbtq-ya-since-ash. Accessed 27 July 2019.

Lo, Malinda. "LGBTQ YA by the Numbers: 2015–16." *Malinda Lo*, 12 October 2017, www.malindalo.com/blog/2017/10/12/lgbtq-ya-by-the-numbers-2015–16. Accessed 15 May 2018.

Lorimor, Stephen D. "It Got Better." Savage and Miller, *It Gets Better*, p. 239.

Love, Heather. *Feeling Backward: Loss and the Politics of Queer History*. Harvard University Press, 2007.

Mahan, Krissy. "Rockin' the Flannel Shirt." Savage and Miller, *It Gets Better*, pp. 71–73.

Mallan, Kerry, and Roderick McGillis. "Between a Frock and a Hard Place: Camp Aesthetics and Children's Culture." *Canadian Review of American Studies*, vol. 35, no. 1, 2005, pp. 1–19.

"The Man Without a Face by Isabelle Holland." *Kirkus Reviews*, 29 March 1972, www.kirkusreviews.com/book-reviews/isabelle-holland-4/the-man-without-a-face/. Accessed 10 January 2014.

Mason, Derritt. "The Earnest Elfin Dream Gay." *Public Books*, 9 November 2018, www.publicbooks.org/the-earnest-elfin-dream-gay/. Accessed 11 November 2019.

Massumi, Brian, with Mary Zournazi. "Navigating Movements." *Hope: New Philosophies for Change*, edited by Mary Zournazi. Routledge, 2003, pp. 210–243.

Mastro, Joseph Odysseus. "A 'Better' Evolution." Savage and Miller, *It Gets Better*, pp. 208–210.

Matos, Angel Daniel. "Queer Consciousness/Community in David Levithan's *Two Boys Kissing*: 'One the Other Never Leaving.'" *Gendered Identities: Critical Readings of Gender in Children's and Young Adult Literature*, edited by Tricia Clasen and Holly Hassel. Routledge, 2016, pp. 59–74.

Matos, Angel Daniel, and Jon Michael Wargo. "Editors' Introduction: Queer Futurities in Youth Literature, Media and Culture." *Research on Diversity in Youth Literature*, vol. 2, no. 1, 2019, pp. 1–17. sophia.stkate.edu/rdyl/vol2/iss1/1/.

McCort, Jessica R., ed. Introduction. *Reading in the Dark: Horror in Children's Literature and Culture*. University Press of Mississippi, 2016, pp. 3–36.

McKinley, Jesse. "Suicides Put Light on Pressures of Gay Teenagers." *New York Times*, 3 October 2010, www.nytimes.com/2010/10/04/us/04suicide.html. Accessed 29 June 2012.

McRuer, Robert. "Reading and Writing 'Immunity': Children and the Anti-Body." Abate and Kidd, *Over the Rainbow*, pp. 183–200.

Mead, Margaret. *Coming of Age in Samoa: A Psychological Study of Primitive Youth for Western Civilization*. 1928. HarperCollins, 2001.

Medovoi, Leerom. *Rebels: Youth and the Cold War Origins of Identity*. Duke University Press, 2005.

Meyer, Michaela D. E., and Megan M. Wood. "Sexuality and Teen Television: Emerging Adults Respond to Representations of Queer Identity on *Glee*." *Sexuality and Culture*, vol. 17, 2013, pp. 434–448.

Meyer, Moe. "Reclaiming the Discourse of Camp." *Queer Cinema: The Film Reader*, edited by
Harry Benshoff and Sean Griffin. Routledge, 2004, pp. 137–150.

Michael, John. *Anxious Intellects: Academic Professionals, Public Intellectuals, and
Enlightenment Values*. Duke University Press, 2000.

Miller, Laura. "*The Fault in Our Stars* Has Been Unfairly Bashed by Critics Who Don't
Understand It." *Salon*, 7 June 2014, www.salon.com/2014/06/06/the_fault_in_our_stars_
has_been_unfairly_bashed_by_critics_who_dont_understand_it/. Accessed 18 June 2018.

Moylan, Brian. "A Parody for Everyone Who Bullies Gays: It Gets Worse." *Gawker*, 11 October
2010. gawker.com/5661326/a-parody-for-everyone-who-bullies-gays-it-gets-worse.
Accessed 30 June 2012.

Muñoz, José Esteban. *Cruising Utopia: The Then and There of Queer Futurity*. NYU Press, 2009.

"My Furry Valentine." *Big Mouth*, special episode, 8 February. 2019, www.netflix.com/
title/80117038.

Neale, Steve. "Questions of Genre." *Screen*, vol. 31, no. 1, 1990, pp. 45–66.

"Negative Space." *OED Online*. Oxford University Press, June 2018, www.oed.com/view/
Entry/125837. Accessed 14 July 2018.

Nel, Philip, and Lissa Paul, eds. Introduction. *Keywords for Children's Literature*. NYU Press,
2011.

Newman, Scarlett. "A Deep Dive into Black Culture and Camp." *Teen Vogue*, 3 May 2019,
www.teenvogue.com/story/black-culture-and-camp. Accessed 13 July 2019.

"New Study: 55% of YA Books Bought by Adults." *Publishers Weekly*, 13 September
2012, www.publishersweekly.com/pw/by-topic/childrens/childrens-industry-news/
article/53937-new-study-55-of-ya-books-bought-by-adults.html. Accessed 18 June 2018.

Nguyên, Ann Thúy, and Maya Pendleton. "Recognizing Race in Language: Why We
Capitalize 'Black' and 'White.'" *Center for the Study of Social Policy*, 23 March 2020,
cssp.org/2020/03/recognizing-race-in-language-why-we-capitalize-black-and-white/.
Accessed 25 May 2020.

Niederkrotenthaler, Thomas, et al. "Association of Increased Youth Suicides in the United
States with the Release of *13 Reasons Why*." *JAMA Psychiatry*, 29 May 2019, doi:10.1001/
jamapsychiatry.2019.0922. Accessed 18 July 2019.

Nyong'o, Tavia. "School Daze." *Bully Bloggers*, 30 September 2010, www.bullybloggers.word
press.com/2010/09/30/school-daze/. Accessed 20 April 2011.

Obama, Barack. "A Message from President Barack Obama." Savage and Miller, *It Gets Better*,
pp. 9–10.

O'Quinn, Elaine J. "Vampires, Changelings, and Radical Mutant Teens: What the Demons,
Freaks, and Other Abominations of Young Adult Literature Can Teach Us about Youth."
The ALAN Review, vol. 31, no. 3, 2004, pp. 50–56.

Parini, Jay. "Feeling 'Gamed.'" *New York Times*, 21 December 2011, www.nytimes.com/
roomfordebate/2010/12/26/the-dark-side-of-young-adult-fiction/teenagers-turn-to
-books-to-get-away-from-the-system. Accessed 5 April 2017.

Patterson, Troy. "The Extreme Puberty of Nick Kroll's 'Big Mouth.'" *New Yorker*, 17 November
2017, www.newyorker.com/culture/culture-desk/the-pre-teen-spirit-of-nick-krolls-big
-mouth. Accessed 27 May 2019.

Pearson, Jordan. "You Can Now Play the First LGBTQ Computer Game, for the First Time."
Vice, 20 December 2017, motherboard.vice.com/en_us/article/ne4nzz/play-the-first
-lgbtq-computer-game-for-the-first-time-caper-in-the-castro. Accessed 12 April 2019.

Penley, Constance. *NASA/Trek: Popular Science and Sex in America*. Verso, 1997.

Pharr, Robert Reid. *Black Gay Man: Essays*. NYU Press, 2000.

Phillips, Adam. *On Kissing, Tickling, and Being Bored: Psychoanalytic Essays on the Unexamined Life*. Harvard University Press, 1993.

"Pillow Talk." *Big Mouth*, season 1, episode 6, 29 September 2017, www.netflix.com/title/80117038.

"The Planned Parenthood Show." *Big Mouth*, season 2, episode 5, 5 October 2018, www.netflix.com/title/80117038.

"The Pornscape." *Big Mouth*, season 1, episode 10, 29 September 2017, www.netflix.com/title/80117038.

Praetorius, Dean. "Jamey Rodemeyer, 14-Year-Old Boy, Commits Suicide After Gay Bullying, Parents Carry On Message." *Huff Post Parents*, 20 September 2011, www.huffingtonpost.ca/entry/jamey-rodemeyer-suicide-gay-bullying_n_972023. Accessed 29 June 2012.

Przybylo, Ela. "Growing into Asexuality: The Queer Erotics of Childhood." *Asexual Erotics: Intimate Readings of Compulsory Sexuality*. Ohio State University Press, 2019, pp. 89–111.

Puar, Jasbir. "In the Wake of It Gets Better." *The Guardian Opinion*, 16 November 2010, www.theguardian.com/commentisfree/cifamerica/2010/nov/16/wake-it-gets-better-campaign. Accessed 20 April 2011.

Puar, Jasbir. "The Cost of Getting Better: Ecologies of Race, Sex, and Disability." *The Subtle Racializations of Sexuality Lecture Series 2010–12*, ICI Berlin, Germany, 7 June 2011. www.ici-berlin.org/events/jasbir-puar-the-cost-of-getting-better/. Accessed 28 May 2012.

Puck Was Here. "[LET'S SOLVE] Caper in the Castro [[Earth's first Queer Videogame!!]]." *YouTube*, 10 January 2018. www.youtube.com/watch?v=Gj29TB9Y1VE. Accessed 19 April 2019.

Pugh, Tison. *Innocence, Heterosexuality, and the Queerness of Children's Literature*. Routledge, 2011.

Pugh, Tison. "'There lived in the Land of Oz two queerly made men': Queer Utopianism and Antisocial Eroticism in L. Frank Baum's *Oz* Series." Abate and Kidd, *Over the Rainbow*, pp. 87–110.

Rasmussen, Mary Louise, Eric Rofes, and Susan Talburt, eds. *Youth and Sexualities: Pleasure, Subversion, and Insubordination in and out of Schools*. Palgrave Macmillan, 2004.

"Raymond Chase Commits Suicide, Fifth Gay Youth To Take Life In Three Weeks." *Huff Post College*, 1 October 2010, www.huffingtonpost.com/2010/10/01/raymond-chase-suicide_n_746989.html. Accessed 29 June 2012.

"Repression." *OED Online*. Oxford University Press, June 2018, www.oed.com/view/Entry/163030. Accessed 14 July 2018.

"Requiem for a Wet Dream." *Big Mouth*, season 1, episode 7, 29 September 2017, www.netflix.com/title/80117038.

Rice, Anne. *Anne Rice*. Facebook.com, 24 February 2014, www.facebook.com/annericefanpage/. Accessed 25 February. 2014.

Rivera, Gabrielle. "Getting Stronger and Staying Alive." Savage and Miller, *It Gets Better*, pp. 45–47.

Robinson, Laura. "Queerness and Children's Literature: Embracing the Negative." *Bookbird: A Journal of International Children's Literature*, vol. 52, no. 1, 2014, pp. v–x.

Rofes, Eric. "Martyr-Target-Victim: Interrogating Narratives of Persecution and Suffering among Queer Youth." Rasmussen, et al., *Youth and Sexualities*, pp. 41–62.

Rose, Jacqueline. *The Case of Peter Pan, or, the Impossibility of Children's Fiction*. 1984. University of Pennsylvania Press, 1993.

Ruberg, Bonnie. "The Arts of Failure: Jack Halberstam in Conversation with Jesper Juul." *Queer Game Studies*, edited by Bonnie Ruberg and Adrienne Shaw. University of Minnesota Press, 2017, pp. 201–210.

Ryan, Caitlin L., and Jill M. Hermann-Wilmarth. "Already on the Shelf: Queer Readings of Award-Winning Children's Literature." *Journal of Literacy Research*, vol. 45, no. 2, 2013, pp. 142–172.

Salerno, Steve. "The Unbearable Darkness of Young Adult Literature." *Wall Street Journal*, 28 August 2018, www.wsj.com/articles/the-unbearable-darkness-of-young-adult-litera ture-1535495594. Accessed 12 July 2019.

Sanchez, Alex, and Lawrence Sipe. "A Conversation with Alex Sanchez and Lawrence Sipe." *Children's Literature in Education*, vol. 39, no. 4, 2008, pp. 263–268.

Sánchez-Eppler, Karen. "Marks of Possession: Methods for an Impossible Subject." *PMLA*, vol. 126, no. 1, 2011, pp. 151–159.

Savage, Dan. Introduction. *It Gets Better: Coming Out, Overcoming Bullying, and Creating a Life Worth Living*, edited by Dan Savage and Terry Miller. Dutton, 2011.

Savage, Dan, and Terry Miller, eds. *It Gets Better: Coming Out, Overcoming Bullying, and Creating a Life Worth Living*. Dutton, 2011.

Savage, Jon. *Teenage: The Prehistory of Youth Culture, 1875–1945*. Penguin, 2008.

Savin-Williams, Ritch. *The New Gay Teenager*. Harvard University Press, 2005.

Scahill, Andrew. *The Revolting Child in Horror Cinema: Youth Rebellion and Queer Spectatorship*. Palgrave Macmillan, 2015.

Schacker, Jennifer. "Unruly Tales: Ideology, Anxiety, and the Regulation of Genre." *Journal of American Folklore*, vol. 120, no. 478, 2007, pp. 381–400.

Schulman, Sarah. *The Gentrification of the Mind: Witness to a Lost Imagination*. University of California Press, 2012.

Scott, A. O. "The Death of Adulthood in American Culture." *New York Times Magazine*, 11 September 2014. www.nytimes.com/2014/09/14/magazine/the-death-of-adulthood-in -american-culture.html. Accessed 18 June 2018.

Sedgwick, Eve Kosofky. *Epistemology of the Closet*. 1990. University of California Press, 2008.

Sedgwick, Eve Kosofky. "Paranoid Reading and Reparative Reading, or, You're So Paranoid, You Probably Think This Essay is About You." *Touching Feeling: Affect, Pedagogy, Performativity*, Duke University Press, 2003, pp. 123–151.

Sedgwick, Eve Kosofky. "Queer Performativity: Henry James's *The Art of the Novel*." *GLQ*, vol. 1, 1993, pp. 1–16.

Sedgwick, Eve Kosofky *Tendencies*. Duke University Press, 1993.

"The Shame Wizard." *Big Mouth*, season 2, episode 3, 29 September 2017, www.netflix.com/ title/80117038.

Shattuck, Kathryn. "Nick Kroll Still Isn't Over Puberty." *New York Times*, 12 November 2017. www.nytimes.com/2017/11/10/arts/television/nick-kroll-big-mouth-netflix-puberty.html. Accessed 10 June 2019.

Shaw, Adrienne. "Caper in the Castro." *LGBTQ Video Game Archive*, 23 August 2015, lgbtqgamearchive.com/2015/08/23/caper-in-the-castro/. Accessed 12 April 2019.

Shepherd, Lynn. "If JK Rowling Cares About Writing, She Should Stop Doing It." *Huff Post Culture*, 21 February 2014, www.huffingtonpost.co.uk/lynnshepherd/jkrowling-should -stop-writing_b_4829648.html?guccounter=1. Accessed 24 February 2014.

Shugerman, Emily. "Critics Praise 'Big Mouth' Planned Parenthood Episode. Conservatives Freak Out." *Daily Beast*, 24 October 2018, www.thedailybeast.com/

big-mouth-planned-parenthood-episode-has-conservatives-comparing-netflix-to-hitler. Accessed 10 June 2019.

Silverman, Karyn. "Two Boys Kissing." *School Library Journal*, 29 September 2013, blogs.slj .com/printzblog/2013/09/29/two-boys-kissing/. Accessed 11 April 2019.

Slaton, Joyce. "Big Mouth." *Common Sense Media*, 29 September 2017. www.commonsense media.org/tv-reviews/big-mouth. Accessed 13 July 2019.

"Sleepover: A Harrowing Ordeal of Emotional Brutality." *Big Mouth*, season 1, episode 4, 29 September 2017, www.netflix.com/title/80117038.

Sleeter, Christine E. Foreword. *Children and Families 'At Promise': Deconstructing the Discourse of Risk*, edited by Sally Lubeck and Beth Blue Swadener. SUNY Press, 1995, pp. ix–xi.

Smith, Andrew. *Grasshopper Jungle*. Dutton Children's Books, 2014.

Smith, Michelle J., and Kristine Moruzi. "Vampires and Witches Go to School: Contemporary Young Adult Fiction, Gender, and the Gothic." *Children's Literature in Education*, vol. 49, no. 6, 2018, pp. 6–18.

smith, s.e. "Book Review: Two Boys Kissing, by David Levithan." *This ain't livin','* 13 October 2013, meloukhia.net/2013/10/book_review_two_boys_kissing_by_david_levithan/ Accessed 11 April 2019.

"Smooch or Share." *Big Mouth*, season 2, episode 9, 5 October 2018, www.netflix.com/title/ 80117038.

Sontag, Susan. "Notes on 'Camp.'" *Camp: Queer Aesthetics and the Performing Subject: A Reader*, edited by Fabio Cleto. University of Michigan Press, 1999, pp. 53–65.

Stebbins, Anne. "What a Shame! Gay Shame in Isabelle Holland's *The Man Without a Face*." *Bookbird*, vol. 52, no. 1, 2004, pp. 34–42.

"Steve the Virgin." *Big Mouth*, season 2, episode 4, 5 October 2018, www.netflix.com/title/ 80117038.

Stiefvater, Maggie. "Pure Escapism." *New York Times*, 21 December 2011. www.nytimes.com/ roomfordebate/2010/12/26/the-dark-side-of-young-adult-fiction/pure-escapism-for -young-adult-readers. Accessed 5 April 2017.

Stockton, Kathryn Bond. *Beautiful Bottom, Beautiful Shame: Where Black Meets Queer*. Duke University Press, 2006.

Stockton, Kathryn Bond. *The Queer Child, or Growing Sideways in the Twentieth Century*. Duke University Press, 2009.

Susala. "It Gets Better." *FanFiction.net*, 17 June 2011. www.fanfiction.net/s/7092736/1/It-Gets -Better. Accessed 18 March 2014.

Sykes, Heather. *Queer Bodies: Sexualities, Genders, and Fatness in Physical Education*. Peter Lang, 2011.

Talburt, Susan. "Intelligibility and Narrating Queer Youth." Rasmussen, et al., *Youth and Sexualities*, pp. 17–39.

Talburt, Susan, and Shirley R. Steinberg, eds. *Thinking Queer: Sexuality, Culture, and Education*. Peter Lang, 2000.

Tarbox, Gwen Athene. "Re: LGBT Visibility." Email received by Derritt Mason, 20 September 2014.

Tatar, Maria. "No More Adventures in Wonderland." *New York Times*, 9 October 2011, www .nytimes.com/2011/10/10/opinion/no-more-adventures-in-wonderland.html. Accessed 18 June 2018.

There_Was_A_Kat. "It Gets Better." *Archive of Our Own*, 19 December 2011, www.archive ofourown.org/works/296322. Accessed 18 March 2014.

Thomas, Ebony Elizabeth. *The Dark Fantastic: Race and the Imagination from Harry Potter to The Hunger Games*. NYU Press, 2019.

Tosenberger, Catherine. "Homosexuality at the Online Hogwarts: Harry Potter Slash Fanfiction." Abate and Kidd, *Over the Rainbow*, pp. 329–353.

Travers, Ben. "'Big Mouth': All Hail the Hormone Monsters, The Only Creatures Nasty Enough to Tell the Truth About Puberty." *Indiewire*, 8 October 2017. www.indiewire .com/2017/10/big-mouth-hormone-monster-nick-kroll-netflix-1201883335/. Accessed 10 June. 2019.

Tribunella, Eric L. "A Boy and His Dog." *Melancholia and Maturation: The Use of Trauma in American Children's Literature*. University of Tennessee Press, 2009, pp. 29–49.

Trites, Roberta Seelinger. *Disturbing the Universe: Power and Repression in Adolescent Literature*. University of Iowa Press, 2000.

Wagner-Martin, Jenn, and Erika Wagner-Martin. "You Will Meet People Who Celebrate You." Savage and Miller, *It Gets Better*, pp. 96–98.

Walcott, Rinaldo. "Reconstructing Manhood; or, the Drag of Black Masculinity." *Small Axe*, vol. 13, no. 1, 2009, pp. 75–89.

Wallace, Kenyon. "School Board Overturns Ban on Gay-Straight Alliance Groups." *National Post News*, Postmedia Network Inc., 19 January 2011, nationalpost.com/news/canada/ school-board-overturns-ban-on-gay-straight-alliance-groups. Accessed 14 November 2012.

Warner, Michael. *The Trouble with Normal: Sex, Politics, and the Ethics of Queer Life*. Harvard University Press, 1999.

Weldon, Glen. "Life, Puberty and the Pursuit of Horniness: 'Big Mouth,' Season 2." NPR, 5 October 2018, www.npr.org/2018/10/05/653657218/life-puberty-and-the-pursuit-of -horniness-big-mouth-season-2. Accessed 10 June 2019.

Weldy, Lance, and Thomas Crisp. "From Alice to Alana: Sexualities and Children's Cultures in the Twenty-First Century." *Children's Literature Association Quarterly*, vol. 37, no. 4, 2012, pp. 367–373.

Westerfeld, Scott. "Breaking Down the 'System.'" *New York Times*, 21 December 2011. www .nytimes.com/roomfordebate/2010/12/26/the-dark-side-of-young-adult-fiction/breaking -down-the-system. Accessed 5 April 2017.

"What Is It about Boobs?" *Big Mouth*, season 2, episode 2, 29 September 2017, www.netflix .com/title/80117038.

"What Is the It Gets Better Project?" *It Gets Better Project*, 2012. Itgetsbetter.org. Accessed 29 June 2012.

Whitehead, Joshua. "'Finding Whe'Wha': Indigenous Idylls in Queer Young Adult Fiction." *Queer as Camp: Essays on Summer, Style, and Sexuality*, edited by Kenneth B. Kidd and Derritt Mason. Fordham University Press, 2019, pp. 223–239.

Wickens, Corinne M. "Codes, Silences, and Homophobia: Challenging Normative Assumptions about Gender and Sexuality in Contemporary LGBTQ Young Adult Literature." *Children's Literature in Education*, vol. 42, no. 2, 2011, pp. 148–164.

Williams, Mary Elizabeth. "Has Young Adult Fiction Become Too Dark?" *Salon*, 6 June 2011. www.salon.com/2011/06/06/wsj_young_adult_literature_too_dark/. Accessed 18 June 2018.

Willis, Ika. "Keeping Promises to Queer Children: Making Space (for Mary Sue) at Hogwarts." *Fan Fiction and Fan Communities in the Age of the Internet: New Essays*, edited by Karen Hellekson and Kristina Busse. McFarland & Co., 2006, pp. 153–170.

Wood, Megan M., and Linda Baughman. "*Glee* Fandom and Twitter: Something New, or More of the Same Old Thing?" *Communication Studies*, vol. 63, no. 3, 2012, pp. 328–344.

Writerbitch92. "It Gets Better." *FanFiction.net*, 18 June 2011, www.fanfiction.net/s/7093797/1/It-Gets-Better. Accessed 18 March 2014.

Yockey, Cynthia. "Tracker McDyke Matches Wits with Dullagan Straightman." *Washington Blade*, 3 November 1989. lgbtqgamearchive.files.wordpress.com/2015/08/caper-in-the-castro-article-november-3–1989-washington-blade.png. Accessed 15 April 2019.

"Youth Risk Behavior Surveillance System (YRBSS)." *Centers for Disease Control and Prevention*, 14 June 2018, www.cdc.gov/healthyyouth/data/yrbs/index.htm?s_cid=hy-homepage-002. Accessed 14 July 2018.

Zurcher, Anthony. "Author Suggests JK Rowling Stop Writing Adult Fiction." *BBC News Echo Chambers*, 24 February. 2014, www.bbc.com/news/blogs-echochambers-26331650. Accessed 25 February 2014.

Index

Abate, Michelle Ann, 27, 89

adolescence: and anxiety, 6, 10–15, 94, 121, 162, 185n4; at-risk, 45; authors, 12; autonomy, 62; and *Big Mouth*, 109, 111, 133; body, 97; closeted, 22, 117, 121, 153–54, 159, 160, 164, 187n14; crisis, 4, 6, 9; development, 138, 168; and dystopia, 21, 23, 88, 89–94, 97, 103; experiences in, 88, 129; and fiction, 54, 184n3; gay, 22, 32, 95; and *Glee/It Gets Better* fanfiction, 160, 164, 167; and HIV/ AIDS, 20; and horror, 23, 105, 121, 133; and identity, 11; incompleteness, 14, 61, 140; and Indigeneity, 181n4; invention of, 10–11, 92, 102; and *It Gets Better*, 136, 142–45, 158, 164; ideal, 11, 90–91; LGB, 47; and literature, 89–90, 181n1; and narrative, 183n17; novel of, 11–12, 181n1; as open psychic structure, 12, 61, 116–17; polymorphous perversity, 133; as promise and threat, 102; protagonist, 162; queerness, 16; queer YA for, 5; queer youth and, 15, 48, 137; reader, 92, 104; real, 90, 96; risk-taking, 6; self-destructive, 103; sexuality, 23, 29, 35, 90, 94–95, 97, 103, 105, 107, 112, 120, 127–28, 167; and shame, 126–27, 132, 133; social issues, 12; and storm and stress, 23, 88, 145, 188n2; studies of, 17, 28–29; subject, 94; suicide, 163; and teenagers, 16; and temporality, 163; themes, 118, 189n3; transition from, 5, 42; turmoil, 169; unruly, 121; and volatility, 89; writing and, 164. *See also* juveniles; queer youth; teenagers; young adults; youth

Adolescence (Hall), 10–11, 188n2

adolescent novel, 11–12, 15, 116, 140, 177, 181n5, 182n6. *See also* children's literature; queer YA; young adult literature

adult anxieties: about adolescence, 94; about adolescent sexuality, 97–98; about childhood, 170, 185n4; and children's literature, 8, 25, 104, 154, 167, 170, 183n15; in *It Gets Better*, 136–37, 150, 154, 158; about power and control, 11; about queer adolescents, 6; and queer YA, 12. *See also* anxiety

adult authors: and anxieties about sexuality, 97; and children's literature, 24–25, 167; of fanfiction, 156, 164; and innocence, 70; of *It Gets Better* stories, 141–42, 146–50, 191n9; of problem novels, 96; of YA, 91

adulthood: avoidance of, 36; between childhood and, 121; death of, 176–78; growth into, 10, 31, 35, 48, 133; happy, 164; heterosexual, 15, 31, 35, 117, 133; as immobilizing, 163; markers of, 62; and positive self-identity, 4; queer, 143; queer question mark of, 163; as reprieve, 136; sanctuary of, 143; sexually resolved, 63; and stability, 5, 42, 142, 158, 163, 167; transition into, 131, 158; as vantage point, 144

adults: and anxiety, 11, 16, 97, 121; approval, 156; attention, 178; and *Big Mouth*, 111, 116–17; care, 169; child relationship, 25, 138–39; and the child's inner life, 10; civilized, 10; content,

About the Author

Image courtesy University of Calgary

Derritt Mason is associate professor of English at the University of Calgary. He is the coeditor, with Kenneth B. Kidd, of *Queer as Camp: Essays on Summer, Style, and Sexuality*. His work has appeared in venues including *Research on Diversity in Youth Literature, Children's Literature Association Quarterly, English Studies in Canada*, and *Jeunesse: Young People, Texts, Cultures*.

de in the USA
Vegas, NV
March 2021